# Turning the World Upside Down Again

D0858542

# Dedication

For Siân, Madeleine, Alastair, Adam, Summer and Marney

# Turning the World Upside Down Again

*Global health in a time of pandemics, climate change and political turmoil*

Nigel Crisp

## CRC Press
Taylor & Francis Group

Boca Raton  London  New York

Second edition published 2022
by CRC Press
2 Park Square, Milton Park, Abingdon, Oxon, OX14 4RN

and by CRC Press
6000 Broken Sound Parkway NW, Suite 300, Boca Raton, FL 33487-2742

© 2022 Nigel Crisp

First edition published in 2010

*CRC Press is an imprint of Informa UK Limited*

*British Library Cataloguing-in-Publication Data*
A catalogue record for this book is available from the British Library

*Library of Congress Cataloging-in-Publication Data*
A catalog record has been requested for this book

ISBN: 9781032212999 (hbk)
ISBN: 9781032212951 (pbk)
ISBN: 9781003267706 (ebk)

DOI: 10.1201/9781003267706

Typeset in Palatino LT Std
by Apex CoVantage, LLC
Printed and bound by CPI Group (UK) Ltd, Croydon, CR0 4YY

# Contents

# Preface

This book is an updated and very extensively rewritten edition of *Turning the World Upside Down* which was published in 2010. The central theme remains the same – that the high-income and powerful countries of the world can learn a great deal about health from lower-income and less powerful ones – but so much has changed.

COVID-19 has hit us, climate change is reshaping our world, and political turmoil has damaged the sense of global solidarity which had seemed so promising only 12 years ago.

Advances in science and technology have brought us new connections, influences, therapies and treatments as well as new dangers and threats. As part of this, social media has emerged as a major influence on what people understand and think about health and on levels of trust in government, science and health systems.

A better understanding of the way society and the environment influence our health has given us new insights into inequalities within and between countries – many of which have grown – and helped expose long-standing and submerged truths about our societies and our world. Black Lives Matter, decolonisation movements, the continuing fight for gender equity and the many struggles by different groups for their human rights are forcing us to examine our own societies and behaviours.

I am very grateful to the people listed below from different backgrounds and countries who have offered me insights and advice and to others whose work I have read or heard about. They have helped me make some sense of what is happening and bring together, however inadequately, some of the new ideas about health from around the world which I believe we must adopt if we are to thrive in the future.

As before, the heroes of this book are the people who are actually doing things, taking practical action to improve lives and communities and creating health in their families, communities, schools, workplaces and wider communities.

## A NOTE ON LANGUAGE

Words matter because they denote how we think and signal to the reader where we are coming from. I have found it difficult to find the right words in some parts of this book.

I have opted to distinguish between countries as being 'low-, middle- or high-income' and often 'lower- or higher-income' countries where the context won't allow me to use country names. This draws attention to a single and measurable difference between countries. I sometimes add 'more powerful' and 'less powerful', and the two concepts of income and power are, of course, closely aligned.

While the meaning is obvious, referring to richer and poorer countries can be seen as ignoring the enormous non-financial riches of people, culture and resources. This book is very largely about those riches and a celebration of the creativity, determination and sense of justice of people everywhere.

Talking about countries as being in the 'Global South' or 'Global North' makes sense to those of us working in health and development, but I hope many other people will read this book. They may well think it odd that this distinction places Pakistan, Thailand and Myanmar in the Global South and Australia and New Zealand in the Global North. Moreover, I don't think that Global South and Global North are always used consistently.

I very much dislike the use of the words 'reverse innovation' to describe innovations coming from people in low-income countries. It is patronising and freighted with prejudice and may suggest that such innovation is somehow second-rate or worse. It isn't, as this book makes clear. Innovations from people in lower-income and less powerful countries are innovations and don't need any further qualification; and like innovations everywhere, some are useful and some are not, some offer long-term solutions and some don't, some bring enormous benefits and some may be actually dangerous.

The term 'reverse innovation' also ignores the plain fact that most innovation comes from outside the mainstream. 'Frugal innovation' is different, however, and has acquired a more technical meaning about being low cost, using materials to hand and ad hoc. Not all innovations are frugal.

Talking about innovation may also obscure the fact that most of the learning I describe in this book is not so much about innovations as about how we see health and the world. It is about behaviours and approaches that work best and, in some cases, the rediscovery of old truths. Innovations in techniques and systems can be very valuable but they are the smaller part of our learning when we turn the world upside down.

I start from the 1948 World Health Organization definition of health as '*A state of complete physical, mental and social well-being and not merely the absence of disease or infirmity*' and explore new ways of thinking about it in the book. I don't attempt to define well-being, which is now quite widely used in different ways.

I am generally meaning the formal health system in a country when I refer to health systems and I also sometimes refer to health and care systems depending on context. Care professionals also have a very important role to play.

## THANK YOU

I am deeply grateful to so many people who I have met and learned from around the world in the last two decades. These include the following who have helped me with my thinking in the preparation of *Turning the World Upside Down Again*:

Rifat Atun, David Aynsley, Maureen Bisognano, Ged Byrne, Jim Campbell, Lincoln Chen, Susana Edjang, Julio Frenk, Liz Grant, Sir Muir Gray, Charlotte Greene, Matt Harris, Heather Henry, Amir Hussain, Oliver Johnson, Penny Jones, Ilona Kickbush, Lord Andrew Mawson, RN Mohanty, Heather Nelson, Francis Omaswa, Gillian Orrow, Agamemnon Otero, Roberta Pike,

Srinath Reddy, Sonia Roschnik, Marc Sansom, Ben Simms, Hazel Stuteley, Shams Syed, Rob Trimble, Nicole Votruba, Sir Mark Walport and Rob Yates.

I am also greatly indebted to very many other people whose work I have read and sometimes quoted in this book. I have learned from many people, traditions and disciplines and their influence can be seen throughout these pages.

I am very grateful to my commissioning editor Jo Koster who suggested this updated edition, her assistant Neha Bhatt, and to Nora Naughton for once again providing such expert editing and proofing.

Above all, I am very grateful to my wife Siân for her ideas, advice and support throughout the whole process of writing and editing this book.

Nigel Crisp
February 2022

# About the author

Nigel Crisp has unique experience of health and health services globally, having run the largest health organisation in the world and subsequently worked in several low- and middle-income countries in Africa and South Asia.

He is an independent crossbench member of the House of Lords in the UK and works and writes mainly on global health.

He was Chief Executive of the English National Health Service (NHS) – the largest health organisation in the world with 1.4 million employees – and Permanent Secretary of the UK Department of Health, from 2000 to 2006. He led major reforms during this period which brought significant improvements to the NHS.

He had previously been Chief Executive of the Oxford Radcliffe Hospitals, one of the UK's leading academic centres, and Regional Director for the NHS in London. His earlier career was in industry and charities.

Nigel Crisp founded the All-Party Parliamentary Group on Global Health and the global campaign on nursing, Nursing Now, both of which he co-chaired. He is on the advisory board of several organisations including the African Centre for Global Health and Social Development and The Walker Institute.

He is an Honorary Professor at the London School of Hygiene and Tropical Medicine, a Senior Fellow at the Institute for Healthcare Improvement and a Foreign Associate of the US National Academy of Medicine. He was formerly a Distinguished Visiting Fellow at the Harvard School of Public Health and Regent's Lecturer at Berkeley.

He has published extensively in academic journals and elsewhere. His books include:

- Crisp N. *Health is Made at Home, Hospitals are for Repairs: Building a healthy and health-creating society*. Billericay: SALUS, 2020.
- Crisp N. *Turning the World Upside Down. The search for global health in the 21st century*. London: RSM Press, 2010.
- Osmaswa F, Crisp N (eds). *African Health Leaders: Making change and claiming the future*. Oxford: OUP, 2014.
- Crisp N. *24 Hours to Save the NHS: The Chief Executive's account of reform 2000 to 2006*. Oxford: OUP, 2011.

# List of Abbreviations

| | |
|---|---|
| AfCFTA | African Continental Free Trade Area |
| AI | artificial intelligence |
| AIDS | acquired immune deficiency syndrome |
| AMR | anti-microbial resistance |
| ANC | African National Congress |
| ART | antiretroviral therapy |
| ASHA | Accredited Social Health Activist |
| BMA | British Medical Association |
| BRAC | Bangladesh Rural Action Committee |
| COP26 | 26th UN Climate Change Conference |
| COPD | chronic obstructive pulmonary disease |
| COVID-19 | coronavirus disease, caused by the SARS-CoV-2 virus |
| CT | computed tomography |
| DAC | Development Assistance Committee |
| EU | European Union |
| FDA | Food and Drug Administration |
| FDI | Foreign Direct Investment |
| GAVI | Global Action on Vaccination and Immunisation |
| GDP | gross domestic product |
| GNI | gross national income |
| GP | general practitioner |
| HIPC | Highly Indebted Poor Countries |
| HIV | human immunodeficiency virus |
| IHI | Institute for Healthcare Improvement |
| IHME | Institute for Health Metrics and Evaluation |
| IMF | International Monetary Fund |
| IPCC | Intergovernmental Panel on Climate Change |
| LBGTI | lesbian, bisexual, gay, transgender and intersex |
| LHS | learning health system |
| M2M | Mothers to Mothers |
| MCN | Movimiento Comunal Nicaragüense |
| MDG | Millennium Development Goal |
| MDRI | Multilateral Debt Relief Initiative |
| MHRA | Medicines and Healthcare Products Regulatory Agency |
| MOOC | Massive Open Online Course |
| MRI | magnetic resonance imaging |

| | |
|---|---|
| MRSA | methicillin-resistant *Staphylococcus aureus* |
| NGO | non-governmental organisation |
| NHS | National Health Service |
| NICE | National Institute for Health and Care Excellence |
| NTD | neglected tropical disease |
| ODA | Official Development Assistance |
| OECD | Organisation for Economic Co-operation and Development |
| ONS | Office for National Statistics |
| PEPFAR | President's Emergency Plan for AIDS Relief |
| ProMED | Program for Monitoring Emerging Diseases |
| PTRA | Penwerris Tenants and Residents Association |
| SARS | severe acute respiratory syndrome |
| SCF | Southcentral Foundation |
| SDG | Sustainable Development Goal |
| STEAM | science, technology, engineering, arts and maths |
| STI | sexually transmitted infection |
| TB | tuberculosis |
| THET | Tropical Health Education Trust |
| UN | United Nations |
| UNAIDS | Joint United Nations Programme on HIV/AIDS |
| UNDP | United Nations Development Programme |
| UNFPA | United Nations Population Fund |
| UNICEF | United Nations Children's Fund |
| VCTF | Village COVID Taskforce |
| VSO | Voluntary Service Overseas |
| WHO | World Health Organization |
| WTO | World Trade Organization |

# Introduction

1

*There are two simple ideas at the very heart of this book – that rich countries can learn a great deal about health and health services from poorer ones and that combining the learning from rich and poor countries can give us new insight into how to improve health.*

These words, the opening sentence of *Turning the World Upside Down*,[1] were fairly radical when I wrote them in 2009 but are now much more widely accepted. They are even more relevant today, although I now use slightly different language and emphasise the importance of power and powerlessness as well as wealth.

*Turning the World Upside Down Again* introduces a third and equally important idea. Not only can high-income and more powerful countries learn from lower-income and less powerful ones but the rich and powerful in any country, the elite, the professionals and the middle classes, can learn a great deal from low-income and disempowered communities in their own country. Real and sustainable progress can be made when we bring together learning and experiences from all parts of the world and all parts of all our communities.

We need that new learning and ideas now more than ever and we need to come together to face the future. The optimistic vision of the Sustainable Development Goals (SDGs) and the Paris Agreement on climate with their shared ambitions and the promise of global solidarity – leaving no one behind – has been punctured by the coronavirus (COVID-19) pandemic, the onset of climate change and global tensions.

There is a greater realism now, not just about the future but about the past too and the contradictions and tensions about race, gender and inequality, for example – often unacknowledged or ignored – that lie just below the surface. Now, in terms of global solidarity, it may appear that the best we can hope for is that nations act together on the shared problems of today through self-interest rather than because of shared beliefs, shared vision and shared moral commitment.

We should not, however, succumb to cynicism and narrow individual concerns – or, worse, to populist politics – but we should try to create a new vision and narrative for health globally that can energise and unify as we work to tackle the great health problems of today.

Such a vision needs to be grounded in reality and not in the puff and pageantry of politicians and their rhetoric. It needs to be about what happens in real life, what people experience, what

DOI: 10.1201/9781003267706-1

1

they believe and what they do. There is too great a gulf between governments and the political and technocratic elites on one hand and everyone else on the other.

Global solidarity may be difficult to imagine now at the national level but it's not hard to find at the individual level – people to people, health worker to health worker – as so many of the stories in this book show. We can all recognise the courage and compassion of health workers rushing to help in dangerous situations all over the world. We have all seen how many communities have pulled together, helping each other as the pandemic struck. We have also seen health professionals learning rapidly from each other across boundaries and scientists throughout the world working collaboratively towards the common good. This should give us all hope for the future.

It is here, I believe, that we should begin to construct a new vision, with individuals and communities and our interdependence at its heart. The starting point for me is that our health as individuals is intimately connected to the health of our communities, the health of wider society and ultimately, to the health of the planet. I go on to suggest in later chapters that we need to think of health in more ecological terms that specifically recognise the relationship between ourselves and our environment and that healthy individuals, communities, societies, and the natural environment can all adapt successfully to external challenges – if they are given the chance to do so.

> Our health as individuals is intimately connected to the health of our communities, the health of wider society and, ultimately, to the health of the planet.

Life has moved on in other ways, too, in the last 12 years. There were marked improvements in health around the world, until the pandemic interrupted progress, and many middle-income countries have developed enormously in recent years. We can all learn from countries such as India and China and we are already importing their ideas and technologies. We are not yet learning, however, from other countries in Asia, Africa and Latin America. Ideas about mutual learning and co-development are discussed more widely than 12 years ago but the evidence suggests attitudes and behaviours haven't yet shifted substantially.

There may have been many improvements globally in recent years but, at the same time, some countries and some communities within countries are falling even further behind. Inequality is growing between and within countries and is a major theme of the book. There are still around a billion people globally who don't have access to a health worker.

My own experiences have shown me that there are creative, passionate local people in countries that have very limited resources, who are innovating, finding solutions and working out how to use the materials at hand to provide the best deal they can for their patients and communities. Unconstrained by the baggage of history, conventions and institutions, they are training people in new ways, creating new types of organisations, involving families and communities, building on older traditions, and concentrating much more on creating health and independence rather than on just tackling disease.

I have seen similar creativity from groups in the UK who are not adhering to customary practice or simply waiting for help to arrive from the authorities but finding new solutions to create health for themselves and their communities. There is no comparison, of course, between the problems to be found in the poorest parts of the world and those in high-income countries like the UK but there are similarities in how they can be addressed and, very importantly, who is in control and decides what needs to be done.

Ill health, poverty, life expectancy and disability are all so much worse in low- and middle-income countries. People die and are damaged by some of the simplest and most treatable or preventable diseases and situations. It is plain to see that science, technology, medicine, professionalism, knowledge and systems, combined with more resources and health workers, are desperately needed.

It is also plain and obvious, however, that health systems in high-income countries are in trouble. While other countries need more of what we in high-income countries have – our science, expertise and resources – we also need more of what they have learned about communities, reaching everyone in need, and taking practical action with the tools to hand.

And we need to work together if we are to tackle pandemics effectively, find ways to stop climate change, manage its consequences, and continue to improve health at a time of great turbulence.

Health and wealth are intimately connected. Poverty damages health and limits opportunity while the health and creativity of our people are arguably the greatest economic and social assets of any country.

Like its predecessor, *Turning the World Upside Down Again* is a search for understanding, an attempt to make sense of the conflicting pressures around health in the world today and to identify some of the practical actions that can make a difference.

## PEOPLE ARE LOOKING FOR CHANGE

Another very noticeable feature today is that many people are actively looking for change. We can see it all around us and among all age groups. It is not just younger people calling for change, although they exemplify the demand for change more than anyone else. Almost all these changes have important implications for health.

We can see this, for example, in the campaigns on climate change, gender, decolonisation, racism, violence against women, and human rights and freedoms. We can see it in a new global emphasis on tackling inequalities and confronting old wrongs from slavery to sexual abuse.

We can see it in the extraordinary bravery of the citizens of Myanmar, Hong Kong and elsewhere fighting for their freedom at great personal cost. We can see it in civil unrest in many countries from France to South Africa to Chile and the US where disaffected citizens are detached from their leadership. And we can see it in the citizens' movements globally that are seeking to preserve civil liberties, taking on the monopolies of the enormous global companies, aiming to force them to pay taxes, be accountable and helping counter abuses of all kinds.

We can also see it in the growth of populist and extremist politics around the world – whipped up by opportunist politicians peddling fear and xenophobia.

There are also plenty of people who are actively anti-science, others are inspired to acts of terrorism, others driven by hatred of particular groups – Muslims, Jews or members of the LBGTI+ communities for example – and there are cultists, conspiracy theorists and conspirators of all sorts.

The internet and social media play an enormous role in all this. It is where most people all over the world now get their understanding and beliefs about health – for better or for worse.

3

Most of these movements are coming from outside traditional politics, from non-political people. It is not as simple as seeing these as overtly political struggles for power. They are more in the nature of protests, taking on a perceived injustice, campaigning for change, and expressing alienation, rather than seeking power for themselves or fermenting revolution. Many people I have spoken to say simply that they want to be counted, for their voice to be heard, to matter, and to influence events.

I suspect that for many people their protests are more about these things than about political revolution, 'the dictatorship of the proletariat' or the replacement of one government and set of politicians with another. However, there are also others who are explicitly looking for the end of capitalism and the economic and social structures that go with it. They envisage a new sort of society growing out of the ruins of the old.

There is in many of these demands for change a hopeful layering of ideas on each other – a recognition that actions to improve health, achieve greater equity and inclusion, and increase sustainable growth and development, environmental protection, education, democracy and fulfilling work can reinforce each other if only we can find ways of bringing them all together. The economy is also vitally important. Rising wealth has brought millions out of poverty in recent years and led to improving health – and improved health in its turn leads to a healthy workforce and an improved economy.

> There is . . . a hopeful layering of ideas on each other – a recognition that actions to improve health, achieve greater equity and inclusion, and increase sustainable growth and development, environmental protection, education, democracy, and fulfilling work can reinforce each other . . .

The politics, tensions and conflicts of late 2021 and early 2022 are, however, a grim backdrop for writing a book about making positive change and improving health and lives.

In 2009, in the aftermath of the credit crunch and financial crisis, I wrote that we were finally reaching the end of the long twentieth century. That, just like at the time of the outbreak of the First World War in 1914, this was the moment when the new century begins to confront itself and turn its back on the long boom that led up to the millennium – exactly as the twentieth century turned away from the long dominance of the British Empire a century before.

Then, as now, there were many tensions and frictions between countries and within countries. The old order was falling apart. For comparison, four great empires fell during the First World War, Gandhi returned to India to begin his fight for independence, and the predecessor of the African National Congress (ANC) was formed in South Africa. Meanwhile, in health, Freud and Jung were writing their revolutionary books and the Flexner Report led to radical reforms in medical education.

Our ideas and our ways of looking at the world will change over the next few years. We must be open to the new. Some treasured old institutions will become irrelevant and vanish as we discover and create new twenty-first century ways of thinking and doing things. Whatever happens, we know from history that it will undoubtedly be a very long and difficult process of change as people and nations give up cherished ideas, assumptions and habits and make way for the new.

I will argue in later chapters that western scientific medicine – and the health and care systems that have developed from it – which have served us so well over many years need radical change. We need to listen and learn if we are to adapt and enhance so it can be fit for the future.

## THE COVID-19 PANDEMIC

Health has always been political, but our more recent understanding of how social and political factors affect our health has brought it still further into the political arena. The COVID-19 pandemic has speeded up this process, just as it has accelerated so many other changes.

The response to the pandemic has been about politics, power and communities as well as about science, resources and the extraordinary commitment and compassion of so many health workers.

The world is still in the grip of the pandemic as I write this in February 2022 and, whatever happens next, it will leave a long legacy. Some of it, perhaps surprisingly, will be good – the advances in science, the acceleration of some positive trends, the strengthening of community in some places – but most will be bad. Damage has been done to lives, physical and mental health, economies, education and the prospects of many young people, and inequalities have widened. The pandemic has also increased divisions in some countries and called into question global cooperation.

The pandemic will feature large throughout *Turning the World Upside Down Again* and we will trace its consequences insofar as they are yet known, look at how people have responded – including, for example, the Village Covid Groups in Uganda – and consider the implications for global institutions and global solidarity in the future.

## CLIMATE CHANGE

The dawning realisation and growing evidence that climate change is upon us, and is not just a distant threat, has also accelerated change.

There were heatwaves and massive forest fires in North America and Turkey last autumn. There were also devastating floods in Germany, China and India, snow in Australia, a developing famine in east Africa and the Gulf Stream was varying its trajectory in Western Europe more than is usual. The sheer number of these one-off or once in a generation or lifetime events shows how deeply our planet is now compromised.

We are already approaching an average increase in temperature globally of 1.5 °C which world leaders agreed as the limit in the Paris Agreement of 2015 and beyond which everything becomes even more unpredictable. The latest scientific results are not looking good, and we must prepare for even worse disruption to come.

We will look in later chapters at the likely health consequences of climate change and discuss the important concept of planetary health. We must also recognise, however, that the whole health industry will also have to change its approach. Estimates suggest that it is responsible for about 4.4% of the world's carbon emissions. If it were a country, it would be the fifth largest emitter in the world.

The major emitting countries agreed in Paris to cut their emissions and to strengthen those commitments over time, but progress has been slow. The 26th UN Climate Change Conference (COP26) was held in Glasgow while I was finishing this book. It has produced a mixed bag of results, as will be discussed in later chapters. There was some positive movement in some areas, but there was still, however, a lack of specific practical commitments – the *how* of bringing about change. There also continued to be disruptive divisions between countries and a failure of high-income countries to support and finance change in low- and middle-income countries.

The position of both China and the USA are vital here. China is the biggest carbon emitter overall and responsible for 28% of the world's carbon emissions, but the USA emits 16 tonnes per capita annually compared to China's 7 tonnes per capita and has made a lower overall commitment to reductions. However, the actions of citizens and governments everywhere will contribute to improving or worsening the position.

## AN UNFAIR EXCHANGE

In *Turning the World Upside Down*, I described the way that richer and more powerful countries import health workers from poorer and less powerful countries and export their ideas and ideologies about health in return as an unfair exchange.

This unfair exchange continues today with a continuing 'brain drain' of people with health and care qualifications migrating in search of a better life. Migration has become an even bigger issue in the last few years, with refugees fleeing conflicts and others travelling for opportunities or work, and it has become a whole new area for concern in health terms as well as social and economic ones.

The export of ideas and ideologies has a long history from, in many countries, colonial times and through the period of structural adjustment led by the World Bank and International Monetary Fund (IMF), which did enormous damage to weak economies and societies in the last quarter of the twentieth century. It has continued through the more recent practices of international development and in the greater commercial activity which has increased as economies grow.

What, I asked in the earlier book, would it be like if we turned this exchange upside down and the poorer and less powerful countries imported health workers to work in their systems under their control and exported their knowledge and learning in exchange? The answer, as I suggest here, is that a very great deal could be gained.

## THE SUSTAINABLE DEVELOPMENT GOALS

There have been some tremendous and highly ambitious campaigns and acts of global solidarity in recent years, none more so than the agreement of the UN's Sustainable Development Goals (SDGs).[2] They were agreed by almost every country in the world in 2015 as the successors to the Millennium Development Goals (MDGs) and run until 2030. There are 17 interdependent goals which are all about developing together and leaving no one behind. Unlike their predecessors, the SDGs are truly global. They apply to all countries, recognising that they all have individual and shared development needs and that we are all deeply interdependent – a theme that runs throughout the book.

We are roughly at the halfway mark in their implementation as I write. COVID-19 has damaged progress, with the UN reporting that 90% of countries have experienced disruptions to essential health services and that the pandemic has halted or reversed progress in health and life expectancy. We need to get back on track as we move on from the acute phase of the pandemic.

The health goal is to '*Ensure healthy lives and promote well-being for all at all ages*', and health is involved in 15 of the other 16 goals. In practice, this means focusing resolutely on more people benefiting from universal health coverage which must embrace mental as well as physical health, protecting more people from health emergencies and, particularly in the light of the pandemic, improving health security.

## HEALTH IS MADE AT HOME, HOSPITALS ARE FOR REPAIRS

Professor Francis Omaswa coined the expression '*Health is made at home, hospitals are for repairs*' when he ran Uganda's health services at the beginning of the century. It contains two very important truths which are both very relevant to the argument of this book. The first is that our health and well-being are shaped by all our experiences and relationships, by our family and home circumstances, our schooling, our work, our community, our culture, and the norms and structures of wider society. The second is the idea that we can *create* health.

The first idea echoes the work of all the health researchers who have worked on the social determinants of health over recent years and shown just how important they are for our health and well-being. We are only at the beginning of understanding how to incorporate these insights into our health and care systems in high-income countries, although, as we shall see, they are often better understood in Uganda and many other lower-income countries.

The second is more radical and invites us to think about the causes of health and not just the causes of disease and ill health. This is an area where everyone has a role to play – parents, families, teachers, employers, designers, businesses and community organisations. All of them can help create the environment and circumstances for us to thrive – as resilient, healthy, capable and confident individuals – and help us to do so.

Many of the stories in this book are about these health creators from outside the health system itself who may engage the health professionals or not in what they are doing. They have an enormous amount to offer for the future, as I describe in Chapter 9.

## AGENTS OF CHANGE

The millions of health professionals globally have the specialist knowledge and expertise to help bring about so many of the changes that are necessary to improve health and health services – both within the health systems and with the health creators and others outside it. They can have a major role as *agents of change*, bringing people together, advising, supporting, and assisting them to improve health as described by the *Lancet* Commission on the Education of Health Professionals for the 21st Century.[3]

There are many such examples. The psychiatrist in India who engages lay people and religious and community organisations in caring for people with mental health problems and the GP in the UK who helps develop health-creating activities in their local community as well as seeing individual patients are both bringing about vital changes. So is the nurse who helps community groups achieve their goals and the midwife who involves traditional leaders in ensuring mothers can deliver their babies in a safe location.

How health professionals see the world and understand their role is one of the most important contributors to improvement locally and globally. I will argue in Chapter 10 that their education and development need to incorporate their role as agents of change as well as their professional and technical knowledge and skills.

## SCIENCE AND TECHNOLOGY

Science and technology are the other great drivers of change in health and health systems, and we can expect enormous advances in many different areas in the coming years. These will lead to changes in diagnosis, treatments, the delivery of care, health workers' education and roles, and the roles of people and organisations outside the formal health system. Big data, machine learning and artificial intelligence (AI) can also be used to analyse and stratify risk in populations and target public health messages and interventions. They can also help build communities.

Later chapters will describe some of the major areas for development but, in line with the theme of learning from lower-income and less powerful countries and communities, they will concentrate on developments in these areas. Countries with weak health systems can find it easier to introduce new developments as they are not replacing existing systems or services, and there are good examples of this in Africa and elsewhere. There is also a great deal of enterprise and creativity worldwide. India is a particularly rich source of digital enterprise with thousands of new developments each year, some of which will find a successful place in health and health systems.

Developments in AI, genomic research, and gene editing and manipulation raise profound ethical, legal and political questions which need to be addressed both within and between countries. They force us to think about the governance of health globally and have implications for global institutions and our ideas about solidarity and cooperation.

## GLOBAL HEALTH AND HEALTH GLOBALLY

I describe global health very simply as being about the issues that affect us all, rich and poor, wherever we are in the world. However, it has become more normal among health professionals and academics to talk about global health in a more focused way as in, for example, the Consortium of Universities for Global Health definition: *'the area of study, research and practice that places a priority on improving health and achieving equity in health for all people worldwide'*.[4]

The term 'global health' has become controversial in the last few years with criticism of the structures and disciplines that have grown around it. It has been critiqued as colonial, top down, western-centric and, to a large extent, maintaining western superiority through different means. In some places, and I caricature it slightly, it appears to have become largely the study of health in low- and middle-income countries by students and researchers in high-income ones.

It has also been very male-dominated, leading to the creation of two campaigns designed to redress the balance. Women in Global Health, founded in 2015, has 25 000 supporters in 90 countries. It argues that *'women make up 75% of the healthcare workforce yet occupy less than 25% of the most influential leadership positions. Their contribution to health systems is monumental, yet the majority of their work is either underpaid or unpaid, leaving women with few opportunities for advancement or to care for their own health. This creates an inequitable health system that impacts the health of all.'*[5]

Similarly, Women Lift Health runs development programmes and an annual conference with the mission to *'expand the power and influence of talented women in global health and catalyze systemic change to achieve gender equality in leadership'*.[6]

These are all very important issues. The central thesis of this book is that we should learn from everyone, everywhere, from different cultures and traditions, and the examples I use in this book reflect this. We can all learn from the experience of weavers in India's Thar Desert and the community health workers in Brazil and from people such as Miriam Were and Edna Adan Ismail in Kenya and Somaliland respectively who have dedicated their lives to achieving practical results for their people.

I critique western scientific medicine in this book and suggest ways in which it needs to adapt, learning from elsewhere, so as to become more effective in the future. For me, one of the most telling points in the various decolonisation movements is that global health as taught and researched in some western universities very largely ignores local knowledge and other knowledge systems by taking western scientific medicine and traditions of public health as its sole starting point. Biology is biology, science is science; but the way it is applied is very culturally and contextually dependent.

> Biology is biology, science is science; but the way it is applied is very culturally and contextually dependent.

I have listened to skilled clinical practitioners who draw on insights from traditional medicine – whether as practised by the First Nations in Canada or in India or Africa – alongside their knowledge of western scientific medicine and been impressed both by the different conceptions of health they bring to bear and their ability to connect with their patients and their communities. I believe that there is a great deal more we can learn from this sharing of knowledge and from the different belief systems and ways of seeing the world, although this goes beyond the scope of the current book.

The criticism of global health rightly draws attention to the importance of understanding history and the forces such as colonisation – and religion, war, politics, economics, environmental factors and inventions – that have, however distantly, shaped the present day and the relationships between peoples and communities.

We also need to recognise the way economic muscle and historical power currently operate. I wrote in *Turning the World Upside Down* about unconscious superiority and how westerners so often outnumbered local people in discussion and decision-making bodies in Africa and Asia. This last was partly because there are more graduates in the West and more people with resources who are able to travel, although this is changing as time moves on and as Zoom and its cousins bring the world closer together.

These were the reasons why Francis Omaswa and I followed up my earlier book by editing *African Health Leaders: Making change and claiming the future.*[7]

As we said in the book, '*most accounts of health and healthcare in Africa are written by foreigners. [This book] . . . redresses the balance. Written by Africans who have themselves led improvements in their own countries.'* As this last sentence says, the book was written by people who had actually led change, not just written about it. The book contains chapters written by 22 Africans from 12 sub-Saharan countries, 12 men and 10 women.

People like these African leaders who are doing things, using the professional and other skills creatively to make improvements and bring about change – not just protesting about things – are the heroes of this book, as they were of the 2009 version.

I believe that the movements to decolonise global health are pointing to problems in global health which do need to be resolved – not with words, policies and token appointments that may degenerate into mere virtue signalling – but with real thought, debate and action. This debate has a long way to go and, as ever, those involved in it need to start by listening to the people who are most affected by it.

In a recent article on decolonising global health, Richard Horton quoted Kwame Nkrumah, the first President of independent Ghana, writing about the need '*to secure a world realignment so that those who are at the moment the helpless victims of a system will be able in the future to exert a counter pressure'.* There is much more at stake here than words, cancellations and culture wars.[8]

COVID-19 has shown that the ambition for greater global solidarity and cooperation in health which is central to most conceptions of global health is too simple and collapses when confronted by the harsh reality of choices about vaccines. It, too, needs far greater thought and recognition of the competing pressures on countries and regions. My own model, as I describe in the next chapter, consists of three parts: our own autonomy, history and independence; our interdependence locally and globally; and the human rights and rule of law that enables us to balance the two.

This approach addresses one of the other dangers with the term 'global health': that it may suggest that the world is one place, with one history, one way of thinking and one way of doing things. It isn't. But, as the argument of this whole book suggests, we can all learn from each other – with all our diversity of knowledge and experience – and work together.

I use the term 'global health' in the subtitle of this book and elsewhere but more often talk about health globally – referring to the things that connect us all – threats, resources, knowledge and the need for shared action.

## TURNING THE WORLD UPSIDE DOWN *AGAIN* – THE STRUCTURE OF THE BOOK

The next six chapters are mainly about understanding the current situation:

- Chapters 2 and 3 offer an overview of health globally. Chapter 2 focuses on the internal world of health and health systems while Chapter 3 describes the wider forces from pandemics and politics to climate change and global initiatives that shape our health and well-being.
- Chapters 4 and 5 go into more detail on respectively health and poverty, and health and wealth.
- Chapters 6 and 7 consider the relationships between countries and the unfair exchange between higher- and lower-income countries. They look in turn at the migration of health workers and the export of western knowledge and ideologies.

The final six chapters are more focused on learning and the future:

- Chapters 8 and 9 discuss in turn what powerful high-income countries can learn from people in lower-income and less powerful countries and from communities in their own countries.
- Chapters 10 and 11 look respectively at people, communities and health workers and at science, equity and systems. They illustrate the sort of practical knowledge we are going to need to tackle the problems of the twenty-first century successfully.
- The last two chapters, 12 and 13, challenge traditional conceptions of health and health systems and propose action. Chapter 12 sets out some new and revived ideas about health creation, adapting western scientific medicine for the future, planetary health, and the critical enabling factors that will help bring about improvements in health globally. Chapter 13 proposes action to accelerate the changes that are already underway in many parts of the world, make them more visible and more coherent and help to improve health globally.

## THE STARTING POINT

There are many movements of people and ideas around the world, none with the monopoly of wisdom, which are helping shape the future. And there are many practical ideas for improvement, preventing disease and creating health and well-being. I have had my old ideas tested and changed by what I have seen and heard in recent years, and I have been reminded that, whatever else is going on in the world, change needs to happen in the most important places of all, namely our minds, our beliefs and our behaviours.

There is a great deal that is very positive that is already happening at the most local level. *Turning the World Upside Down Again* is about celebrating the people who are doing things – acting and not just talking about it – and seeking to accelerate progress. Its focus is on practical action and taking control for ourselves, however unpromising the wider environment.

Our starting point must surely always be to listen to the people who are most affected by the problems and changes we are dealing with.

What if we listened more to the mothers of Liverpool and of Zimbabwe, of Sao Paolo and of Bangladesh?

What if we listened more to the young people of Sweden and Pakistan, the well-known ones like Greta Thunberg and Malala Yousafzai, but also the unknown young nurses of Zimbabwe and Indonesia, Munashe Nyaka and Alenda Dwiadila who I have met, and others like them who care passionately about the future and are using their skills and knowledge to make their part of the world a better place to live?

I was reminded of how difficult it can be to listen – and the wide gulf between the technocratic approaches of the professionals and the lives of most people – by an encounter I witnessed between a very bright, well-meaning and experienced researcher and a group of women who were active on their housing estate in southern England. The researcher said something about them being deprived. They reacted by saying they weren't deprived.

'*What should we call you then?*' the researcher asked. '*Needy?*' she suggested as an alternative.

'*No,*' they replied. '*We are kind, members of the community, we look out for each other, and we want to make the place better.*'

We need to find better ways to overcome this gulf. Our health as individuals is intimately connected to the health of communities, the health of wider society and, ultimately, the health of the planet.

We are all involved in the problems, and we all need to be able to participate in the solutions.

## REFERENCES

1. Crisp N. *Turning the World Upside Down: The search for global health in the 21st century*. London: CRC Press, 2010.
2. https://sustainabledevelopment.un.org/content/documents/21252030%20Agenda%20 for%20Sustainable%20Development%20web.pdf (Accessed 8 November 2021).
3. Frenk J, Chen L, Bhutta ZA *et al*. Health professionals for a new century: transforming education to strengthen health systems in an interdependent world. *The Lancet*, December 2010; **376**(9756): 1923–58. doi: 10.1016/S0140-6736(10)61854-5.
4. Koplan JP, Bond TC, Merson MH *et al*. Towards a common definition of global health. *The Lancet*, June 2009; **373**(9679): 1993–5. doi: 10.1016/S0140-6736(09)60332-9. PMID 19493564. S2CID 6919716.
5. https://www.womeningh.org/ (Accessed 8 November 2021).
6. https://www.womenlifthealth.org/ (Accessed 8 November 2021).
7. Omaswa F, Crisp N (eds). *African Health Leaders: Making change and claiming the future*. Oxford: Oxford University Press, 2014.
8. Horton R. The real meaning of decolonisation. *The Lancet*, 27 November 2021. doi: https:// doi.org/10.1016/S0140-6736(21)02687-8 (Accessed 30 November 2021).

# Overview (1) – health and health systems

**2**

Perhaps the most striking thing about health in the twenty-first century is that the whole world is now so interconnected and so interdependent.

As we now know all too well from our own bitter experience, diseases travel; the COVID-19 coronavirus that boards a plane in Wuhan in the morning can be in Washington before the sun has set. As I write, the virus has now arrived back in China to infect people in Wuhan and other cities having travelled around the world and mutated en route. As we also know, the internet provides information and knowledge but also spreads ignorance, prejudice and superstition to every part of the world. Science and technology, too, create enormous benefit but can also bring new environmental and biological perils, which, like climate change, are already affecting us all.

This interdependence is changing the way we see health, creating a new global perspective and affecting the way we need to act. At the same time, there has been a growing understanding of the importance of context and localness and of how the environment, economy, society and political systems affect our health and well-being. This has been accompanied by recognition of the links between human and animal health and the environment – the so-called 'One Health' approach – in everything from zoonoses, where infectious diseases have crossed from animals to humans, to the use of antibiotics and the impact of farming on climate change and health.

Meanwhile science and technology are moving on at pace and creating new possibilities in all aspects of health and well-being.

*Turning the World Upside Down Again* is a search to understand what is happening and what it means for us. It is based on my own journey from running the largest health system in the world to working in some of the poorest countries, and it draws on my experiences in community work as well as health to explore new ideas, trends and innovations from around the world.

These next two chapters set the scene. This chapter focuses on health and health systems, describing some of the differences between countries and introducing the ideas of mutual learning and co-development. Chapter 3 provides an overview of the big global issues of pandemics, politics, climate change and solidarity.

This chapter argues that western scientific medicine, which has been such a dominant and successful force in the world, is no longer by itself capable of continuing to improve our health and there need to be radical changes in the health systems that are based on it. We also

DOI: 10.1201/9781003267706-2

need to understand how to make the best use of our ever-improving scientific knowledge and technology within a much wider context. And, unless we take account of the new global, social and political dimensions, we will be in constant danger of using twentieth-century ideas and tools to tackle twenty-first-century problems.

This chapter concludes with a discussion about our independence, our interdependence and the way human rights and the rule of law can help us achieve a balance between them. These ideas are expanded in the following chapter into a more ecological approach – linking human, community and planetary health.

## LIFE IN THE HILLS AND VALLEYS OF SOUTH WALES – HEALTH IN HIGH-INCOME COUNTRIES

A story of one family illustrates just how successful western scientific medicine has been in the past and how much health has improved for the populations of rich western countries in the last century.

Life in the hills and valleys of South Wales was much tougher in the 1920s and 1930s than it is today, and life expectancy was shorter. Half the population didn't reach retirement age, about 1 in 250 women died in childbirth, there was no health system for the poor and tuberculosis (TB) was rampant. It must have seemed to many people that things would never improve.

Ben Jenkins owned and operated a timber yard in Brecon with his brother and lived next door to it with his wife Ethel and their nine children and a maid. They were a relatively prosperous family and lived a very different life from the miners in the valleys below, who were constantly at risk from work-related diseases and the dangers of the coal mines. They were not poor and could afford to call the doctor; nevertheless, the Jenkins family faced tragedy.

Trevor, the eldest child, caught TB while working away from home and died aged 21 in 1929. Tragically, he had brought the disease home with him and most of the family became infected. Several were sent to sanatoria higher in the hills and two went to Switzerland in an effort to recover or escape the disease altogether. The treatment was only partially successful and both their daughters, Winifred and Betty, died of TB in the following years.

> The treatment was only partially successful and both their daughters, Winifred and Betty, died of TB in the following years.

David, the seventh son and youngest child, recalls being sent to a sanatorium for six months at the age of 9. His mother, who by this time had seen all her other children sicken, couldn't bear to say goodbye to another one, possibly for the last time, so the small boy found himself sent away with strangers to a vast hospital, not knowing what was happening to him and unable to communicate with his family.

The other children lived but the mother died early, of a broken heart according to family legend, although in reality of a brain tumour, in the week that her youngest child, David, went off to join his remaining brothers at war in 1942.

It was not just TB that was such a killer at the time. The story in those Welsh hills was that one funeral led to another. Standing hatless in the rain, mourners were at risk of pneumonia, still a regular killer in those pre-antibiotic days.

Today, having survived the risks of TB, pneumonia and war, my father-in-law David Jenkins is 98. He had three elder brothers still living when he turned 90. The Jenkins family can trace the story of how health has been transformed in the UK through the history of their own family, where the eldest died tragically young and the youngest survives. Sadly, the others have died.

The experience of the Jenkins family is by no means unique and life expectancy in the UK has increased by 30 years in the last century. That is 3 years in every decade or almost 8 hours more for every day that we lived. One need only translate this through into one's own life to see how significant this is. My life expectancy at birth was about 65. It is well above 80 for my grandchildren. We are truly very grateful to all concerned.

It's not just about life expectancy, of course. We are healthier and fitter in our 50s, 60s, 70s and 80s and beyond than our parents were at the same age. We have 'wonder' drugs that allow us to manage our heart disease and other conditions and we have replacement hips, knees and lenses that give us so much more freedom from our disabilities. We are much richer now as a society in the UK and therefore much more able to acquire labour-saving, life-enhancing devices and drugs than at any time in human history. And there is the promise of more to come thanks to spectacular advances in science and technology.

## HEALTH SYSTEMS THAT ARE INCREASINGLY UNFIT FOR PURPOSE

We can see how health in the UK has improved enormously over the last century, but we can also see that continuing growth in health services and funding is now only producing marginal benefits. It is the same story in many rich countries where massive increases in expenditure in recent years, planned as in the UK or unplanned as in the USA, have led to improvements but have not transformed health services. At the same time, the public is becoming more assertive, harder to please and less willing simply to follow medical advice and be passive and patient.

Life expectancy in the UK fell for the first time since the Second World War in 2018 due to an increase in non-communicable diseases. Other high-income countries saw similar falls and gains plateaued in many other high-income countries around the world. COVID-19 caused dramatic falls, with a report for the American National Academy of Science projecting that '*COVID-19 will reduce US life expectancy in 2020 by 1.13 years. Estimated reductions for the Black and Latino populations are 3 to 4 times that for Whites. Consequently, COVID-19 is expected to reverse over 10 years of progress made in closing the Black–White gap in life expectancy and reduce the previous Latino mortality advantage by over 70%.*'[1]

These figures illustrate both a reversal in the previously improving trend and growing inequalities. As we shall see in later chapters, the pandemic is not the only reason why inequalities are growing around the world.

Part of the reason for the wider health system problems and the dissatisfaction of the public is that the most significant diseases of the twenty-first century in richer countries are different from those in the twentieth century so that our health services have to deal with different problems.

With the obvious exception of a pandemic such as COVID, we are no longer generally so affected by communicable diseases such as TB; infections are better controlled, there is less injury and accidental death and many cancers are becoming manageable chronic conditions. It is now these long-term conditions and non-communicable diseases, such as cancers, heart disease and diabetes that require the most attention and use the most resources. There are more comorbidities, particularly among older people, and mental health has become more high profile and is being given higher priority in many countries.

The mismatch between current services and these changing needs is leading to increasing problems of quality and safety at the same time as there is rising public and professional concern about both. Using twentieth-century methods to deal with twenty-first-century problems is costly and inefficient but also risky and potentially very dangerous.

There need to be new and very different ways of dealing with these diseases – with more services created outside hospital, more involvement of the patient and much greater integration into other aspects of the patient's life such as education, employment and leisure activities. Many, perhaps most, clinicians and health workers have tried to change their practice accordingly. However, as I can describe from my own experience in the National Health Service (NHS), it is very difficult in practice to change the way healthcare is delivered.

> Using twentieth-century methods to deal with twenty-first-century problems is costly and inefficient but also risky and potentially very dangerous.

A major part of the difficulty in the UK and other countries with well-developed health systems is that the very factors that led to such improvements in the twentieth century – the essential features of western scientific medicine: scientific discovery, greater professionalism, commercial innovation and massively increased funding – are so invested in maintaining and developing the old models of delivery and behaviour that they make it difficult to create new ones and have themselves become part of the problem.

We have built up over the years such tremendously strong health systems that they condition what we can do in practice and, in effect, dictate what happens when people are ill. As a result, we may end up in hospital when we don't need to. We may be overinvestigated, overmedicated and, in all likelihood, overspent.

More problematically, these features of western scientific medicine have also conditioned our mindsets so that we have a very simple model in our minds of what good treatment looks like. We have come to expect treatment by doctors with the latest equipment and drugs in specialist facilities and hospitals, whether or not this is actually what we need for our particular problem or illness. Good treatment for our condition may actually be something else altogether.

The dominance of this way of thinking among politicians, health leaders and the public is so great that most attempts at reforming health systems in high-income countries have concentrated on getting the best out of the existing model, through improving the existing arrangements, incentivising doctors differently and making more productive use of equipment and facilities. These reforms have not, despite great rhetoric, generally led in any major way to designing completely different services and systems suitable for the longer-term conditions and chronic diseases we now face, let alone produced a major swing towards health creation and disease prevention.

> The dominance of this way of thinking . . . is so great that most attempts at reforming health systems in high-income countries have concentrated on getting the best out of the existing model.

Economic language and thinking have come to the fore as costs have risen and systems become stronger. We talk of supply and demand not services and needs, incentivising health workers not motivating them – or recognising that they have their own professional motivations – and tend to turn to financial and market levers to drive reform. It is curious how, particularly in the UK, discussion of reform almost always centres on the funding model and costs and not on what we are trying to achieve and how best to achieve it. It is a category mistake in which a complex health problem is reduced to a simple financial one.

Existing power structures and vested interests reinforce this dominant way of thinking at every turn. Almost any change, any innovation and any improvement will disadvantage somebody. Moving services to the community reduces hospital income. The empowerment of nurses and patients, which may be necessary to improve health, reduces the power of the doctors and commercial companies.

As I shall describe in later chapters, while many doctors, hospital chief executives and businesses are leading innovators and driving many of the improvements in the world, their professional and business associations recognise the threat to their power bases and react accordingly by opposing the change. This has happened time and again over the years, as when the UK's British Medical Association (BMA), the doctors' trade union, opposed the establishment of the NHS in 1948 until they were bought off, their *'mouths stuffed with gold'* in the words of the NHS founder Aneurin Bevan.

This history shows that it requires not only great political leadership and resolve to drive change in a complex field such as health but also consummate political skill to generate support and energy and negotiate around the obstacles. Politicians around the world know to their cost just how difficult this can be.

The problems with current health systems are growing. Looking to the future, health systems need to change radically. They need to give the same priority to mental health as they do to physical, and to recognise many people have needs in both areas. They also need to address the social aspects of health referred to in the World Health Organization (WHO) definition and take account of all the complex social, economic, economic, environmental and political determinants of health as *'A state of complete physical, mental and social well-being and not merely the absence of disease or infirmit'*[2] and therefore we need to be able to see health in the round in all its aspects and work with others outside the health system on all aspects of care, disease prevention and health creation.

> The problems with current health systems are growing. Looking to the future, health systems need to change radically.

There has been growing understanding of the social, economic, environmental and political determinants of health since the publication of the WHO's Commission on the Social Determinants of Health report in 2008, which has led to reviews being undertaken in many countries.[3]

Similarly, 'Health in All Policies'– an approach which assesses the health implications of policy decisions in all sectors in order to improve health and health equity and builds on ideas developing since the publication of the Ottawa Charter in 1986 – is now becoming widely accepted.[4]

However, neither of these approaches has as yet had a substantial impact on the way health systems are organised and operate in most countries. Existing institutions and power structures are proving unable and/or perhaps unwilling to adapt to these approaches. The COVID-19 pandemic, which, as we have already noted, has disproportionately affected poorer, more disadvantaged groups and ethnic minorities and deepened inequalities, may prove a turning point by spurring governments into action.

Ilona Kickbush has been a leading exponent of both these closely related approaches and established a programme on health diplomacy at the Graduate Centre in Geneva that seeks to take this wider understanding of health deep into government and into foreign policy and international relationships.[5]

Lasting change will require political leadership as well as changes in mindsets in all sectors.

There is an enormous amount of innovative and creative activity underway throughout the world which is attempting to take on these challenges. Some of this is about human relationships, the anthropology and sociology of health, and understanding the dynamics of health as a system and creating learning health and care systems. There are also advances in AI, science and technology that can help to bring about transformation, disrupting current practice and introducing new models and approaches. We should note, however, that these advances can also be used to reinforce the existing system and behaviours.

Underpinning all this potential for change is the education and development of health workers and the evolution of their roles in the future. How the professionals conceive and think about health will shape the future. Their role as agents of change in leading, shaping services and facilitating others will be crucial, as described in an important report led by Julio Frenk and Lincoln Chen, the title and subtitle of which very effectively describe its contents: *Health professionals for a new century: transforming education to strengthen health systems in an interdependent world.*[6]

We also need to recognise the intimate links between health and wealth. Increasing wealth enables countries to spend more on health and improving health promotes productivity and the economy. Dame Sally Davies, the former Chief Medical Officer for England, described *'health as one of the primary assets of our nation'* in her 2018 report.[7]

In an interview, she went on to say that *'(health) . . . is often perceived as a cost to the public but we must reposition health as an investment. If employers invest in their staff's health, productivity will increase, sick days will reduce and the economy will grow. Investing in health is a win for everyone.'*[8]

## FROM WALES TO BANGLADESH – HEALTH IN LOW- AND MIDDLE-INCOME COUNTRIES

Turning to low- and middle-income countries we find that, in some of them, just like in Wales in the 1920s, half the population today does not reach their equivalent of retirement age, 1 in 220 women in low-income countries died in childbirth in 2017,[9] there is no health system for the poorest and TB is rampant. It must seem to many people that things will never improve.

I recalled the Jenkins family history as I flew back from Bangladesh in 2008 and thought about the poverty and the illness I had seen there. What were the chances of a similar transformation in Bangladesh, I wondered? More importantly, why wasn't it already happening? We know what to do clinically about all the most common diseases and problems. There has been an enormous investment in aid and development. It seemed outrageous that it wasn't just happening. What was getting in the way?

I had begun to think about these issues when the Prime Minister, Tony Blair, had asked me to consider what more the UK could do to use its experience and expertise to help improve health in developing countries.[10] I had reported to him in 2007 but had remained involved in health globally. On this occasion, as Chair of the UK charity Sightsavers, I had been visiting eye services in Bangladesh and had been reminded by my visit of the enormous contrast there was between health in richer and poorer countries.

I had spent more than 5 years as the Chief Executive of England's NHS. It is the largest integrated health service and the fourth biggest organisation in the world, with 1.3 million employees and a turnover by 2021 of around £150 billion a year. Only the Chinese Army, the Indian railways and Walmart have more employees.

In some ways, these organisations seem to reflect the countries themselves. They draw attention to China's power, India's size and the links between its million villages and its great towns and cities, and America's love of commerce. For the UK, the NHS undoubtedly represents something about us as a nation. It is a universal system; mainly tax-funded, which is designed to offer services to every citizen, equally, regardless of their ability to pay. Love it or hate it, the NHS says something about the British and our ideas about fairness and compassion.

On that flight from Bangladesh I was coming home from a country that has a very different way of life and a very different health system, where many of the services provided for the poor aren't run or sponsored by the government but by the Bangladesh Rural Action Committee (BRAC). BRAC is a voluntary organisation, possibly the largest non-governmental organisation (NGO) in the world, which brings together hundreds of thousands of Bangladeshis in local groups to plan and organise its services and activities.

BRAC doesn't just deal with health; it deals with education and other public services as well. It runs empowerment groups for women, teaching them how to take action to better their lives and those of their families. It has its own microfinance bank to provide small loans to enable people, mainly women, to earn a living, allowing them to purchase seed or farming tools or to buy goods that they can sell on in the local markets. It runs a university and shops and is prepared to be involved and invest in any practical approaches that benefit the poor.

BRAC is a remarkable example of people who are not prepared to wait for others to help them but have taken the future into their own hands and are creating their own solutions. The way they do things challenges the top-down, professionalised and commercialised mindset that is so common in high-income countries. Even this short description shows just how differently services are organised in Bangladesh from the model described earlier.

> The way they do things challenges the top-down, professionalised and commercialised mindset that is so common in high-income countries.

Funding is also managed differently. In Bangladesh, as in several other low-income countries, I saw microfinance systems paying out loans for healthcare and a system of cross-subsidy in place where those who were able to were expected to pay for their services, while the poorest got them free. Everyone, however, received the same attention and the same clinical service – except for the elite, of course, who went elsewhere, possibly out of the country altogether.

BRAC, like the NHS, represents an idea, an ideal and a sense of justice and community. It was founded in 1972 during the country's struggles for independence from Pakistan and embodies the values of self-determination and self-sufficiency of that period. At the very same time that we had been agonising in the NHS over issues such as the proper use of new and expensive technology and how to get the best value from major new expenditure, BRAC was struggling in Bangladesh with the consequences of poverty and neglect and the problem of providing even the most basic healthcare to a large part of their population.

Self-determination and local control, so well exemplified by BRAC and other organisations, is a major theme of *Turning the World Upside Down Again* and will be referred to in later chapters. For the moment, however, let us return to my own question of why, despite the efforts of inspiring organisations like BRAC and despite the years of aid, big improvements were not already happening? Three reasons stand out. There are three levels of problems to confront at the same time; each is formidable and together they show how extremely difficult it is to make a truly transformational change.

First, dealing purely with health issues, there is simply very much more disease and very many more causes of disease, injury and death than we now see in high-income countries. Communicable diseases such as malaria, TB and human immunodeficiency virus (HIV)/acquired immune deficiency syndrome (AIDS) are rife in many countries, the non-communicable diseases are becoming more common, and injury and death from conflict, traffic accidents and employment are widespread.

At the second level, poverty affects health in myriad ways and makes it much harder to make improvements. Around 700 million people around the world were living in extreme poverty (defined as less than US$1.90 a day in 2015), while close to 46% of the world's population was living on less than US$5.50 a day. It is not, of course, as if these few dollars are available every day: some days it may be more, some days less or nothing. They are living on the edge and can easily be pushed over it into destitution, famine and death by disease, drought or war.[11]

The health of many of the poorest people in the poorest countries is truly dreadful. The statistics are now so often repeated that they can easily be ignored; unless, of course, you decide to make it personal by thinking about your own children or relatives when you hear that 1 in 13 children dies before the age of 5 across the whole of sub-Saharan Africa, with some countries having 1 child dying in every 7 before their fifth birthday.[12]

It is almost worse to know that most of these deaths could so easily be avoided, even in the poorest countries, if there were clean water, insecticide-treated mosquito bed nets, adequate food and housing and better access to simple treatment, advice and education. All of these contribute to health while their absence leaves the way clear for illness, disability and death. People need more than just health services to improve their health.

People need more than just health services to improve their health.

Poverty also means that, in many countries, there is no health system to speak of, with few facilities and with difficulties in staffing and providing drugs, particularly in rural areas. Where health systems in richer countries may be too strong, they are often perilously weak in poorer ones and access to care may be haphazard, of uncertain quality and, where available, very costly.

At the third and deepest level, we can also see how social, economic and political factors – and the exercise of power – both within a country and globally affect health profoundly. The education of women is crucial in securing the health of their children while their own position in society often dictates whether they can – or are allowed to by their men folk – get access to trained health workers or whether they must instead use traditional healers and remedies. This contributes to the fact that over a quarter of a million women each year die in low- and middle-income countries in childbirth or as a result of pregnancy.[9]

Maternal death is the very epitome of a twenty-first-century problem. It is about social and economic factors as much as it is about the availability of appropriate treatment and healthcare. Indeed, given that the clinical care and treatment of pregnant women is so well understood, the social factors are the most significant and intractable barrier to improvement. It is a statement of the obvious that mothers are crucial to good health. Each death is a personal tragedy for themselves and their families. They protect the health of their families. They educate and train their children in healthy habits. They lead health improvement efforts in any community. Their death or absence almost always means the absence of emotional security and stability and has long-term detrimental effects on their children.

> Maternal death is the very epitome of a twenty-first-century problem. It is about social and economic factors as much as it is about the availability of appropriate treatment and healthcare.

Power is exercised globally very largely by the high-income countries of the West and the major powers of China, India and Russia, acting individually or together through the G7, G20, UN Security Council or other groupings. The pandemic has shown the stark reality of power, and the many ways it operates, with vaccines being developed and manufactured almost exclusively in these countries and distributed first to their citizens.

There are many other social, economic and political factors which make it harder for lower-income countries to grow and develop. The other obvious example is the way economic and trade relationships are concentrated among the wealthiest regions of the world. They keep the money flowing and growing largely among themselves to the exclusion of poorer countries.

The whole continent of Africa, for example, still plays only a marginal role in world trade. African trade in goods and services has stayed at around 3% of global exports and imports on average for several years.[13]

The countries of sub-Saharan Africa, the far larger part of the continent, account for little more than 2% of world trade. These countries also have a heavy dependency on imports. In Mozambique, for example, trade represents 96% of GDP with exports at only 26%. Moreover, as Evita Schmieg reports, 'Sub-Saharan Africa's exports to the rest of the world remain dominated by raw materials; almost two-thirds comprise fuels, ores and metals, and another 15 percent agricultural products. Only 16 percent are finished products, whose export is crucial for value creation and employment in these economies. In this respect there has been little change since colonial times.'[14] Around 67% of imports to sub-Saharan African countries, on the other hand, are high-value finished products.

Moreover, the bigger economies are also better able to subsidise their own producers at the expense of others. To take one example, the USA subsidised its own agricultural producers by US$22.4 billion in 2019. This rose to US$46.5 billion or 39% of net farm income in 2020, reflecting increases due to aid for the pandemic.[15] These subsidies help drive down international prices in commodities such as cotton to the disadvantage of many much poorer countries. For comparison, the USA's total overseas development aid amounted to US$35.5 billion in 2020, net of bilateral debt relief.[16]

In addition, lower-income countries have little access to capital, are worse affected by trade fluctuations and don't have the power and the positions in world organisations to lobby and negotiate effectively.[17] Their citizens generally have the poorer and less well-paid jobs in international organisations and processes, although there has been considerable progress on this in the last decade. However, they are still disproportionately the miners not the manufacturers, the farmers not the processors and, in the worst cases, the exploited child and adult labour not the protected workforce.

The African Union's adoption of a free trade area which is designed to address some of these problems is described in Chapter 7.

In health itself, as we shall see later, there is a particularly unfair import–export business where higher-income countries import trained health workers from lower-income countries and export their ideas and ideologies about healthcare to them in return. It is not a fair trade. Trained workers from lower-income countries emigrate to find their fortunes, leaving their homeland the poorer for the loss of the investment in their training as well as their talent.

High-income countries, in turn, export their ideas and ideologies about health and medicine alongside their aid. In many cases, these ideas and ideologies are inappropriate and may be out of date and discredited in their countries of origin. It is not just in health, of course, that ideas and ideologies are exported with aid and development.

> High-income countries, in turn, export their ideas and ideologies about health and medicine alongside their aid.

The major donors and development agencies have moved, in recent years largely, beyond the idea of simple charity and doing things to and for people towards the idea of helping them to do things for themselves. There is a great deal written by donors about country-led plans and country-led development, but in reality there is still very often a largely one-way relationship with donors and development agencies deciding what happens in a country, sometimes regardless of the wishes of the country itself, and attaching their own conditions to the support. They attach their own conditions to the financial support in order to secure accountability to their own government, but there is still little idea of accountability to the recipient country and virtually no conception of mutual benefit.

International aid and development is itself going through a period of great change. The established agencies and donors, largely from western democracies, have created one pattern of giving that, in theory at least, is consistent across the world. Even they, however, have had their differences, with the largest donor, the USA, remaining outside this broad consensus until the recent change of administration.

The other great and emerging powers of China, India, Russia and, to some extent, Brazil have different ideas and are engaging in bilateral negotiations with poorer countries often to gain preferential trade agreements and secure natural resources. Oil and minerals are great attractions for investors, but so, too, are land and the food it can produce. Sudan, Ethiopia, Congo and Pakistan are among the countries that have leased over 20 million hectares of farmland, an area almost half the size of Spain, to foreigners who use it to grow food for their own populations and not for the locals, however hungry.[18]

China has become a very active development partner with its Belt and Road initiative and invested US$47 billion in 2020, a COVID-19-induced fall of 54% from over US$100 billion in 2019.[19] This provides funding without the sort of conditions imposed by western aid agencies but on a more commercial basis, where failure to pay back loans can lead, for example in Zambia – where debts amount to a possible US$23 billion – to China owning large parts of the infrastructure.[20]

## TURNING THE WORLD UPSIDE DOWN – LEARNING FROM LOWER-INCOME AND LESS POWERFUL COUNTRIES

We can all learn from people and organisations in lower-income and less powerful countries – BRAC is a wonderful example and there are many others. There are, for example, countries in South East Asia such as Vietnam which have shown how, in the right circumstances, enormous change can be made. They follow on from the established economic success of others such as the Republic of Korea and Singapore. As importantly, there is an evident can-do spirit in much of Africa, with new health leaders and scientists emerging and a ferment of new ideas and applications. Overall, many millions have been lifted out of poverty in recent years. However, very sadly, COVID-19 has reversed some of this gain.

There is another way of looking at the world in which we turn it upside down and ask what would it be like if the import–export business in health workers and ideas described earlier was reversed? What if poorer countries exported their ideas and experience rather than their health workers, and what if richer ones exported their health workers while learning from poorer ones?

Some months before I visited Bangladesh, I had been in Ethiopia, where I met a young British consultant, Dr Martin Beed. He was working in Jimma University Hospital in southern Ethiopia for a short period as part of a partnership scheme with Nottingham University Hospital in the UK. Every year for the last 15 the hospitals had been exchanging small groups of staff for up to a month at a time. The original idea (and still the main purpose) was to help train and educate health workers from the Jimma Hospital both in Jimma itself and on their visits to the UK. Increasingly, however, it had become obvious that the British people also benefited, learning about Ethiopia and about themselves at the same time.

It had become obvious that the British people also benefited, learning about Ethiopia and about themselves at the same time.

Jimma University Hospital is fairly typical of the larger old African hospitals with a few modern buildings of three or four storeys, used mostly by the University, surrounded by mainly single-storey wards and departments. It was in reasonable repair, although the concrete blocks, bare plaster and curtainless windows contrasted sharply even with Nottingham's oldest buildings.

I asked Dr Beed why he had decided to work there. He told me that one of the reasons he had wanted to join the scheme was because there had been a large increase in TB where he worked in Nottingham. There had been five cases in the intensive care unit in the previous year and he wanted to go somewhere where they understood the disease well and he could gain more experience of it.

In the event, he had learned about TB, but he had also been surprised to see that the local staff had such good clinical skills, better than many, if not most, UK doctors. By this he meant that, in the absence of all the equipment, nurses and doctors needed to look at the patient properly, talk to them, assess the feel and texture of their skin and pulse and make a clinical judgement from their verbal and other responses. All this had to be done without the instruments British doctors would have relied on at home.

I asked what else had surprised him in Ethiopia. He told me that he was teaching on a direct-entry anaesthetics course, where people with high school education were trained to use a range of anaesthetics after 4 years' training. This is very uncommon in the UK or other rich countries, yet it is the backbone of the anaesthetic service in many sub-Saharan African countries. We generally require full medical training before anyone can give anaesthetics.

Moreover, he had been intrigued to see the way that education in Jimma University was so entirely community-based. At every stage and at every opportunity, students of every discipline from agriculture to healthcare were linked to local communities and learned their profession and skills in the field rather than just in the classroom.

As Dr Abraham Haileamlak, the Vice President for Clinical Service at Jimma University explained, he wanted to train people who could and would practise in the real conditions of rural Ethiopia. The three Medical Schools in Addis Ababa, he told me, used American curricula and produced doctors better suited to emigrate than to work in their own country. Here in Jimma he trained them for their own country.

These things challenged our preconceived ideas. Dr Beed and I could have seen this as just being a sad story of students who didn't have proper equipment and facilities and who were therefore being forced to learn, inadequately, from what was at hand. But we didn't see it like that at all, although we knew, of course, that more money, more people and more equipment would make an enormous difference.

We realised that we were meeting able people who were getting a good grounding in their professions by learning from their patients and their communities as well as from their professors. We saw, too, that their education was based on knowing what was needed locally. It was based on their context and their circumstances. As Dr Beed put it in a later article: *'Although resource-poor, the medical staff were far from knowledge-poor.'*[21]

Although resource-poor, the medical staff were far from knowledge-poor.

*Dr Martin Beed*

If we only try to look, we can find many more examples where richer countries can learn from importing the ideas and experience of poorer countries. In countries as different as India and Uganda, health leaders are using the natural strengths of their countries, the sense of community and family and the desire for self-determination, to promote health and provide healthcare. They are supporting their women as the natural health leaders, linking microfinance schemes and health insurance and finding ways to reconcile local traditional medicine and its practitioners with the western scientific tradition.

There is no shortage of ideas and examples to copy. In Brazil, Mozambique and elsewhere, governments are educating health workers to meet the needs of the country and not just of the professions. Local health workers, often called clinical officers, are trained in 3 years to deal with specific tasks such as undertaking caesarean sections or cataract operations, which require a full professional education elsewhere. Meanwhile, as we shall see later, international good practices in conditions as different as HIV/AIDS and club-foot have been developed from experience in Africa. The potential for learning from low- and middle-income countries is discussed in more detail in Chapter 8.

Health workers from high-income countries can also make valuable contribution to low- and middle-income countries. There is a long and important tradition of partnerships between hospitals and communities in richer and poorer countries and many people have travelled as paid workers, researchers or volunteers, individually or through organised schemes, to work in poorer countries. They and the country can both benefit.

There are thousands more health workers in rich countries who would gladly offer their skills to poor countries if the circumstances were right. They could support local people and institutions, train thousands more health workers in their own countries and help transform the lives of whole populations. Groups from the diaspora, the migrants themselves and their children, are often also keen to help and can make a distinctive contribution.

In return, they would learn for themselves how to see their own world differently and to challenge the old assumptions of the industrialised health systems. Lower-income countries, precisely because they have so few resources, have to learn how to engage patients and communities in their own care, how to prioritise prevention and health creation over tackling illness, how to deploy new technologies effectively and how to manage the ever-growing burden of costs. These are exactly the sorts of issues that need to be grasped in high-income countries as they come to terms with the diseases and long-term conditions of the twenty-first century. There is much that they might learn from experience in these lower-income countries.

I have been very struck by the way that some leaders in lower-income countries, without either having the resources or being burdened by the established practices of the high-income countries, have created new approaches and new ways of dealing with old problems. It is equally evident that many health workers from high-income countries who find themselves dealing with patients in lower-income countries without all their usual resources frequently find different ways of doing things. They learn for themselves and, if their home country were more receptive, might bring these ideas back home to great effect.

> They learn for themselves and, if their home country were more receptive,
> might bring these ideas back home to great effect.

I have also been impressed by the way that many young health professionals, the students, doctors, nurses and others that I have met in the UK and the USA, see their careers very differently from their parents' generation and are nurturing new ideas and approaches. While their elders are preoccupied by running complex health systems and struggling to work out how to pay for all the new high-tech and high-cost treatments that industry can develop, many young professionals are interested in health globally and in how society, the economy and the environment shape our health and our lives.

There is now a very considerable focus on inequalities which has been reinforced by the experience of COVID-19 and a demand for understanding the roots of inequalities and injustice – whether this is about racism, gender, class or simply poverty – and for tackling them. As already noted, there is nothing more unequal than a difference in life expectancy of 10 or 20 years or even more between different parts of a country or between whole countries. These differences in life expectancy are accompanied by differences in health with greater morbidity, sickness and suffering more likely in lower-income countries and communities.

Both groups, the leaders in low-income countries and the young professionals everywhere, are creating a new way of thinking about health. They are developing a new and explicitly global outlook that recognises our interdependency and its implications but also stresses the uniqueness of each situation and the way that the local blend of social, political, economic and environmental circumstances affects health.

This approach respects the evidence of science and seeks to understand how things get done in practice and what role patients and the public play alongside scientists and clinicians. It doesn't start, as western medical education has traditionally done, by studying the science and then applying it to society but, rather, turns the world upside down, starts with understanding society and seeks to apply the findings from both the natural and the social sciences. It is a profound difference that influences the way that clinicians think and behave.

> It doesn't start . . . by studying the science and then applying it to society but . . . turns the world upside down and starts with understanding society and seeks to apply the findings from both the natural and the social sciences. It is a profound difference that influences the way that clinicians think and behave.

This approach of learning from lower-income countries and younger people when combined with the new sciences and technologies – where the internet, genomics, AI and engineering are already turning our world upside down – will help us confront and tackle the challenges of the future.

I have spent some time in the last 3 years meeting with people in different communities in my own country, when the pandemic allowed, in an effort to understand how they are improving their communities and creating health. There are striking similarities with low- and middle-income countries in the way that UK authorities, planners and officials attempt to intervene in and improve these communities. They, too, frequently plan for the communities and not with them, producing top-down solutions and failing to listen to local concerns and ideas.

Conditions in low- and middle-income countries are, of course, generally much worse than in the UK. However, a remark made by Hazel Stutely, the co-founder of C2 Connecting Communities, that *'Communities know how to heal themselves'*,[22] is very reminiscent of the question I have heard many people ask: *'Why don't development workers support us in what we know needs doing rather than imposing their own ideas?'*

> Communities know how to heal themselves.
>
> *Hazel Stutely*

In the UK and other countries, we can also learn from our own poorer communities and groups representing or working with particular parts of the population. We can also see in high-income countries how disability campaigners, social entrepreneurs and community activists are using concepts of human rights and responsibilities to challenge traditional thinking and redesign services. They provide interesting parallels, with activity and activists in lower-income countries working towards self-determination and building their own future for themselves. They are showing us that the future is about rights and human justice not charity.

A great deal of technology, knowledge and basic resources need to be transferred from the rich world to the poor if the health of the poorest is to be improved. However, at the same time and partly due to their very poverty, pioneers and leaders in lower-income countries are developing new ideas and new approaches to health that may have real relevance and application in high-income countries. We can all learn from each other.

This exploration of examples and experiences around the world allows us to start to identify the practical knowledge of people and societies, science and systems that will be necessary for the future, the twenty-first-century knowledge that will equip our health workers and ourselves to address the needs of the twenty-first century. They no longer need to work with the ideas and tools of the twentieth century.

## INDEPENDENCE, INTERDEPENDENCE AND HUMAN RIGHTS

We can see the beginnings of a new approach here. The authorities of the old system, the vested interests that keep it in place, may not understand it, but the world is shifting around them. There is a movement of people and of ideas and, as we explore further, three ideas seem to be central to it.

It is, firstly, concerned with independence, control and self-determination. Personal, cultural and social issues determine what people value and how they want to live their lives and manage their health. Health is no longer seen simply as the absence of disease or a sense of well-being, but as independence and the ability to live lives we have reason to value, whether we are rich or poor, old or young, disabled or dying. We want our lives back when we are ill, we want to retain our independence when we are old, and we want to be the judges of our own quality of life.

Secondly, it is based on our interdependence and on mutuality. It values the contributions of laypeople alongside professionals and the public sector alongside the private, and stresses the importance of family and community, with the leading role of women at its heart. It embraces the understanding that, when countries work together, everyone gains. Benefits are mutual. There are opportunities for shared learning and co-development and – in our present troubled world – for tackling our great shared problems.

Thirdly, it embodies the belief that health is a basic human right and that the rule of law should be upheld. People are entitled to expect their governments to safeguard and promote their health just as they expect them to defend the country and ensure public safety, the education of children and economic stability. They also expect them to create a fair and just society and tackle inequalities wherever they are found. This is accompanied by a demand for greater openness and accountability at every level of authority. We no longer take everything on trust. We want to see the evidence.

Figure 2.1 shows the three central ideas of independence, interdependence, and human rights and the rule of law. We will explore these further in the following chapters.

---

**Independence** – and the ability to live the life we have reason to value
**Interdependence** – family, community, mutual learning and co-development
**Human rights and the rule of law** – government safeguarding our independence and our interdependence

---

**Figure 2.1** Independence, interdependence, human rights and the rule of law.

## REFERENCES

1. Andrasfay T, Goldman N. Reductions in 2020 US life expectancy due to COVID-19 and the disproportionate impact on the Black and Latino populations. *PNAS*, February 2021; **118**(5) e2014746118, doi: 10.1073/pnas.2014746118. https://www.pnas.org/content/118/5/e2014746118 (Accessed 10 November 2021).
2. https://www.who.int/about/governance/constitution (Accessed 6 February 2022).
3. WHO. *Closing the Gap in a Generation: Health equity through action on the social determinants of health*. Geneva: WHO, August 2008. https://www.who.int/publications/i/item/9789241563703 (Accessed 10 November 2021).
4. WHO. Health in All Policies (HiAP) Framework for Country Action. https://www.who.int/healthpromotion/hiapframework.pdf (Accessed 10 November 2021).
5. Kickbusch I, Nikogosian H, Kazatchkine M, Koeny M. *A Guide to Global Health Diplomacy: Better health – improved global solidarity – more equity*. Geneva: Global Health Centre, 2021. https://www.graduateinstitute.ch/sites/internet/files/2021-02/GHC-Guide.pdf (Accessed 10 November 2021).
6. Frenk J, Chen L, Bhutta ZA *et al*. Health professionals for a new century: transforming education to strengthen health systems in an interdependent world. *The Lancet*, December 2010; **376**(9756): 1923–58. doi: 10.1016/S0140-6736(10)61854-5.
7. https://assets.publishing.service.gov.uk/government/uploads/system/uploads/attachment_data/file/767549/Annual_report_of_the_Chief_Medical_Officer_2018_-_health_2040_-_better_health_within_reach.pdf (Accessed 10 November 2021).
8. https://www.health.org.uk/news-and-comment/newsletter-features/investing-in-health-is-a-win-for-everyone (Accessed 10 November 2021).
9. https://www.who.int/news-room/fact-sheets/detail/maternal-mortality (Accessed 10 November 2021).

10. Crisp N. Global Health Partnerships: the UK contribution to health in developing countries. 2007. https://www.who.int/workforcealliance/knowledge/resources/global healthpartnerships/en/ (Accessed 10 November 2021).

11. https://www.worldbank.org/en/news/press-release/2018/10/17/nearly-half-the-world-lives-on-less-than-550-a-day (Accessed 9 November 2021).

12. https://www.who.int/news-room/fact-sheets/detail/children-reducing-mortality (Accessed 10 November 2021).

13. https://www.wto.org/english/res_e/publications_e/strengthening_africa2021_e.htm (Accessed 10 November 2021).

14. https://www.swp-berlin.org/publications/products/arbeitspapiere/Afrika_Globalisierung.pdf (Accessed 10 November 2021).

15. https://www.cato.org/commentary/examining-americas-farm-subsidy-problem (Accessed 10 November 2021).

16. https://data.oecd.org/oda/net-oda.htm (Accessed 10 November 2021).

17. Crump L, Maswood SJ. *Developing Countries and Global Trade Negotiations*. Oxford: Routledge, 2007.

18. Land deals in Africa and Asia: cornering foreign fields. *The Economist* [Online] 21 May 2009. https://www.economist.com/leaders/2009/05/21/cornering-foreign-fields (Accessed 10 November 2021).

19. https://green-bri.org/china-belt-and-road-initiative-bri-investment-report-2020/ (Accessed 10 November 2021).

20. https://globalriskinsights.com/2020/12/the-curse-of-the-white-elephant-the-pitfalls-of-zambias-dependence-on-china/ (Accessed 10 November 2021).

21. Crisp N. *Turning the World Upside Down. The search for global health in the 21st century*. London: RSM Press, 2010.

22. https://www.c2connectingcommunities.co.uk/ (Accessed 10 November 2021).

# 3  Overview (2) – pandemics, politics, climate change and global solidarity

There is a very large agenda of shared health issues globally. The most obvious, of course, is our shared vulnerability to infectious diseases, but interdependence goes far wider and deeper. This chapter examines some of the ways in which we are interdependent, from pandemics and geo-politics to shared knowledge and a mobile health workforce.

The experience of COVID-19 is already bringing about long-term changes in our health systems and societies and has forced us to recognise the importance of inequalities and re-examine our ideas about global solidarity. The impact of climate change will be even more dramatic. This chapter looks at how both will affect health globally and how health systems need to respond.

The chapter concludes with a discussion about how we might think about health in ecological terms and introduces the idea that we should focus on the causes of health as well as the causes of disease.

How we think about health is very important and we can see it through a variety of lenses, none of which can give us the whole picture. We can view it in purely epidemiological terms, describing diseases, prevalence and impact. We can see it through the biology of genetics, proteins, viruses and evolution. We can think of it in psychological terms about the impact on individuals and their behaviour. We can take sociological, cultural or anthropological lenses and consider the impact on societies and communities and how health is defined and valued.

Public health and population health bring many of these perspectives together. However, as noted in the last chapter, health is very commonly talked about in the West in economic terms, with discussion of costs and benefits and the use of terms borrowed from economics such as supply and demand instead of services and needs, assets instead of people, and incentivising rather than motivating health workers. This fits well with the business world and seeing health as an industry, people as consumers and health as a commodity to be handled in the same way as any other within a capitalist framework. This one-dimensional version of health, however, doesn't fit well with people's experience, beliefs or fears – and doesn't fully meet their needs.

DOI: 10.1201/9781003267706-3

Health is all these things and is also, of course, political, and it is no surprise that different approaches to health are a sharp political dividing line in many societies. Decisions about health policy are very often political decisions, sometimes to the total exclusion of other perspectives.

*Turning the World Upside Down Again* uses different lenses at different times. They all offer insights. It is important to know about costs and power, and it is also important to understand culture and beliefs and how they impact on successful care and treatment. There is a discussion in Chapter 10, for example, of the idea that the primary diagnosis is almost always social.

Here, we start with a discussion of epidemics, which are distinguished from pandemics only by scale: an epidemic affects a large number of people within a community, population or region while a pandemic is an epidemic that's spread over multiple countries or continents. I suspect that COVID-19 was viewed by us all initially purely as a dangerous virus, but we rapidly had to realise that it has much bigger economic and social ramifications.

Some commentators have described COVID-19 as a 'syndemic', meaning it is a coming together of a biological threat with an underlying social crisis – here one of inequality – which amplifies its impact and effect. Merrill Singer, who coined the expression in the 1990s, is quoted as saying: *'It means we have to consider not just biological issues but the social structural forces that propel disease interaction, population vulnerability and unequal access to healthcare, including, once we have them, Covid-19 vaccines.'*[1]

It seems to me, however, that all epidemics and perhaps all diseases are like this. They need to find their social niche in which they can thrive most effectively. COVID-19 has found its perfect place in a modern world with great communications, unhealthy populations and social conditions which put large numbers at risk.

The idea of a syndemic is useful, however, in drawing attention to the way we need to think about epidemics, using all the lenses at our disposal.

## EPIDEMICS

Recent experience of epidemics and pandemics, including severe acute respiratory syndrome (SARS) in 2003, H1N1 (swine flu) in 2009 and Ebola in 2014, should have prepared us better for COVID-19. There were plenty of warnings from experts which I echoed in *Turning the World Upside Down*. I also added in words that I hope are not too prescient: *'we can also easily imagine how terrorists or, indeed, rogue governments and armies could use biological agents to blackmail, disable and kill.'*

Some of the countries most directly involved learned lessons from these earlier epidemics, but many governments failed to prepare and reacted very slowly at the beginning of the current pandemic – or downplayed or even denied the dangers. Now, however, health security, our ability to reduce and manage these natural and man-made threats, has become a matter of concern to us all. Governments are beginning to understand fully what many public health experts have told us for years, that the health of one nation affects its neighbours and that we need to share our knowledge and build our defences together. We are only as strong as our weakest part, wherever that may be.

**We are only as strong as our weakest part, wherever that may be.**

We have seen this demonstrated starkly in the last few months as new variants emerge in countries where very few people have been vaccinated and spread globally. High levels of vaccination in richer countries had appeared to be holding the disease in check, but these new variants are causing great concern. It will be 2023 before most of the world is vaccinated and many more years before the long-term impact of the pandemic begins to fade. Even then, some things will have changed for ever.

There are still so many things we don't know about COVID-19: what further mutations we will see, what will be its long-term effects on body systems, what long COVID is, how effective the vaccinations will be in the long term, and what side effects they will have. The most hopeful view is that COVID-19 will fade into the background in the next 2 or 3 years and become, like the causes of earlier pandemics, just one of the coronaviruses circulating around the world and causing variants of the common cold. The least hopeful is that the lengthy period before the large majority of the world's population is vaccinated will provide many more opportunities for new and dangerous variations to emerge.

Whatever happens, it will leave behind a trail of destroyed lives, mental health problems, damaged economies and a very large number of people with other diseases who have been untreated during the pandemic, some of whom will not recover while others will be added to waiting lists of record lengths. The damage to the economy will bring with it further damage to health as people lose jobs, business models change and spending on many public services is reduced. Children and young people have missed important parts of their education, homelessness is growing, and disrupted supply chains are causing shortages.

COVID has revealed all too starkly the problems at the heart of governments and in the partnerships and international organisations that bring peoples and countries together globally to fight disease and create health.

The pandemic has also highlighted differences in attitudes and behaviours within as well as between countries, widening some divisions and creating others. It has shown us very clearly the way inequalities and social circumstances affect health. It has affected the poorest and most vulnerable in all societies more than the more affluent and secure. Those countries and groups who were further behind are being left further behind, a point we return to later in the chapter.

There have been some positive consequences of the pandemic. The way in which some communities have come together, strengthening local bonds, has been impressive, as is the way many businesses have reacted, finding new openings and opportunities. Science is benefiting, and there is a new emphasis on research and development with the rapid development of vaccinations and treatments, greater use of technology and some unfreezing of attitudes that will undoubtedly lead to greater innovation and creativity in the future. We have also seen in some countries a new respect for health workers and an increase in people wanting to join the health systems and the professions.

The legacy of COVID-19 will be with us for years to come and its impact will be discussed in more detail later in the chapter. First, however, we will look briefly at other global epidemics that are having massive impacts now and will continue into the future.

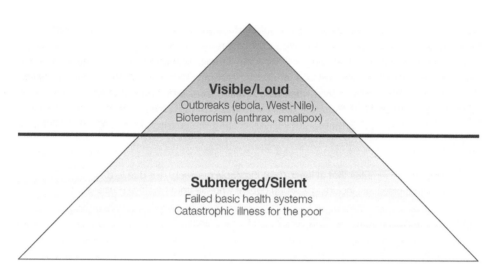

**Figure 3.1** The iceberg of hidden epidemics and developing crises. From Lincoln Chen and Vasant Narasimhan.[2]

Lincoln Chen and Vasant Narasimhan drew attention to the existence of hidden epidemics in 2002. They point out that, under the very visible health threats that we can all understand – such as disease outbreaks and bio-terrorism – there are much larger hidden epidemics of more common diseases and health failures which already exist and particularly affect poorer people and communities. If these are not tackled, they can breed personal and national insecurity and, of course, incubate new strains and diseases. They illustrate this with the analogy of an iceberg: part is visible; a larger part is hidden, as shown in Figure 3.1.[2]

We see this very clearly in the way that new strains of multidrug-resistant and extremely drug resistant TB are spreading rapidly around the globe. These are variants of the disease that killed the older Jenkins siblings in Wales in the 1920s, as described in Chapter 2, and are no longer treatable with our ordinary antibiotics but require the development of new generations of drugs. TB, which was once beaten in most of the world, will have to be beaten again. It had become a disease of the poor, forgotten and invisible to the rest of the world in the 'submerged' part of the iceberg described by Chen and Narasimhan. Now it is a real threat to us all and, 'visible' once again, requires a massive effort to limit its reach and reduce its potentially devastating impact.

Some strains of TB are becoming drug-resistant and are part of the bigger issue of anti-microbial resistance (AMR). The WHO describes this very simply as being when *'bacteria, viruses, fungi and parasites change over time and no longer respond to medicines making infections harder to treat and increasing the risk of disease spread, severe illness and death'*.[3]

If it were not for COVID-19 and climate change, AMR would be given even greater priority both in human health and in agriculture where many antibiotics are used in animal health. It threatens us all with a return to the time more than 80 years ago when every operation or medical procedure held the risk of uncontrolled infection and infectious diseases were the great killers in every part of the world. Modern treatments such as chemotherapy would become dangerously risky. The three enormous threats are, of course, linked, and actions to improve the situation with one can help improve it for all three.

The WHO estimates that at least 700 000 people die each year due to drug-resistant diseases, including 230 000 people who die from multidrug-resistant TB. It says: *'More and more common diseases, including respiratory tract infections, sexually transmitted infections and urinary tract infections, are untreatable.'*[4] There are also enormous costs involved, with the US Center for Disease Control estimating that in 2019 it was costing the country more than US$4.6 billion annually.[5]

> The WHO estimates that at least 700 000 people die each year due to drug-resistant diseases, including 230 000 people who die from multidrug-resistant TB.

The Global Action Plan on AMR centres on five key areas:[6]

- Raising awareness of the issues
- Strengthening the knowledge and evidence base
- Reducing infections
- Optimising the use of antibiotics
- Developing capacity in countries in human and animal health to tackle the issue.

Implementing this plan involves many different people all over the world and, in health, this arguably means every health and care worker as a minimum.

AMR is a very good example of something that has been developing for years in the submerged part of the iceberg in Figure 3.1. There were people warning about it for years before it had developed into such a full-blown crisis that could no longer be ignored. Climate change is another such crisis, although it developed more in the public eye. Both examples, however, show how important it is to pick up on problems early and plan for the future. Both, too, are examples of how inventions and discoveries of great value, whether it is drugs or fossil fuels, can be used and abused to such an extent that they damage human life.

THET, the Tropical Health Education Trust, ran a study with some of its partners in Ghana, Tanzania, Uganda and Zambia to explore good practice in antimicrobial stewardship and infection prevention and control and to understand how, at a very practical level, they could influence policy at regional and national levels. One partner explained what they were tackling: *'The real challenge is trying to translate that kind of thing into clinical policy, when there's a real disconnect between national policy creation by people who aren't necessarily directly involved with clinical work.'*

Their study and the learning from it are just one example of the detailed work that will be needed in every part of the world in order to change practice and manage this enormous problem. Technical solutions will be needed – new drugs, new methodologies and new equipment – but, ultimately, it is behaviour change that will make the difference.

## GLOBAL INTERDEPENDENCE AND SOLIDARITY

Global interdependence in health goes far beyond our shared vulnerability, important as this is. We are becoming more interdependent, for example, in terms of regulation, with many international bodies attempting to set standards for everything from disease prevention to professional practice and the sharing of medical records. There is an international convention on the control of tobacco, standard definitions of health professions adhered to in large parts of the world, and an overwhelming amount of advice available on how to deliver services from authorities of all sorts.

> Global interdependence in health goes far beyond our shared vulnerability, important as this is.

We are interdependent, too, in terms of key health resources. We are dependent on the same relatively few pharmaceutical companies for certain drugs and the development of vaccines and, equally crucially, on the same pool of trained health workers, who may migrate from country to country. There is growing pressure internationally to share both these drugs and these health workers more equitably between the populations of the world. COVID-19, however, has shown us just how difficult this is, with countries looking after their own populations first.

Most profoundly of all, perhaps, we are connected together through shared knowledge about health, shared assumptions and shared behaviours. Over the last century western scientific medicine has become the dominant world model, moulding minds, habits and institutions in its image. It has largely rolled over and ignored other traditions, whether they are Islamic, Chinese or local, and become the model of choice on every continent. The environment is now changing, however, with a resurgence of interest in other ideas and the recognition that western scientific medicine cannot by itself solve every problem and deal with every situation.

There have been some wonderful examples of a global response to some of these issues over recent years. Several very important global organisations and programmes have been established and are tackling some specific issues: Gavi, The Vaccine Alliance and the Global Fund (The Global Fund to Fight AIDS, Tuberculosis and Malaria), for example. Other UN bodies such as the United Nations Children's Fund (UNICEF) with its focus on children, United Nations Development Programme (UNDP) dealing with development and the World Trade Organization (WTO) all play an important part in health.

Even more importantly, almost every country in the world signed up to the UN's SDGs in 2015. These are enormously ambitious goals for development across the world as a whole, tackling everything from poverty and gender equity to climate change and health, as shown in Figure 3.2.[7]

The SDGs replaced the MDGs,[8] which were a more limited set of global goals current from 2000 to 2015 which similarly had massive global support and addressed some vital health issues including maternal and child mortality, TB, malaria and HIV/AIDS. The MDGs led to some major improvements – although maternal mortality did not improve as much as the other health indicators – and lessons were learned which were applied to the SDGs.[9]

A problem with the MDGs was that the overall position in a country on, for example, child mortality, could improve so that the country met its target but that there was less improvement in the lowest income groups and among other groups such as disabled people and ethnic minorities. I think of this as the averages and aggregates trap: if we focus on averages and

35

**Figure 3.2** The United Nations Sustainable Development Goals (SDGs).[7]

aggregates, we miss the fact that the health of some groups and individuals in a population may actually get worse even if the average and aggregate improve. In other words, we can miss the inequalities.

> The averages and aggregates trap: if we focus on averages and aggregates, we miss the fact that the health of some groups and individuals in a population may actually get worse even if the average and aggregate improve.

This trap applied across the MDGs and inadvertently led to widening the gap between the better off and the more disadvantaged and increasing inequalities. This, in turn, led to a call to *'leave nobody behind'* and to the creation of indicators for the SDGs, which disaggregated data and differentiated between groups in a population so that the position in any country could be better understood.

Importantly, the SDGs, unlike the MDGs, apply to all countries, recognising that they all need to make improvements against these indicators. This implicitly gets rid of the increasingly irrelevant distinction between developed and developing countries – which is, in any case, slightly absurd in appearing to suggest both that some countries are developed (and not presumably in need of further development) and that there is a clear development path which all countries follow. It is, however, important to maintain the UN's Human Development Index which brings together country-level data on, for example, life expectancy, education and national income.[10]

The SDGs also recognise the interrelationships and dependencies between the different goals. The ability to improve health, where the goal is *'Ensure healthy lives and promote well-being for all at all ages'* is both dependent on and an influence on improvements in other areas such as poverty, gender equity and climate change.[7]

Universal health coverage – the aim to provide a level of health services to all people everywhere – is at the centre of most countries' efforts to achieve the SDG health goal and it is central to WHO's 'Triple Billion' targets. These inform all its current activities and are to have by 2023 compared to a base line of 2018:

- 1 billion more people benefiting from universal health coverage
- 1 billion more people better protected from health emergencies
- 1 billion more people enjoying better health and well-being.[11]

The SDG goals are all interlinked and, looking further afield, health globally is affected by much wider considerations of economics and international relationships. Like COVID-19, the financial crisis of 2007/2008 or credit crunch swept around the world very rapidly, after a long incubation in the excesses of the 1990s and early 2000s. It led to several years of austerity in many countries and declines in the growth in health expenditure in both rich and poor countries. Austerity damaged health in clearly measurable ways, which will be discussed in Chapter 5.

International relations are complex and changing as we move to a multipolar world where the US is not the only great power and other countries such as China and India are coming into their own. Some, such as Russia, are unsettled, disputing borders and sowing discord. The only thing that is clear is that there will be change. A telling point is made by Martin Jacques: *'the Chinese do not think of themselves as a nation but a civilization'*.[12] The changes we can expect are not just about economics and power but will be about how power is exercised and about ideas and culture and behaviour. It won't just be a straight swap of superpowers; the rules of the game will change. It is interesting to note, that Xi Jinping, the Chinese Premier and senior colleagues have regularly spoken about the importance of global unity in recent months. The Beijing Communist Party Secretary, for example, spoke of *'building a community with a shared future for mankind,'* at the opening of the winter Olympics in China in 2022. These are words an American President might have used in earlier years but with a very different vision of what that future would look like.[13]

> The changes we can expect are not just about economics and power but will be about how power is exercised and about ideas and culture and behaviour. It won't just be a straight swap of superpowers; the rules of the game will change.

These changes and uncertainties raise fundamental questions about the future role of the great international institutions such as the UN and its constituent bodies, including the WHO, and the 'Bretton Woods' institutions such as the World Bank and the IMF. These were all designed under US leadership in the wake of twentieth-century crises in order to bring peace, economic and financial security, and sustained development to the world on terms agreed by the great powers of the time.

Life has moved on. Power is shifting and the unchecked hegemony of the West appears to be over. The USA's unilateral and abrupt pulling out of Afghanistan in August 2021, leaving its allies to scramble behind it, is indicative of the changes underway.

In 1975 when the G7 was established, the seven countries represented around 70% of world gross national income (GNI); now it is below 40% – with the countries of Asia, none of which are part of the G7, now having more than 50%. It has some important achievements to its credit, including the establishment of the Global Fund and the Paris Accord on Climate, but its latest meeting in the UK in 2021 when the leaders of the western world came together achieved little or nothing at a time of great global crisis.

The G20 is much more representative. Its countries create about 80% of global GNI but even it under-represents Africa and includes the European Union (EU) but not the African Union. It has grown in stature since its formation in 1999 and in 2009 declared itself the primary venue for international economic and financial cooperation. It does not yet, however, have a permanent secretariat: its agenda and activities are established by the rotating Presidencies, in cooperation with the membership.

It is possible that the G20 may play a greater role in the future, particularly if it acquires a permanent secretariat. However, it will be doing so in what is clearly becoming a multipolar world with multiple different agreements being made between different countries and regions to address specific issues. The old rhetoric is all there in public pronouncements about creating a better world, partnerships, friendships and mutual benefits but decisions are now much more openly pragmatic and driven by self-interest and power.

It is not at all clear how this will play out over the next few years. There is clearly a need for a redesign of the global architecture, this time with the emerging powers playing a bigger role in the new configurations and the ways they work – but how and when it will stabilise and what it means for health is anyone's guess.

Global solidarity is not just something for governments and politicians. Scientists have for years worked closely together and, as Jeremy Farrer describes, it was scientists working together through the long-established voluntary network of the Program for Monitoring Emerging Diseases (ProMED) who first shared information about the infections in Wuhan.[14]

Global solidarity is also something that health workers and institutions can express in their own way without deferring to anyone in doing so. The elected government of Myanmar was overthrown in a military coup on 1 February 2021. Health professionals were among the leading protesters and, as a result, they and health institutions were targeted by the military. Health services have been dreadfully disrupted at a time when, alongside everything else, the country was fighting the pandemic. Many health professionals have had to practise away from their clinics and hospitals in community facilities.

> Global solidarity is not just something for governments and politicians. . . .
> Global solidarity is also something that health workers and institutions can
> express in their own way without deferring to anyone in doing so.

There are a number of long-standing partnerships between UK health professionals and institutions and their counterparts in Myanmar. Within days of the coup, a group of about 40 began regular virtual meetings convened by THET to provide support to their colleagues in the country. Seven months on and guided throughout by the principles of medical neutrality outlined by UN Council Resolution 2286, they have achieved a great deal with initiatives in four areas: medical education and quality improvement, communications, advocacy and fundraising.

They have established a range of different mechanisms for supporting the Myanmar professionals, all of them things that have been specifically asked for by clinicians trying to carry on

- Established a website with clinical guidance resources for Myanmar health workers with a userbase of 3000 to date
- Delivered 21 Medics4Myanmar webinars on emergency treatment that have attracted over 500 doctors and nurses in Myanmar
- Supported the continuation of medical education for up to 1000 junior doctors by UK Myanmar diaspora
- Coordinated the development of an online medical school undergraduate degree curriculum
- Completed virtual training for over 600 nurses and midwives across Myanmar on needs identified by the group
- Provided continuing support to over 100 GPs in 50 townships in Myanmar, including Training of Trainers training for 30 GPs to host final-year medical students, allowing them to gain practical experience in patient treatment and care

**Figure 3.3** Support for Myanmar clinicians.

their work in very difficult conditions. This has included creating a website which contains clinical guidelines in Burmese and English, running webinars on emergency treatment, maintaining medical education and providing personal advice and support, as detailed in Figure 3.3.

The group has also helped secure jobs and clinical attachments in the NHS for more than 140 Myanmar doctors who would otherwise be deported, lobbied for support from the UK government, raised funds and used both social and traditional media to maintain the public profile of the dire situation in the country.

## COVID-19

The impact of the COVID-19 pandemic is devastating in so many different ways and at so many different levels. We need to see it through a number of different lenses including: the purely scientific and epidemiological to understand the disease itself; the organisational and its impact on health services; the psychological and its impact on the population; the social consequences, the economic, the political and no doubt others. These impacts are so numerous and so large that the pandemic features in every chapter of this book and the experience of the pandemic will directly inform our approach to health and health services for many years to come.

This section provides an overview of the main issues as they appear today in February 2022 and is written with the caveat that the pandemic may well provide more surprises for us in the coming months and years. This account, in line with the purpose of the book, is less about the disease itself and the management of the pandemic and more about international relationships and what the experience of the pandemic means for how we think about health and health systems in the future.

There is so much that is already known about the virus and so much yet to know. Methods of transmission have become clearer, mutations have been identified, treatments and patient management have improved, and vaccines have been developed. Technologies for analysing variants and testing have moved on fast and public health methodologies, sampling, modelling and tracking methodologies as well as preventative and behavioural strategies have all advanced.

Scientists, unlike politicians, have worked together globally, sharing and learning together, but there is still much to understand. The long-term effects it will have on patients, for example, are unknown, both for those who have long COVID and those with organs damaged by the virus. Important questions about how long vaccines will remain effective and whether they will be able to do more than mitigate the effect of the virus are unknown. Or whether, as noted earlier, it will fade into the background and become just one of the many coronaviruses that contribute to the common cold. COVID-19's origins still remain unclear, but that is now largely a political matter and may never be resolved.

Looking back more than 2 years to events in Wuhan in late 2019, we can see how different countries reacted. China predictably behaved with secrecy and determination, several South East Asian countries familiar with epidemics planned cautiously for the worst, and the West behaved complacently, apparently believing somehow that this was a faraway local issue that would not affect them. '*Magical thinking,*' as Ilona Kickbusch told me.

Most governments and populations were not prepared. As reality dawned in the West in February and March 2020, there was panic buying of equipment, emergency training of staff, and the creation of temporary hospitals to meet demand. Some of the countries hit worst in those early days suffered terribly. In Italy, for example, where the virus arrived early, the death toll of health workers as well as patients was horrendous.

The Independent Panel on Pandemic Preparedness set up in September 2020 was damning in its report to the WHO in May 2021: '*The Independent Panel has found weak links at every point in the chain of preparedness and response. Preparation was inconsistent and underfunded. The alert system was too slow – and too meek. The World Health Organization was under-powered. The response has exacerbated inequalities. Global political leadership was absent.*'[15]

> The Independent Panel has found weak links at every point in the chain of preparedness and response. Preparation was inconsistent and underfunded. The alert system was too slow – and too meek. The World Health Organization was under-powered. The response has exacerbated inequalities. Global political leadership was absent.
>
> *Independent Panel on Pandemic Preparedness*[14]

The UK and other countries will hold their own inquiries into why they were unprepared and, as importantly, how decisions were made in the crucial few weeks in early 2020 when there had been a chance to stave off the worst.

I know from my own experience that governments have to make trade-offs and never have all the information they might want to make a decision. I remember from my time that we were criticised for stockpiling drugs at the time of SARS – and we were also criticised, quite rightly, for not doing enough about the 'silent' epidemic of methicillin-resistant *Staphylococcus aureus* (MRSA). With COVID-19, however, there was an evident reluctance by the UK and some other governments to take the impact of the virus seriously and the delay in taking action was not due to any deliberative process of decision making. Worse still, delays were repeated time and again.[16]

Many governments' reputations have suffered but there has also been some damage to science through its association with government. The political process, with its lack of transparency and desire to spin every announcement in the government's favour, makes it easy to accuse them and their scientific advisers of distortion and hiding the truth. Trust in the authorities – whether they are governments or doctors – has been identified as one of the factors that differentiated the countries with the most effective responses to the pandemic from the others. Rebuilding lost trust will be difficult and time-consuming.

Any loss of trust will have serious long-term consequences in, for example, people's willingness to tackle some of the major issues of today, including AMR and climate change. Dr Oliver Johnson, from London's Kings College, who played a significant role in tackling Ebola in Sierra Leone in 2014, pointed out to me that vaccines which are at the heart of so much controversy and concern today will grow in importance in the years to come. It is very likely that new vaccines for some of the main infectious diseases that affect the world, such as malaria and HIV, will become available in the next decade or so. We need to find ways to repair any damage to science and prepare for managing their introduction based on our current experience.

Health and care workers and scientists are the great and visible heroes of the pandemic. They have been under enormous strain now for 2 years, with no obvious let-up to come in the near future, and almost all have reacted magnificently despite the personal stress and the heartache of lost patients and lost colleagues. Hospitals, surgeries and clinics have been hard hit and forced to reorganise and regroup time after time. The two extremes of intensive care units and care homes have perhaps been the worst affected.

The effect on health services has been profound. Most non-COVID patients have had their care delayed, with long waiting lists building up, and there has been an inevitable impact on outcomes, with acute conditions becoming chronic, diagnoses made late and greater mortality as well as morbidity. There is an associated increase in mental health problems among both staff and patients. There are particular problems with 'burnout' among health workers subjected to pressure for very long periods and this will undoubtedly affect the retention of staff. The evidence of the impact is already being seen in some areas. In addition, as Charlotte Greene, a doctor in training in Edinburgh, pointed out to me, many final-year medical and nursing students were brought into service roles earlier than usual and have missed out on some of their education.

But it is not just health services that have been affected by the pandemic. Children and young people have lost large parts of their education and feel that opportunities are being taken away from them. In some cases, they will also take years to recover. The long months of home schooling and virtual lessons have proved inadequate for many and widened gaps between those whose families have the education, money and space to support them effectively and those living in far more difficult circumstances.

> The long months of home schooling and virtual lessons have widened gaps between those whose families have the education, money and space to support them effectively and those living in far more difficult circumstances.

Many health services have also gone online, providing virtual and phone consultations and greater availability of information. It has been in effect a trial of the effectiveness of these methods. Some will no doubt be maintained for the longer term but there will have to be a return to a greater level of face-to-face consultations than at present to meet the needs of some groups in the population such as elderly or disabled people and where a clinician needs to examine their patients in person or to create the right environment for confidential and difficult discussions. There have also been some gains from better teamwork both within the health service and, in the UK's case, between the NHS and social services and other public and voluntary services externally.

Another positive area has been the way that communities and groups in the general population have responded to the crisis. This seems to have been true in many countries and certainly here in the UK any number of community groups, village WhatsApp groups, volunteer schemes and bigger, more ambitious programmes sprang up. More than 1 million people volunteered for an official government scheme, four times as many as the target, with most never being asked to do anything, and NHS Charities Together raised more than £150 million to provide support for NHS and care workers and patients. I describe some of these schemes and others in Chapter 9, which deals with learning from communities and health creation.

There were other heroes, too, less visible than the health workers, among the people who kept the other vital services going: power, refuse disposal, supplies, food production, deliveries, water and all the utilities. They, too, need to be recognised. Many businesses have contributed too, not just supporting their workers but making donations of food and other goods to NHS staff. Many thousands of others demonstrated extraordinary creativity in adapting their plans and products in efforts to stay afloat.

As many as possible of these gains and as much as possible of the community spirit generated need to be held onto as health systems, businesses and wider society reset for the future. However, by far the biggest task is to deal with the damage the pandemic has caused and to address the enormous social issues and inequalities that it has brought into the open. The old normal that some of us may be longing for simply wasn't good for everyone.

Older people, people who are overweight and those with underlying health conditions have been worse affected than others by the pandemic and have suffered higher hospitalisation and mortality rates. However, only a few months into the pandemic it became apparent that people from ethnic minorities of all ages were being worse affected than those from the majority population. A mix of economic and social factors were overlaying each other: poor housing and multigenerational households, jobs where people were exposed to risk, education levels, cultural beliefs and misinformation were combining to increase the likelihood of infection. It was the beginning of the realisation that COVID-19 was thriving on and increasing inequalities in society and that they could no longer be ignored.

> It was the beginning of the realisation that COVID-19 was thriving on and increasing inequalities in society and that they could no longer be ignored.

The pattern was repeated globally. In the US, as noted in the last chapter, life expectancy in 2020 is estimated to have fallen by 1% in white populations, and up to 3% among Black and Hispanic populations.[17] These are long-term chronic issues which will not be resolved easily and which have long been half-hidden and largely ignored in our societies. I have heard it said that the experience of COVID-19 for the middle classes was of staying in our nice houses and gardens, working from home, while other people delivered food and other goods to our doors.

Different people have certainly experienced it in very different ways: from someone who is stuck in a small flat with small children and an abusive partner to a street trader in India forced to walk home destitute to their village or an elderly and confused person in a care home whose relatives can't visit.

A recent study from Professor Rifat Atun and colleagues shows clearly that in Brazil it was these social factors rather than age and morbidity that were the better determinants of whether or not people died from COVID-19.[18]

Another study, which has the WHO Director General among its authors, focuses on the impact of *'pervasive gender inequalities, with profound consequences, especially for women, girls, and people of diverse gender identities'*. It points to an increase in gender-based violence, increasing risk of child marriage and female genital mutilation, and a greater burden of unpaid care work being provided by women. It also shows how actions to control the pandemic have included less access to healthcare services, less employment and reduced income. *'Women'*, it says, *'have borne the brunt of marginalisation, particularly those working in the informal sector.'*[19]

> . . . pervasive gender inequalities, with profound consequences, especially for women, girls, and people of diverse gender identities.
>
> Fisseha S, Sen G, Ghebreyesus TA et al.[19]

The economic impacts of the pandemic have been enormous, with falls everywhere in GNI and in global trade. The high-income countries of the world have been able to mitigate the impact for their citizens with grants, allowances and furlough schemes that subsidise their employers to keep them on their books. They have also been able to create recovery funds. The USA set up a US\$1.9 trillion American Rescue Plan in January 2021 which, among other things, gave a US\$1400 cheque directly to every household.[20] Governments have generally become more interventionist, many of them reversing long-held political positions in doing so.

Low-income countries do not have these options. They cannot pay for furlough or recovery funds, and many have seen their incomes drop as world trade has fallen. The World Bank estimates that as many as 150 million people have fallen into extreme poverty as a result of the pandemic, undoing the excellent progress over many years.[21] Some countries have increased overseas development funding in response to COVID-19 but the UK Government, shamefully in my opinion, has reduced its contribution by £4 billion. This is a large sum but little more than 1% of the £372 billion the UK Treasury committed to COVID-19-related measures up to 31 March 2021.[22]

> The World Bank estimates that as many as 150 million people have fallen into extreme poverty as a result of the pandemic, undoing the excellent progress over many years.

Clearly, the world needs to prepare better for pandemics, but there is an even bigger point here about the importance of strong health systems and different ways of thinking about health and behaving that are good in themselves and will help make us more resilient to future pandemics.

Professor Srinath Reddy, President of the Public Health Foundation of India, summed it up for me very clearly by outlining the four key elements that are needed:

- Strong and equitable health systems able to function effectively
- Strengthened public health based in primary care

- Good community participation enabling a collective response
- Decentralised data analysis and technology enabling local decisions to be made.

This is, of course, the description of an effective system that is needed anyway, regardless of pandemics.

Other policymakers and commentators agree with these comments. Professor John Ashton, for example, former North West regional public health director in the UK, describes how the UK's regional and local public health structure has been weakened and side-lined over the last 70 years and was not involved in contributing significantly to decision making.[23]

Community participation is another of the elements missing in many systems. The Ugandan Government set up a Village COVID Taskforce (VCTF) in every village. The taskforce involves the Village Chairperson and Council with the Village Health Team of five or more members, one of whom will be a full-time paid Community Health Worker, together with representatives of every sector and part of the community.

The taskforces' responsibilities are for surveillance and case detection, community case management including drug distribution, contact tracing, shielding vulnerable people, communication and education, maintaining the village health register, and responding to other health needs. It is a comprehensive approach to community participation and data analysis and, very importantly, is linked into the professional health workers available in the local clinics, hospital and beyond.

Professor Francis Omaswa who chairs the National Committee that oversees this whole National Community Engagement Strategy has argued for just such a paid community health worker role for more than 20 years. A global disaster has finally brought it into being.

Sir Andy Haines argued at the onset of the pandemic that the UK should employ community health workers to help, based on models from Brazil and Africa.[24] It didn't happen, although a pilot scheme has now been set up in Westminster and is described in Chapter 8. Francis Omaswa reminded me of some of the specifically local features in Uganda and some other African countries. Many rural children, for example, go to boarding schools and were either without education for a year or more or away from home for that period.

Dr Oliver Johnson played a key role in setting up the first Ebola isolation ward in the main hospital in Sierra Leone's capital Freetown during the 2014 epidemic in West Africa and has written very graphically about it with a colleague. He reminded me that health workers had been violently attacked in the country by local people who objected to the way their sick relatives were isolated and bodies were buried without all the normal ceremonies and mourning. It was another reminder about the importance of context and of involving the community.

Oliver Johnson also told me about the sheer racism of the response to Ebola. Africans were left to die in a tent in a field, he said, while westerners were sent home for treatment. There are many echoes of this in the response to COVID-19.

The Our World in Data website tracks vaccinations on a daily basis. Today, 6 February 2022, 61.3% of the world population have received at least one dose of a COVID-19 vaccine. Over 10.18 billion doses have been administered globally, and 17.75 million are now administered each day. Only 10% of people in low-income countries had received at least one dose.[25] It is a phenomenal achievement but also extraordinarily unfair.

> Today, . . . Over 10.18 billion doses have been administered globally, and 17.75 million are now administered each day. Only 10% of people in low-income countries have received at least one dose. It is a phenomenal achievement but also extraordinarily unfair.

There will be a political and cultural backlash against this situation which, as already noted, is threatening global solidarity and the willingness of nations to work together. The refusal of western countries to suspend intellectual property rights on vaccines and treatments and allow others to manufacture their products, something advocated by several countries and supported by the Independent Panel on Pandemic Preparedness, has made the situation worse.

Many countries are now considering how to set up their own facilities as part of a general move in all countries to achieve self-sufficiency and control their supply chains.

The Panel also called for new arrangements and structures to make this truly 'the last pandemic'. They are part of a general questioning of the global structures that provide a governance framework for health. The WHO is at the centre of this and has been caught in the crossfire between the global powers of China and the USA and their developing rivalry. As the Panel says, the WHO lacks the clout to force countries to provide data and take action. The International Health Regulations which were developed to manage health crises that cross boundaries are legally binding but lack the power of a treaty.[26]

A number of proposals have been put forward for changing the whole global governance structure, including introducing a treaty, setting up pandemic specific structures, or utilising the G20, which has the political power the WHO lacks, in some way. The ensuing arguments will take years to resolve.

In the meantime, we are left with a pandemic that is still driving the agenda and there is mounting civil unrest in countries around the world about pandemic restrictions. We are already having to face up to the task of recovery and redevelopment, getting economies back onto an even keel and building greater resilience. There are difficult decisions to make about priorities and tough times ahead.

There is much talk of building back better and many calls for creating a better and fairer world. Klaus Schwab, founder of the World Economic Forum, and Thierry Malleret in a book published in July 2020 say that *'the post-pandemic era will usher in a period of massive wealth redistribution from the rich to the poor, and from capital to labour'* and that *'COVID-19 is likely to sound the death knell of neoliberalism.'*[27]

Their book is a call to arms from an unlikely place at the centre of the business world. The authors argue that the world needs a reset in a more positive direction and that *'doing nothing, or too little, is to sleepwalk towards ever-more social inequality, economic imbalance, injustice and environmental degradation'*.

> Doing nothing, or too little, is to sleepwalk towards ever-more social inequality, economic imbalance, injustice and environmental degradation.
> *Klaus Schwab and Thierry Malleret*[27]

These words apply as much to climate change as they do to COVID-19. There are obvious links between the two.

Low-income countries will be worse affected by climate change, at least initially, and have little ability or the resources to adapt to and mitigate the problems. Sub-Saharan Africa will suffer the loss of fertile country and water and parts of Bangladesh will probably disappear permanently beneath the sea. There will be lower food yields, reduced biodiversity, less drinkable water, increased movement of populations, conflict over resources and higher sea levels.

Equally, however, some of the actions taken to manage the pandemic and create resilience for the future are the same as those needed to address climate change. Policymakers, advisers and researchers are increasingly making the point that action to tackle pandemics, climate change, inequalities and the growth of non-communicable diseases not only needs to be aligned but can actually be the same thing. In every case, the actions advocated by Srinath Reddy above of strong health systems, based in primary care and public health, with community participation and developed data and decision making, are foundations for resilience and sustainability.

## CLIMATE CHANGE

COVID-19 is a rapid-onset crisis, which has to be dealt with today, while climate change has had a slower progression, which has allowed governments to put off decisive, and unpopular, action until tomorrow. Tomorrow has now arrived and with it the need for action by all of us.

There is a global framework in place. The SDGs link action across multiple different areas from water to health and gender to climate. Data and analysis have been being collected in a consistent fashion since the Intergovernmental Panel on Climate Change (IPCC) was set up in 1988 within the UN to *provide the world with a clear scientific view on the current state of knowledge in climate change and its potential environmental and socio-economic impacts*.[28]

There has also been a legal basis for action since the agreement in 1992 of the UN Framework Convention on Climate Change, which aims to *stabilize greenhouse gas concentrations in the atmosphere at a level that would prevent dangerous anthropogenic interference with the climate system*.[29]

Global awareness of the seriousness of the problem has grown over the years – partly thanks to the campaigners – and has been massively reinforced for people everywhere by the catastrophic weather-related events they are now seeing all over the world. The narrative has changed from debates about whether climate change is happening to what we need to do about it.

> The narrative has changed from debates about whether climate change is happening to what we need to do about it.

This doesn't mean that all disputes are settled and that opposition to action has disappeared. Far from it. There are enormous, vested interests at stake. The coal and oil producers of the US have a powerful grip on their politicians, with jobs and trillions of dollars at stake. China, the largest carbon emitter of all, is maintaining its rapid pace of economic development and has announced that its emissions will grow to a peak in 2030 and then fall to net zero by 2060.

The global picture is all about power. As with COVID-19, the high-income and powerful countries hold all the levers and can determine not just what happens in their own countries but what is agreed globally. There is an understandable resentment among some people elsewhere that the high-income countries caused all the problems and are now attempting to stop others developing their own countries and their economies.

COP26, held in Glasgow in November 2021, was the opportunity for governments throughout the world to come together to take decisive action to mitigate the impacts of climate change and keep warming below 1.5 °C above pre-industrial levels. The UK, which chaired the conference, had four key objectives summarised as coal, cash, cars and trees – ending coal power generation, supporting developing countries with their green transition, promoting electric vehicles and phasing out gasoline- and diesel-powered vehicles, and reversing deforestation.

The resulting Glasgow Climate Pact does not achieve any of these goals fully, but some progress was made with all of them and in many other areas from the involvement of the private sector and the development of green finance to agreements on reducing methane emissions. All of these issues affect health and the failure of the richer countries to deliver their pledge of US$100 billion for developing countries to manage their green transition between 2020 and 2025, putting it back until at least 2023, also affects the trust and global solidarity needed to manage so many shared health issues.

One outcome of the conference was that countries agreed to update their plans by the end of 2022 and reconvene for renewed negotiations in 2023. This provides a further opportunity not only for progress but also to keep the pressure on politicians everywhere to deliver on their promises and go further to implement practical changes with the urgency needed.

There is clearly room for a greater focus on health and the impact of the whole health industry worldwide in future discussion and action.

The impacts on health are also becoming clearer. The WHO states that '*Climate change affects the social and environmental determinants of health – clean air, safe drinking water, sufficient food and secure shelter.*' It estimates that between 2030 and 2050 this will lead to 250 000 additional deaths per year, from malnutrition, malaria, diarrhoea and heat stress.[30]

In 2016 the IPCC published its assessment of the impact on health resulting from increased heat, diminished food production and the spread of disease, as shown in Figure 3.4.[31] I am sure that this year's events will have increased these risks and the confidence levels shown, which is itself a sign of how rapidly change is now moving.

- Greater risk of injury, disease and death due to the more intense heat waves and fires *(very high confidence)*
- Increased risk of undernutrition resulting from diminished food production in poor regions *(high confidence)*
- Consequences for health of lost work capacity and reduced labour productivity in vulnerable populations *(high confidence)*
- Increased risk of food and water-borne diseases *(very high confidence)* and vector-borne disease *(medium confidence)*
- Modest reductions in cold-related mortality and morbidity in some areas due to fewer cold extremes *(low confidence)*
- Geographical shifts in food production and reduced capacity of disease-carrying vectors due to exceedance of thermal thresholds *(medium confidence)*
- These positive effects will be increasingly outweighed, worldwide, by the magnitude and severity of the negative effects of climate change *(high confidence)*

**Figure 3.4** IPCC assessment of the major effects on health if climate change continues as projected. Based on the *IPCC Fifth Assessment Report*.[31]

The growing crisis and the interconnectedness of the health of the planet and human health has led to the development of the concept of planetary health, defined as: *'the achievement of the highest attainable standard of health, wellbeing, and equity worldwide through judicious attention to the human systems – political, economic, and social – that shape the future of humanity and the Earth's natural systems that define the safe environmental limits within which humanity can flourish. Put simply, planetary health is the health of human civilisation and the state of the natural systems on which it depends.'*[32]

This explicitly ecological approach has created a whole new field of enquiry that tries to understand how the best balance between the human systems and the natural systems can be achieved. It raises questions about what policies are needed and what actions must be taken. At a deeper level, it is also making us think about the way in which we conceive health and health systems.

The Rockefeller Foundation–*Lancet* Commission report that set out this definition of planetary health argued that *'Solutions lie within reach and should be based on the redefinition of prosperity to focus on the enhancement of quality of life and delivery of improved health for all, together with respect for the integrity of natural systems.'*[32]

> Solutions lie within reach and should be based on the redefinition of prosperity to focus on the enhancement of quality of life and delivery of improved health for all, together with respect for the integrity of natural systems.
> *The Rockefeller Foundation–Lancet Commission*[31]

Economist Kate Raworth also describes this balance in *Doughnut Economics* where she sets out a twenty-first-century vision of economics where the single goal of GDP growth is replaced by targeting a doughnut – a solid ring bounded on the inside by *'a social foundation of wellbeing that no one should fall below'* and on the outside by *'an ecological ceiling of planetary pressure that we should not go beyond. Between the two lies a safe and just space for all.'*[33]

It is always encouraging when thinkers from different disciplines reach similar conclusions and start to change the received orthodoxy within their own field. These comments and the quotation from Schwab and Malleret noted earlier chime with other thinkers and developments elsewhere. Perhaps we are here moving towards some new thinking that will help define the twenty-first century.

Climate change will impact on health, but health systems also impact on climate change. It is estimated that the healthcare climate footprint is equivalent to 4.4% of global net emissions (2 gigatons of carbon dioxide equivalent) and likely to grow further without action.[34]

Sonia Roschnik, the International Climate Policy Director of the aptly named Health Care Without Harm, believes that every health professional as well as every health institution needs to take on the challenge of reducing emissions locally. She and colleagues have created a road map which sets out seven high-impact actions, the headlines of which are described in Figure 3.5. Looking at the list, most of it seems eminently possible from the use of renewable energy and purchase of local produce to circular waste management and carbon neutral buildings – although all will take time and investment to achieve.[35]

The Road Map includes making improvements to health system efficiency and effectiveness, including developing greater resilience in the community. It explicitly links improved health

1. 100% clean renewable energy
2. Zero emissions buildings and infrastructure
3. Zero emissions transport
4. Healthy, locally sustainable food
5. Incentivise low-carbon medicines and treatments
6. Implement circular economy principles
7. Improve health system efficiency and effectiveness

**Figure 3.5** The Road Map for reducing health system emissions. Based on Health Care Without Harm's Road Map.[35]

with tackling climate change. Sonia Roschnik has a vision for green universal health coverage which will integrate providing access to healthcare for everyone while ensuring sustainability of resources and zero impact on climate.

> A vision for green universal health coverage which will integrate providing access to healthcare for everyone with sustainability of resources and zero impact on climate.

She gave me the example of rural clinics in India powered by solar energy which enabled them to operate in the most rural areas and, incidentally, provide some power for local people. These, she said, were only isolated examples at the moment but she envisaged there being enormous scope to take the idea much further.

Meanwhile, the National Academy of Medicine in the US has set up a working party on Decarbonizing the US Health Sector, and the NHS in England is about to launch a campaign to engage every health worker in carbon reduction.

It will be difficult to shift these great health organisations in this direction because they have so much else on their agenda and will be consumed with the long tail of pandemic-related difficulties for years to come and, despite the health benefits, will need some outside encouragement and help.

Agamemnon Otero, with a background in medicine and architecture, has spent more than 10 years developing ways to improve community well-being. The NGO he has created, Energy Garden, supports communities to improve biodiversity, grow food and generate electricity around transport infrastructure. There are now 34 energy gardens around London, growing food and generating power at railway stations and bringing people in the community together.

He has explicitly used income generated from renewable energy to support these schemes and has much bigger plans for the future. He is now at the point where he can offer hospitals fully funded schemes to install solar panels on their vast roof areas in return for using some of the savings in running cost to support local groups. His primary focus is on well-being and his work provides a wonderful example of a win–win for everyone involved.

## AN ECOLOGICAL APPROACH TO HEALTH

These discussions naturally raise the question of how far we can think of health in ecological terms – another of the many lenses that can provide its own unique insights.

An article in 2011 by Machted Huber and others challenged the 1948 WHO definition of health as a complete state of physical, mental and social well-being as being out of date in a time when non-communicable diseases had become the dominant burden on societies. They argue that this definition sets too high a standard in describing 'a complete state' of well-being. They suggested that we think about health very differently: *'just as environmental scientists describe the health of the Earth as the capacity of a complex system to maintain a stable environment within a relatively narrow range, we propose the formulation of health as the ability to adapt and to self-manage.'*[36]

This approach links with the concept of homeostasis defined as an organism's ability to regulate various physiological processes to keep internal states steady and balanced. These processes take place mostly without our conscious awareness.[37] Examples include the body's ability to maintain temperature and blood sugar levels within stable parameters. It is why, for example, we sweat when we are hot or shiver when we are cold. The approach also recognises that, in some situations, clinicians are explicitly assisting the body or the mind to heal itself – creating the conditions for healing to take place whether dealing with psychological trauma or a broken leg or strengthening the immune system. The interventions of the professionals are needed when the body cannot adapt and self-manage and heal itself – as good a definition of ill health and injury as we will find.

As we noted in the last chapter and will discuss further in Chapter 9, there are also important ways in which communities know how to heal themselves – if they are given the support to do so. Moreover, human health is seen as intimately connected with the health of society and of nature. More recently, different groups around the world have been developing these sorts of ideas and taking them further in ways which stress the relationships between individuals and their social, cultural and physical environment.

Invivo Planetary Health, for example, is just such a global group, based in Australia, which describes itself as *'a collaborative network for Planetary Health'*. It argues that *'to restore human health we must restore the health of our society and our relationship with the natural environment – with a greater sense of unity, place and purpose.'*[38]

Now seems to be the ideal moment to learn from low- and middle-income countries – and from people everywhere – rather than to go backwards to the habits and thought patterns of the past.

First, we look in the next two chapters respectively at the relationship between health and poverty and health and wealth.

## REFERENCES

1. https://www.ft.com/content/34a502b1-5665-42ff-8a8d-1298b71f1e7b (Accessed 11 November 2021).
2. Chen L, Narasimhan V. Human security and global health. *J Hum Dev*, 2003; **4**: 2, 181–90. doi: 10.1080/1464988032000087532.
3. https://www.who.int/health-topics/antimicrobial-resistance (Accessed 11 November 2021).
4. https://www.who.int/news/item/29-04-2019-new-report-calls-for-urgent-action-to-avert-antimicrobial-resistance-crisis (Accessed 11 November 2021).
5. https://www.cdc.gov/drugresistance/biggest-threats.html (Accessed 11 November 2021).

6.  https://www.who.int/publications/i/item/9789241509763 (Accessed 11 November 2021).
7.  UN. The Sustainable Development Goals. Washington DC: United Nations, 2015. https://sdgs.un.org/goals (Accessed 11 November 2021).
8.  https://www.un.org/millenniumgoals/ (Accessed 11 November 2021).
9.  https://www.who.int/news/item/08-12-2015-from-mdgs-to-sdgs-who-launches-new-report (Accessed 11 November 2021).
10. http://hdr.undp.org/en/content/human-development-index-hdi (Accessed 11 November 2021).
11. https://www.who.int/data/triple-billion-dashboard (Accessed 11 November 2021).
12. Jacques M. *When China rules the world: The rise of the middle kingdom and the end of the western world.* London: Allen Lane, 2009.
13. https://abcnews.go.com/Sports/live-updates/beijing-olympics-opening-ceremony/?id=82644432#82671993 (Accessed 6 February 2022)
14. Farrar J, Ahuja A. *Spike: The Virus vs the People – The inside story.* London: Profile Books, 2021.
15. https://theindependentpanel.org/wp-content/uploads/2021/05/COVID-19-Make-it-the-Last-Pandemic_final.pdf (Accessed 11 November 2021).
16. Horton R. *The COVID-19 Catastrophe.* London: Polity, 2020.
17. Andrasfay T, Goldman N. Reductions in 2020 US life expectancy due to COVID-19 and the disproportionate impact on the Black and Latino populations. *PNAS*, February 2021; **118**(5): e2014746118; doi: 10.1073/pnas.2014746118. https://www.pnas.org/content/118/5/e2014746118 (Accessed 11 November 2021).
18. Rocha R, Atun R, Massuda A *et al*. Effect of socioeconomic inequalities and vulnerabilities on health-system preparedness and response to COVID-19 in Brazil: a comprehensive analysis. *The Lancet Global Health*, June 2021; **9**(6): e782–92. doi: 10.1016/S2214-109X(21)00081-4. Epub 2021 Apr 12.
19. Fisseha S, Sen G, Ghebreyesus TA *et al*. COVID-19: the turning point for gender equality. *The Lancet*, August 2021; **398**(10299): 471–4. doi: 10.1016/S0140-6736(21)01651-2.
20. https://www.whitehouse.gov/briefing-room/legislation/2021/01/20/president-biden-announces-american-rescue-plan/ (Accessed 11 November 2021).
21. https://www.worldbank.org/en/news/press-release/2020/10/07/covid-19-to-add-as-many-as-150-million-extreme-poor-by-2021 (Accessed 11 November 2021).
22. https://www.nao.org.uk/covid-19/cost-tracker/ (Accessed 11 November 2021).
23. Ashton J. *Blinded by Corona*. London: Gibson Square, 2020.
24. Haines A, Falceto de Barros E, Berlin A *et al*. National UK programme of community health workers for COVID-19 response. *The Lancet*, April 2020; **395**(10231): 1173–5. doi: 10.1016/S0140-6736(20)30735-2.
25. https://ourworldindata.org/covid-vaccinations (Accessed 11 November 2021).
26. https://www.who.int/health-topics/international-health-regulations#tab=tab_1 (Accessed 11 November 2021).
27. Schwab K, Malleret T. *COVID-19: The Great Reset*. Geneva: Forum Publishing, July 2020, p. 78.
28. http://www.ipcc.ch/organization/organization.shtml (Accessed 11 November 2021).

29. https://unfccc.int/files/essential_background/background_publications_htmlpdf/application/pdf/conveng.pdf (Accessed 11 November 2021).

30. https://www.who.int/news-room/fact-sheets/detail/climate-change-and-health (Accessed 11 November 2021).

31. Smith KR *et al*. Human health: impacts, adaptation, and co-benefits. In Field CB *et al*. *Climate Change 2014 – Impacts, adaptation and vulnerability. Part A: Global and Sectoral Aspects. Working Group II Contribution to the IPCC Fifth Assessment Report*. Cambridge: Cambridge University Press, 2014, pp. 709–54.

32. Whitmee S, Haines A, Beyrer C *et al*. Safeguarding human health in the Anthropocene epoch: report of The Rockefeller Foundation–*Lancet* Commission on planetary health. *The Lancet*, November 2015; **86**(10007): 1973–2028. http://dx.doi.org/10.1016/S0140-6736(15)60901-1 (Accessed 11 November 2021).

33. Raworth K. *Doughnut Economics*. London: Penguin Random House, 2017.

34. https://noharm-global.org/sites/default/files/documents-files/5961/HealthCaresClimate Footprint_092319.pdf (Accessed 11 November 2021).

35. https://healthcareclimateaction.org/roadmap (Accessed 11 November 2021).

36. Huber M, Knottnerus JA, Green L *et al*. How should we define health? *BMJ*, 2011; **343**: d4163. doi: 10.1136/bmj.d4163.

37. https://www.verywellmind.com/what-is-homeostasis-2795237 (Accessed 11 November 2021).

38. https://www.invivoplanet.com/ (Accessed 11 November 2021).

# Health, poverty and powerlessness

# 4

Take the death of this small boy this morning, for example. The boy died of measles. We all know he could have been cured at the hospital. But the parents had no money and so the boy died a slow and painful death, not of measles, but out of poverty.[1]

These words, spoken by a man in Ghana, show just how intimately poverty and ill health are linked. In 2019 alone, 6.1 million children under the age of 15 died – including 5.2 million children under the age of 5. Most of these deaths can be avoided.[2] The leading causes of childhood deaths – pneumonia, diarrhoea, malaria and measles – are easily prevented with a few basic things such as clean water, insecticide-treated bed nets, oral rehydration and immunisations. All these diseases can be linked back to poverty.

Each of these children is an individual, someone's child. A good part of a generation has grown up as orphans in southern Africa because their parents died of AIDS, leaving them to fend for themselves, be taken into orphanages or be cared for by already overburdened relatives.

In India, where the Taj Mahal stands as a memorial to an Emperor's wife, Mumtaz Mahal, who died in childbirth in 1631, women in 2016–2018 had a lifetime chance of dying in childbirth or as a result of pregnancy of about 1 in 330.[3] In comparison, a woman's lifetime risk of maternal death in high-income countries is 1 in 5400, but it is 1 in 45 in low-income countries.[4]

This chapter continues the search to understand what is happening globally by asking why these personal and community tragedies are still happening. Why, after all the effort and the aid that has been put in by national governments, countless NGOs, the WHO and so many donors, is the situation still so dreadful?

## THE THREE HEADLINES

Low- and middle-income countries are not all the same, any more than rich ones are. Africa is not a single place, nor is Latin America or South East Asia. Environment, culture and the economy all matter. There have been extraordinary successes in some countries,

DOI: 10.1201/9781003267706-4

their economies and their populations thriving, and awful failures in others. Nevertheless, as I have discovered from visiting a number of countries and talking to many people, it is possible to identify some common themes and problems in most of the poorer and less powerful countries of the world.

There are two simple headlines and a third more complex one. Different observers may put more stress on one than the others, but all three are connected and all need to be addressed, separately and together.

The first is that there is much more ill health, early death and disability in these countries than in richer ones and many more causes for the problems. Sub-Saharan Africa easily emerges as the region with the greatest problems and the widest range of problems. Communicable diseases such as HIV/AIDS and malaria, non-communicable ones such as diabetes and heart failure, childbirth, war, violence and accidents all take their toll.

The second headline is that poverty and everything associated with poverty makes matters worse and, of course, ensures that there aren't the resources to deal with any of the health problems properly. Health problems are reinforced and magnified by a wide range of factors associated with poverty including low levels of education, unstable societies, conflict, hunger, dirty water, bad nutrition, high birth rates, housing conditions, unemployment, crime, violence, unsafe working environments and, in some cases, corruption and the absence of the rule of law – in other words, all the social and political determinants of health.

Poverty means that the poorest region of the world, Africa, with about 16% of the population of the world in 2015 and 23% of the world's burden of disease, had only about 4% of the world's health workers and 1% of the world's health expenditure.[5] This is a massive disadvantage. It means that African health systems are trying to deal with 50% more disease than the global average with 25% of the average number of health workers and 6% of the average budget. The sums don't add up.

For individuals, the costs of healthcare for themselves and their families can be catastrophic. The WHO and the World Bank calculated in 2017 that over 100 million people are impoverished each year because they have to pay for healthcare.[6] Others simply don't get healthcare because of their and their country's poverty.

This takes us on to the third and more complex headline. This is that national and international social, economic and political structures, between and within countries, generally keep the rich rich and the poor poor. They maintain the status quo. Wealth and power go hand in hand.

We see this internationally, where richer countries by reason of historic power, alliances and, often, language and culture occupy the powerful positions in international organisations from the Security Council to the World Bank and effectively determine the way international relationships work and business is conducted. As a result, the terms of trade, as discussed in Chapter 2, favour more powerful countries and richer people to the disadvantage of low-income countries and poorer citizens around the globe, and even development aid, as we shall see in Chapter 7, comes with its own ideological and cultural baggage.

Prosperity is very fragile in many of these countries and people live their lives on the edge and are very dependent on others. To put it at its simplest, in countries where a single export dominates their economy, such as Zambia with copper or Haiti with sugar, a fall in world commodity prices can be disastrous.

The international situation is mirrored nationally where poorer people tend to be marginalised and powerless within their own country. They are often unable to help themselves, let alone secure the services they need. Cultural and social issues may generate tensions in some societies and family and tribal groups may dominate politics and the economy. These cultural and social issues as we shall see may have a very significant effect on health.

> The international situation is mirrored nationally where poorer people tend to be marginalised and powerless within their own country.

These differences between rich and poor, the haves and the have-nots, which are visible enough even in high-income countries, are magnified many times over in lower-income countries where very often a small elite coexists with a large and very poor population with poorer education, worse nutrition and less opportunity to advance.

Many governments in lower-income countries lack the checks and balances and accountability arrangements prevalent in longer established countries and corruption remains a major problem in many of them. Another quotation, this time from a man in Eastern Europe, shows that this is not lost on poorer people. *'What type of government do we have? One hand gives and the other takes away!'*[1]

Low-income countries and their poorest citizens are struggling against all the odds.

## SUCCESS AND ACHIEVEMENT

Most of this chapter is devoted to looking at the problems that people face in lower-income countries. It shows how the problems of health, poverty and society intersect at every level and how solutions need to address all three. It necessarily paints a gloomy picture.

It would be a mistake, however, to think that everything is awful. There are great successes to talk about, from the well-publicised growth of many Asian countries to the continuing rise of Latin American countries and the less well-known renaissance that has been underway for some years in many African countries.[7] It would also be a mistake to think that further improvements are going to come mainly from aid and development support and the actions of richer countries and international organisations. Sustainable change comes from within.

*Turning the World Upside Down Again* contains many stories of great leadership and achievement. There is evident innovation, activity and energy in almost every country, and it is no surprise that authoritative figures like Professor Francis Omaswa, who has played a leading role in Ugandan, African and global health organisations, spoke in 2009 about hope and of there never having been a better opportunity to make improvements. Today, in 2022, he is still hopeful in part because Africans are now talking much more openly about their problems and acknowledging them and determining how they will deal with them. He also pointed to the years of growth in the economy but, in doing so, he sounded a warning that wealth was not trickling down, and that it needed to be inclusive.

We need to see the problems in context. There have been substantial improvements over the years, and we need to make sure that the sheer scale of the remaining problems doesn't disguise this fact or lead to unnecessary despondency about the possibility of improvement.

One of the remarkable features in recent years is how the world has come together to address health and social issues and how health and development have risen so high on the agenda at meetings of world leaders. The Millennium Development Goals (MDGs) undoubtedly played a major part in galvanising action that led to very large reductions in child mortality and to increased treatment for HIV/AIDS, TB and malaria between 2000 and 2015. There was, however, less good progress made in the goal to achieve improvements in maternal mortality.

McArthur and Rasmussen report that *'The foremost result is that an estimated range of 21.0 million to 29.7 million additional lives were saved during the MDG era, compared with pre-MDG trajectories.'* Africa accounted for about two-thirds of these saved lives with at least 14.1 million saved. Reduced child mortality accounted for 8.8 million to 17.3 million lives saved, improvements in HIV/AIDS treatment for 8.7 million lives, reduced TB deaths for an estimated 3.1 million deaths averted, and faster progress on maternal mortality for 0.4 million to 0.6 million lives saved.[8]

> . . . an estimated range of 21.0 million to 29.7 million additional lives were saved during the MDG era, compared with pre-MDG trajectories.
>
> *McArthur and Rasmussen[8]*

The MDGs were replaced by the Sustainable Development Goals (SDGs) which have as one of the goals to *'Ensure healthy lives and promote well-being for all at all ages'.*[9] In addition, 15 of the other 16 goals relate in some way directly to health. There are 13 targets within the health goal and indicators for success.

They have been agreed against a background where life expectancy in low- and middle-income countries has increased faster than in high-income ones over the last 50 years, albeit from a lower base, where economies in many of these countries have been growing fast and where there have been successful campaigns in many parts of the world to tackle diseases such as cholera and polio.

Figure 4.1 shows how life expectancy at birth has changed between 1961 and 2019 in different regions of the world. The size of the regions does, however, mask big differences between countries; so, for example, the worsening position in Russia and parts of Eastern Europe disguises the high and growing life expectancy in the west of the region. The table also obscures the starting point of regions – Europe and North America were very far ahead of other regions at the start of this period. All the others are catching them up and parts of Asia have overtaken them.[10]

The figure shows very clearly the spectacular scale of improvements with South Asia increasing by 62%, the Middle East and South Asia and the Pacific by 56% and sub-Saharan Africa by 50% in these 58 years. However, the gains in life expectancy are not spread evenly through the population. The poorest sectors have, as always, fared worst.

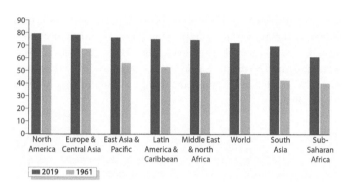

**Figure 4.1** Life expectancy in low- and middle-income countries has grown faster than in high-income countries between 1961 and 2019. Source: https://ourworldindata.org/

These substantial improvements have come from a mixture of action taken to improve health and the impact of economic growth and improved wealth. It has been estimated that half of the improvement observed in poorer countries resulted from growing wealth but that a significant part came from specific health interventions such as eliminating polio in Latin America and the Caribbean and controlling TB in China. Overall, much of the improvement has come from very big reductions in deaths among newborn and small children.[11]

COVID-19 will, of course, have a significant impact which is as yet difficult to estimate globally, although the estimated fall of more than 1 year in life expectancy in the US – with a fall of 3 years in some parts of the population – may give us some indication.[12]

## THE FIRST HEADLINE – THE BURDEN OF DISEASE

Lower-income countries simply have more disease than high-income ones and more causes of ill health, disability and death. Here, we will look in a little more detail at what that means in practice and at how non-communicable diseases such as diabetes have become major problems, alongside communicable ones. We will also look at how women and children and people with disabilities are affected.

Much of the data used here comes from specialist international organisations and national sources but a good part of it, including the analysis of global trends, comes from another remarkable international collaboration. The Institute for Health Metrics and Evaluation (IHME) was launched in 2007 with the goal of providing an impartial, evidence-based picture of global health trends to inform the work of policymakers, researchers and funders.[13] It has since then begun to build up a comprehensive picture of disease globally through an extraordinary collaborative effort.

In December 2010, the IHME published The Global Burden of Diseases, Injuries, and Risk Factors Study 2010 (GBD 2010), a comprehensive study of disease globally which covered the years 1990 to 2010, in *The Lancet*. This was the result of an extraordinary collaborative effort of 488 researchers from 303 institutions in 50 countries, covering 187 countries, 20 age groups, 21 regions, 291 diseases and injuries, and 67 risk factors.

The Institute has continued to publish reports covering the globe as a whole, as well as others which address particular regions, countries or issues. Most recently, the Global Burden of Disease report (GBD 2019) was published in October 2019. It analysed 286 causes of death, 369 diseases and injuries, and 87 risk factors in 204 countries and territories and revealed how well or not the world's population was prepared in terms of underlying health for the impact of the COVID-19 pandemic.[14]

## COMMUNICABLE AND NON-COMMUNICABLE DISEASES

The communicable diseases such as HIV/AIDS, malaria and TB are still among the biggest killers in much of sub-Saharan Africa, while malaria and TB cause enormous suffering in parts of South Asia. There are as yet no reliable figures for deaths from COVID-19 and the pandemic is, of course, far from over.

A few simple facts speak for themselves and illustrate the depth of the problem. Malaria killed 409 000 people in 2019, mostly children under the age of 5.[15] TB kills 1.4 million people each year.[16] HIV/AIDS has had an even more shocking impact in sub-Saharan Africa. Life expectancy fell by 12 years in South Africa and 18 years in Swaziland between 1990 and 2005, largely due to HIV/AIDS.[17]

These figures help explain why Africa has seen such a relatively low increase in life expectancy compared to the rest of the world. Even now that progress has been made and new cases of HIV/AIDS are reducing, these diseases are not yet beaten and there is a real danger that progress will stall as attention moves to other diseases and other threats. It is worth noting that malaria has been 'beaten' in a number of countries before returning.

Prevalence of HIV/AIDS in South Africa remains very high at 19% in 2019.[18] There are new cases every year and the threat of multidrug resistance in TB and malaria is on the horizon. Even where these diseases are well managed and controlled, they complicate every other aspect of healthcare from childbirth to mental health. They remain the dominant factors in health system planning in every country that has been badly affected. Like COVID-19, the legacy of the HIV/AIDS epidemic will be with us for decades to come.

These major and widespread communicable diseases have caught the world's attention but there are others which are locally widespread and have devastating effects. There are now 14 diseases, including river blindness, sleeping sickness and leprosy, which have been officially classified as 'neglected tropical diseases' (NTDs) and all of which present significant problems, in part because they have been neglected. They have sometimes been called the diseases of neglected people. They affect more than 1.5 billion people in the world but, as diseases of the poor, they do not represent a good market for the drug developers.

> Neglected tropical diseases have sometimes been called the diseases of neglected people.

There has been major progress with most of these in recent years thanks to long-term funding from a number of philanthropic organisations and donor countries. One billion people received treatment in 2019 and, most importantly, 34 countries have eliminated at least one NTD since 2012.[19] The UK has played a significant role, particularly in tackling blinding trachoma and river blindness (onchocerciasis), but cut its entire funding for them in its cut of almost 30% in development aid in 2021 in response to COVID-19.

Communicable diseases have been, and remain, a dreadful scourge in Africa and elsewhere, but the growing problem is non-communicable disease. The biggest causes of death globally now are the non-communicable diseases, and most significantly, diseases of the heart and vascular systems, cancers and diabetes.

These diseases tend to increase as populations grow richer and adopt new lifestyles with different diets and less physical activity. This is part of what academics call the epidemiological transition from diseases of the poor to the so-called 'diseases of affluence'.[20]

Non-communicable diseases place a particular burden of constant illness and suffering that weighs very heavily on individuals and their families and on the economy and functioning of their country. Sub-Saharan Africa and South Asia face a double problem of both communicable and non-communicable diseases and a high burden of disability resulting from maternal, perinatal and nutritional causes. They also place a great burden on Europe and Central Asia, reflecting the very unhealthy environment and lifestyles in the former USSR and its satellites.

There are, however, differences in the way diseases manifest themselves in different countries and what impact they have. Diabetes, which now affects 415 million people worldwide – or a staggering 11% of the world's adult population, most of whom live in low- or middle-income countries, is generally manageable in richer countries.[21] It can, however, quickly be fatal in poor countries, where it may go undiagnosed and where insulin may not be available.

Delivering healthcare is very different in different parts of the world. The diseases and their presentation and causes may be different. The main health risk factors for most high-income countries are poor diets, smoking and alcohol intake. In low-income countries, however, for example in Sierra Leone, the top risk factors include child wasting, household air pollution, unsafe water source, poor sanitation, and the lack of access to handwashing facilities. For countries where HIV/AIDS is a major health burden, such as South Africa and Kenya, unsafe sex is the top risk factor.[22]

> Delivering healthcare is very different in different parts of the world. The diseases and their presentation and causes may be different.

In addition, complications need to be taken into account, where, for example, expectant mothers have malaria or HIV/AIDS leads to mental illness. The availability of resources and the physical, social and cultural environments also affect what can be done. These factors tend to make it more difficult to deliver healthcare in poorer countries and mean that it is not possible simply to transfer the procedures and skills learned in wealthier countries to poorer ones. There is the need to understand the local context in all its aspects.

One feature that is important in many countries is the differences between rural and urban areas with, on the one hand, rural areas often very far from any health services or advice and, on the other, urban areas and particularly the slums where poor people live being both dangerous and, very often, ideal locations for spreading disease. Different approaches to improving health will be needed in the different locations.

Professor Sir Eldryd Parry, who has worked in African countries for more than 40 years, has developed a deep understanding of medicine in these environments and influenced many people, including me. Together with colleagues, he has written the definitive textbook on medicine in Africa, which places its practice firmly in the local context of the local diseases and their local manifestations, the local resources and the local culture.[23] Reading it, one is left wondering if a similar volume is also needed in richer countries, where diseases, resources and culture may also be very different from the scientific norm. Certainly, clinicians and health service planners need to understand the local context and expression of diseases and the culturally and contextually appropriate ways to manage them.

## WOMEN AND REPRODUCTIVE HEALTH

Social and cultural issues come to the fore when we examine the health of women and children, who, in general, bear the greatest burden of morbidity and mortality in the poorest countries. This is partly due to the risks of childbirth and the sheer vulnerability of children. However, it is also about society and the way in which both women and children may be neglected in favour of feeding and looking after the adult males and the current and future breadwinners.

It has been estimated that there are 200 million fewer women in the world than you would expect, given the normal distribution of births and deaths.[24] In South Asia, West Asia and China, the ratio of women to men can be as low as $1:0.94$ and it varies widely elsewhere in Asia, in Africa, and in Latin America. Part of this is due to poor nutrition and lack of healthcare. Many girls are given less food than boys and are less likely to receive healthcare. This leads to problems later in life, with undernourishment making childbirth more risky and increasing the susceptibility to a number of diseases. Matters are made worse by the preference for male children in some societies and, in some of them, the abortion of female foetuses and murder of female babies.

These essentially social and cultural factors contribute very substantially to the fact that more than a quarter of a million women die each year of pregnancy-related causes and thousands more are injured.

Mothers are essential for the healthy and safe upbringing of their children. Studies show that a mother's education profoundly affects how likely her children are to live. Two multinational surveys showed that children of mothers with no education had 2.2 times higher mortality than those whose mothers had had education. They also showed that rural mortality was 1.5 times higher than urban, reflecting the different conditions and poorer access to education and services, and that poorer children overall had 2.5 times higher mortality.

A mother's education profoundly affects how likely her children are to live.

Paradoxically, the world knows what it can do about maternal deaths. The technical healthcare solutions to the problem are understood. Any of the major international agencies from UNICEF to United Nations Population Fund (UNFPA) can list the same small set of interventions that would deal with much of the problem. These include universal access to family planning, focused primary and antenatal care, attended delivery and postpartum care and access to emergency obstetric care.[17] The outstanding problems lie in the lack of resources and health systems needed to deliver this care and in the prevailing social and cultural attitudes.

One of the biggest resource problems is the lack of skilled birth attendants. Only 10% of mothers had a skilled health worker attending them at delivery in Ethiopia in 2012.[25] The average in Africa is less than 50%. Anything less than 100% in rich countries would be regarded as shocking, unless the mother has specifically chosen to give birth without this support.

More generally, pregnant women need a health system that functions well across the whole range of services, from community care to the most specialised hospital treatment, if they are to thrive and survive. This means in practice that maternal health is the best indicator of the health of an entire health system and suggests that improving the system for pregnant women is likely to improve it for everyone else.

Underpinning everything are the social issues and the value placed on the lives of women and children. To take one simple example, in parts of Nigeria women cannot leave the house without the permission of their menfolk and do not generally go to a clinic or hospital to give birth. Elsewhere, women are expected to manage with the help of an untrained traditional birth attendant, as their mothers and grandmothers did. Their chances of surviving a problematic labour are massively reduced as a result.

## DISABILITY, DAMAGE AND DEPENDENCY

The scale and impact of disability in poorer countries can easily be overlooked by contrast with the drama of trying to save and treat people with high-profile diseases, yet it is a profound human and economic problem. These very diseases add to the long-term problems of disability and dependency. The HIV/AIDS epidemic has produced thousands of people who are now weakened and dependent on drugs while malaria causes recurring bouts of sickness, and heart disease can cripple as well as kill. The reality of these diseases is very often poorer lives, stunted growth, lower resistance to other diseases and a reduced ability to earn a living.

While some sorts of physical injury are often very visible, other types of disability are not. The millions of people depressed and stressed by illness or other causes including COVID-19, the people who are deaf or blind, the women damaged in childbirth and the thousands affected by the aftermath of illness may not be immediately obvious to an outside observer. There is social stigma attached to mental health and disability in many poor countries, just as there is in rich ones. The blind man, the disabled girl, the child unable to learn and the demented old woman are often hidden away in their own homes or kept out of sight in the family village.

'*Mental illnesses are killer diseases. They need to take their place among the other killer diseases for investment and priority.*' These are the words of Sir Graham Thornicroft, a leading figure in mental health research and service provision globally.[26] He points out that in high income countries, men with severe mental health problems die up to 20 years and women up to 15 years earlier than people without these problems. This life expectancy gap is less well researched in low- and middle-income countries but is likely to be even larger.

> Mental illnesses are killer diseases. They need to take their place among the other killer diseases for investment and priority.
>
> *Sir Graham Thornicroft*

According to the GBD 2019 report, mental health problems account for about 13% of the world's disease burden and make up about a quarter of the years that people live with disability globally. In recent years, mental illness has become a real focus of effort globally and the UK declared that it would give it parity of esteem with physical health; however, even here, it has not yet achieved anything like parity of resources. Mental illness has less priority in poorer countries with about 2% of their very limited budgets allocated to it and very limited service provision. Sadly, there are still examples of people suffering from mental illnesses being chained or restrained in other ways and abused, their human rights ignored.

As in other areas, COVID-19 has made the situation much worse. A recent report calls for a radical change in the way services are provided and the way specialist workers operate.[27] These changes are a very important part of the transformation in health workers' roles and education that are called for in later chapters.

Disability campaigners in high-income countries have had to fight hard to get some level of equal treatment and to gain access to education and jobs as well as to services and buildings. Their counterparts in lower-income countries have an even greater struggle. The latest figures show that more than 32 million children with disabilities worldwide are deprived of education, representing about one-third of the out-of-school population.[28]

Local campaigners with whom I spoke in one Ugandan village had decided to do something about making disability both very visible and very audible. They started a disabled band and dance troupe. I watched them perform in exuberant style on a patch of land beside the local school. Blind performers, white sticks in hand, danced vigorously while those unable to walk played instruments or sang. The schoolchildren, dressed, boys and girls alike, in a bright pink uniform, sang and danced around the edges. They allowed some people without disabilities to join the group and it had become a real institution in the area, a source of local pride as well as entertainment.

The performance over, I was taken to a single-roomed building that housed a branch of a microcredit bank that had been established specifically to cater for disabled people, although it, too, was open to others. Here, disabled people were able to save and to borrow money to start small ventures. The bank implicitly recognised that poverty can lead to disability and disability to poverty and had been established to help break the link locally. I later met blind men and women caring for animals and looking after crops who had been funded by the Bank, disabled people leading active lives and contributing to society.

Part of the tragedy is that so much of the disability as well as the disease could be prevented. Around 450 000 people died as a result of accidents and injuries and other non-natural causes in sub-Saharan Africa in 2017; 250 000 of these deaths were due to homicide, suicide, conflict, drowning, crime and violence while road injuries killed 162 000 people.[22] It is perhaps no surprise that so many vehicles in many African countries carry religious slogans such as 'In God We Trust' and 'Trust No Other'.

> Part of the tragedy is that so much of the disability as well as the disease could be prevented.

Although health and safety legislation may sometimes seem an unreasonable burden in high-income countries, the absence of any such controls in most poor countries leads to a devastating toll of death and injury every year from falls from buildings, exposure to poisonous chemicals and mining. Physical trauma is a significant cause of death and disability in Africa and has enormous knock-on consequences.

As a result of the high level of disability, the ratio of disabled people dependent on other people to those able to work is about 10% in sub-Saharan Africa and 7% elsewhere.[29] In sub-Saharan Africa, a significant proportion of this is due to disability and illness among working-age people. In other parts of the world, where people live longer, dependency due to disability is more often due to age. This has a very big impact on the economic capability of the region as well as on the health and welfare of its inhabitants. In addition, Africa has a high dependency ratio of those aged under 15 and over 64 to the whole population – this was 78% in 2018, reflecting the very high birth rate – although this will unravel with time and bring a demographic dividend of a far larger working population.[30]

Disability and dependency have, perhaps not surprisingly, taken a lower priority than the immediate task of dealing with the big killer diseases. However, they will increasingly need to be the focus of attention and policy as the individual diseases are brought under control and renewed emphasis can be given to the overall health and productivity of the population.

These high levels of disability and dependence have a major economic impact. Poor health, poverty, disability and high birth rates all affect the economy. Conversely, improvements in health can have a significant impact on the economy. The physical and emotional capacity of a population and its scope for positive independent and productive activity will be a key for the future.

## HEALTH AND POVERTY – THE SECOND HEADLINE

The earlier discussion has already brought out the close relationship between health and poverty and revealed that there are many wider factors in the environment that determine health. These linkages mean that health policies need to be integrated with others dealing with education, agriculture, employment and economic growth in order to make health improvements.

Between them, these factors affect the health and prospects of millions of people. There is now clear evidence from many studies that reducing birth rates, improving education for girls, better nutrition, less crime and increased household incomes all contribute to improving health.[23] While the absence of these factors can lead to a downward spiral of poor health and poor prospects, their presence can lead onwards and upwards to better things. Figure 4.2 illustrates this.

Looked at in this way, the crucial question becomes how to convert the downward spiral into an upward one so that health and other benefits flow towards those most in need. What can be done practically to achieve this?

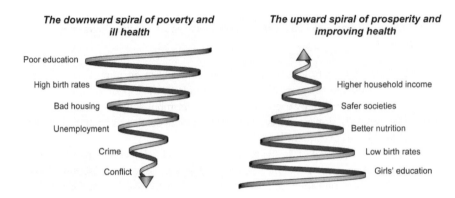

**Figure 4.2** The relationship between health and poverty.

Part of the answer seems fairly clear and involves a pragmatic and practical approach to health improvement. So much of the death, disease and disability seen in poor countries is preventable and a little knowledge, clean water, protection from mosquitoes, the adding of micronutrients to food and a small range of drugs could work wonders. This has been well understood for years and has led health policymakers and planners to focus on primary care and prevention, working across sectors and with people in their own communities to prevent and treat early disease there rather than treating the fully developed disease in, often distant, hospitals.

The Alma Ata Declaration of 1978 enshrined this as international policy. It defined primary healthcare in very wide terms to include education about health, nutrition, safe water and sanitation, maternal and child healthcare, family planning, immunisation against major infectious diseases, prevention and control of local diseases, treatment of common diseases and injuries, and provision of essential drugs.[31] It was an integrated and essentially common-sense approach. The Declaration was revisited on its 40th anniversary in 2018 when governments and development agencies committed themselves to this approach as a vital part of achieving universal health coverage.

It has proved very difficult to make this shift to primary care over the years. It is self-evidently sensible and appropriate, not only in low-and middle-income countries, but it has never gathered the necessary momentum and political will. The reasons are largely to do with the way that health systems operate and all the vested interests that are involved, from the professions to the institutions to the commercial sector. These have already been outlined in Chapter 2 and will be discussed in more detail in relation to richer and more powerful countries in Chapter 5.

Politics and public opinion have also played their part. Acute emergencies and the 'blue light services' are very visible and the public demands action is taken. Politicians need to respond to public demand and can also see for themselves the value in building hospitals and creating specialist services which are such visible and tangible symbols of progress.

Another idea that has had a very long gestation is the concept of a package of essential services. As long ago as 2001, the Commission on the Macroeconomics of Health advocated the community-based provision of an essential package of care, very much in line with Alma Ata, that it costed at US$34 per person per year. This set out a plan for poor countries based on the best analysis and evidence available.[32]

As with primary care, this approach adopts a very broadly based approach to the services required in a country and points to the importance of strengthening general health systems, not just investing in individual priority services. Like primary care, it has largely been ignored, although it, too, has been resurrected as part of the wider drive for universal health coverage.

> This approach . . . points to the importance of strengthening general health systems, not just investing in individual priority services.

In Zambia at one point in the 1990s, more than half the country's health budget was being spent in the main Lusaka hospital. More recently, in 2007, 90% of donor aid in Zambia was directed towards specific diseases rather than to supporting general health services or primary care.[33] The Alma Ata and Macroeconomics models are not being followed.

A significant part of the problem relates to the assumptions inherent in western scientific medicine, which has become the dominant model among professionals, planners and politicians in most of the world, that good healthcare revolves around doctors, hospitals and technical treatments. It undervalues the role of the community and family, lifestyles, culture and behavioural and social factors.

Poverty means that there is also a chronic shortage of resources of all kinds for healthcare and results in the inability to create effective health systems to deliver these improvements. Perhaps the most significant shortage in poorer countries is of trained health workers who can bring their expertise and skills to bear on the problems. In many cases, even a little knowledge can help prevent disease or save a life. The WHO estimates that the shortage of health workers globally in 2013 was 17.4 million and that, on current trends, this will reduce to 14.5 million in 2030.[34] This is evident everywhere in poor countries. At a meeting of African Health Ministers in 2006, the Honourable Marjorie Nguange from Malawi told me that she had three pharmacists in the country and wanted four; the Tanzanian Minister said that the most effective thing the UK could do would be to provide him with nurse tutors. Others demanded compensation for the professionals they had trained at local expense who now worked in the UK.

This theme of staffing and migration is dealt with at length in Chapter 6, where I argue that the UK and other countries that have benefited by this migration should provide compensation by supporting training in these countries.

The shortage of staff manifests itself not just as a shortage of doctors, nurses and other clinical staff but is revealed in the absence of all the managerial, administrative, maintenance and logistical staff that are needed to keep a system going. It turned out when I questioned Minister Nguange that she wanted pharmacists to supervise the distribution of drugs. It was a logistical and stock management problem. Her Ministry bought drugs centrally but was unable to ensure their safe distribution with the result that drug cupboards in hospitals and clinics were all too often bare.

The problems of logistics, lack of maintenance of equipment, inadequate supply mechanisms and slow decision making are endemic in many countries. The position is further complicated by the way in which services are provided by a whole range of different providers – governments generally provide the basic service while charities, international NGOs, traditional healers and others contribute in different ways with very often little coordination or commonality of standards of quality. The fragmentation and unpredictability of services adds to the problems.

> The problems of logistics, lack of maintenance of equipment, inadequate supply mechanisms and slow decision making are endemic in many countries.

Underpinning these problems is the sheer shortage of money. The funding of health systems is a very complex issue in itself with a great deal of variation between countries. There are, however, a few general points that are worth drawing out here to help our understanding of the distinctive problems faced by low-income countries.

The starting point is that funding levels are very low compared to high-income countries. The average health spending in low-income countries was only US$41 per person in 2017, compared with US$2937 in high-income countries – a difference of more than 70 times.[35]

An obvious question to ask would be how much more money is actually needed in the poorer countries of the world? What is the funding gap?

It is hard to estimate the amount of additional money needed to deliver improvements, partly for methodological reasons and partly because it depends on what improvement is being aimed for. One credible estimate is that an additional US$274371 billion spending on health is needed per year by 2030 to hit the SDG3 target on health, a range of between an extra US$41 and US$58 per person per year by the end of that period.[36]

We also need to consider who pays. Out-of-pocket expenditure, as opposed to that paid for by insurance or the state, averaged 13.7% of all health expenditure in high-income countries in 2018, while it was 33.6% in sub-Saharan Africa and 62.4% in South Asia. It is precisely this sort of expenditure that leaves the individual open, without government funding or insurance, to catastrophic costs from any illness.

The good news is that the proportion of out-of-pocket expenditure has been falling in all these groups for many years. In 2000, the figure for sub-Saharan Africa was 52%, with most of the 18% fall coming in the last 3 years.[37] This appears to be the result both of economic growth and of policy changes. There is a consistent trend over many years which shows that countries spend more of their wealth on health as their economies grow.

## FOOD SUPPLY, NUTRITION, WASTING AND STUNTING

The developing food crisis is partly about supply of food and food security and partly about quality and costs. Food and nutrition are rapidly becoming an even more high-profile issue: COVID-19 and climate change have combined to make it much more political, with increased emphasis on carbon emission, the best use of land and shortening supply chains to increase country self-sufficiency in the face of future pandemics and global crises. The growth in world population to 9 billion in 2050 will require a massive increase in food production; meanwhile, climate change may reduce crop yields by 25%.[38]

This is an enormous subject in its own right with low- and middle-income countries likely to be particularly affected by shortages and rising prices. A few statistics describe the main health consequences. Stunting or chronic malnutrition – where a child experiences a prolonged period of malnutrition or repeated infections – affected around 149 million children under 5 in 2020. Over 79 million of them live in Asia and most of the rest, 61 million, in Africa. Severe wasting or acute malnutrition associated with a recent period of starvation or disease affected 13.6 million children under 5, almost two-thirds of children affected living in Asia and almost a third in Africa. Meanwhile, 38.9 million children under 5 were overweight and, again, the largest numbers were in Asia (about half this number) and a quarter were in Africa.[39]

Levels of stunting and wasting have been falling in recent years while the number of children being overweight or obese has been growing. COVID-19 has deepened the food crisis and is very likely to have increased the numbers in all three categories, with more children falling into poverty and more being confined to their homes with less scope for exercise and physical activity.

These are desperately sad statistics. Stunting affects brain development as well as other physical characteristics and severely limits children's potential and life chances. Food and nutrition are vital parts of a country's health strategy and need to be fully integrated into their wider approaches to social, economic and environmental development.

## THE THIRD HEADLINE – CHANGING THE NATIONAL AND GLOBAL STATUS QUO

Discussion earlier in this chapter has already begun to bring out the ways in which national and international social, economic and political structures and processes affect health.

International institutions, relationships, trade and aid have been created by the richer countries and operate on the basis of their assumptions and preferences. Unsurprisingly, they maintain the status quo. Trade was discussed in Chapter 2 and we will explore the international position in some detail in Chapters 6 and 7, when we look at the so-called 'brain drain' of skilled workers from poorer to richer countries and at the ideas and ideology that rich countries export alongside their aid.

Here, we will only note how the different aspects mesh together so effectively, with richer countries sharing aspects of culture and history, creating treaties and alliances and raising capital and promoting trade between themselves. Each part works with the others, as illustrated in Figure 4.3.

What happens within a society or a country is also very important. We have already noted how women's rights affect their access to healthcare, how a mother's education affects her children's chances of life and how social attitudes towards disabled people affect their opportunities at every turn. Health, education, tradition and legislation interact within every culture in a myriad different ways particular to the locality.

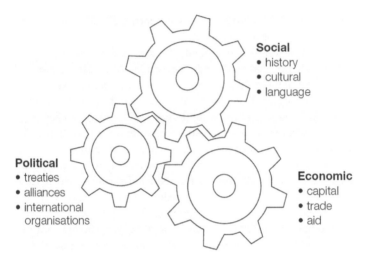

**Social**
- history
- cultural
- language

**Political**
- treaties
- alliances
- international
  organisations

**Economic**
- capital
- trade
- aid

**Figure 4.3** Social, political and economic structures work together to maintain the status quo.

Another important issue is the treatment of minorities of different kinds, whether they are ethnic groups or, for example, people from lesbian, bisexual, gay, transgender and intersex (LBGTI) communities. As a single example, the treatment of people from LBGTI groups in many countries – in some of which they are criminalised – is appalling and not only breaches their human rights but drastically affects their health and wider life chances.

These issues about minorities are not by any means confined to low- and middle-income countries. Minorities such as Gypsy, Roma and Travellers are discriminated against and have poorer health status in countries in Europe; Black Americans have lower life expectancy and poorer health outcomes than the white population.

The Commission on the Social Determinants of Health undertook a very wide-ranging review of how social issues affect health, bringing together the facts and exposing the fictions.[40] It analysed and described in considerable detail the ways in which social organisation, behaviours and structures determine the mental and physical health of individuals and groups in society. It showed, among other things, that there is a social gradient, with a person's relative position in society affecting their chances of better or poorer health.

> There is a social gradient, with a person's relative position in society affecting their chances of better or poorer health.

Its recommendations, published in 2008, were very straightforward. If we are really to be serious about improving health for everybody, we must improve daily living standards and tackle the inequitable distribution of power, money and resources both nationally and internationally. These recommendations explicitly address social, economic and political issues and have been seen by some people and governments as being far too partisan a political agenda. They take us into areas of social justice and rights that we will return to for further discussion in later chapters.

The Commission's investigation of the evidence for links between economic growth and health is valuable, however, whatever the political context, in looking at whether it is sufficient simply to promote economic growth in order to improve health. It demonstrates that, while economic growth is raising incomes in many countries, increasing national wealth alone does not necessarily increase national health. It depends how the wealth is used. It shows that there will not automatically be a 'trickle-down' effect to benefit the poor.

Some low- and middle-income countries such as Cuba, Costa Rica, China, the state of Kerala in India and Sri Lanka have achieved levels of good health despite relatively low national incomes. Others have failed to improve the health of their whole populations despite increased wealth.

This demonstration is particularly important where health ministers have to argue hard within their government both for increased expenditure on health and for their share of the proceeds of growth. Countries need health infrastructure and spending as well as other public infrastructure. Free markets and economic growth will not simply provide for the millions still living in poverty. COVID-19 is leading to a reappraisal of this in many countries and governments are taking a more active role in investment and services.

Turning to government and governance, it is a sad fact that government in low-income countries can often be a byword for corruption, bureaucracy and disorganisation. The rhetoric of democracy, accountability and good governance all too often does not match the reality for both economic and social reasons. The Kenyan writer Binyavanga Wainaina describes the problem: *'We are often guilty of using words like leadership, government, parliament and institutions as if they represent solid realities . . . But in truth, all these structures are about as solid as free-floating gases . . . we watch our Government float above us like a helium balloon tethered by the flimsiest of strings.'*[41]

> . . . we watch our Government float above us like a helium balloon tethered by the flimsiest of strings.
>
> *Binyavanga Wainaina*

Many countries simply do not have the resources and infrastructure or the outlook and culture necessary to hold governments and officials to account and make these institutions work effectively. Democracy and, in particular, democratic elections are extremely expensive and, more generally, all the apparatus of good government and accountability does not come cheap. Elections may even be counterproductive, with autocrats learning to bribe, intimidate and cheat their way into power – becoming just another tool for controlling the population.[42]

Creating good governance and government is a very long-term process for any country. Outsiders may help, but the leadership must come internally. There had been improvements with regards to governance in recent years. However, there is evidence that this is declining. The Mo Ibrahim Foundation's Index of African Governance has seen a slowing rate of improvement since 2015 and the first actual drop in 2019. The Foundation suggests that COVID-19 is likely to increase that fall in the area of security and the rule of law.[43]

A positive indicator is that, between 1960 and 1992, the period immediately after most countries became independent from the colonial powers, only three heads of state in Africa relinquished power voluntarily; but since then, many more have. There are concerns, however, that the tide is turning again as many leaders have abolished two-term limits so that they can be re-elected time after time.[44] This is not, of course, an African issue; there are now de facto dictators and autocrats of different sorts in about 50 countries around the world.

Governance and corruption remain very significant issues. I wrote in 2009 that several serving and former Kenyan Ministers are being accused of corruption and the Zambian Ministry of Health is under investigation for allegedly using health department' money to support the government campaign for re-election. Today I have another list: the South Africa Minister of Health is suspended amid allegations of giving COVID-19-related contracts to relatives and friends and suspicions of COVID-19-related corruption currently hang over the UK government.

We need, however, to be careful to understand how culture and family and ethnic links shape behaviour. In many countries, family loyalties are very important; elsewhere, communities are the first loyalty for many people. Outsiders need to be careful about imposing their own values on how societies behave, particularly in countries that were created for their own purposes by the colonial powers and frequently cut across tribal boundaries or forced two or more incompatible peoples together. There are, of course, some clear boundaries between corruption and normal cultural behaviour. Theft, bribery and demanding money with menaces are clear crimes, while networking, making friends and building alliances are natural and reasonable ways of behaving in any society. Cronyism and family ties operate in grey territory.

The boundaries of what constitutes reasonable behaviour are constantly shifting in all societies. There is an increasing expectation, in western countries at least, that more and more decisions, from the size of an ex-banker's pension and the amount of expenses claimed by MPs to the evidence used to go to war, should be open to public scrutiny. At the same time, however, more and more effort is going into keeping things secret. COVID-19 has raised the stakes still further on both freedom of information and civil liberties, with greater demands for openness and transparency.

> COVID-19 has raised the stakes still further on both freedom of information and civil liberties with greater demands for openness and transparency.

A look back into the history of any of today's high-income countries will show us governments and societies that became rich and powerful through means and methods they would now disown, and that economic growth and democracy did not always go hand in hand.

Leaders from poorer countries understand these issues very well and have had to face up to and fight corruption throughout their lives. I recall watching the Honourable Professor Sheila Tlou, then Minister of Health in Botswana, berate colleagues at a meeting about stamping out corruption. They couldn't blame the richer countries or expect them to tolerate it, she said. '*No excuses, we have to deal with it,*' she said. She was not prepared to be a victim.

In January 2009, I asked a senior African leader what the election of a man of partly Kenyan heritage to the Presidency of the USA meant for Africa and Africans. '*It's great,*' he said and paused for maximum effect. '*And now we have to behave ourselves!*'

And we in the West have to do so as well.

## THREE LEVELS FOR ACTION ON HEALTH

This chapter has described three levels of problems and showed that health improvement needs to be tackled through confronting the health issues themselves, through alleviating poverty and through changing some of the social, political and economic structures that maintain the status quo.

In my exploration of these issues I have met people who advocate dealing with only one level of these problems saying, for example, that unless the world's trade relationships are sorted out, nothing else matters or that all we can do is offer practical help with health problems or that economic growth is the answer.

The truth is that these problems need to be tackled together to have greatest effect. Many countries have drawn up national development plans and poverty reduction plans that attempt to balance action in each of these areas. Table 4.1 offers an example of the sort of actions that countries are taking to improve health in the context of their overall development. It has been put together from real examples from a number of different countries.

There is a more general point here relevant to the whole book. Wherever possible we should be looking for actions that reinforce each other across different sectors and domains. Actions on health, for example, that help address climate change, actions on climate that help tackle health issues – as Sonia Roschnik was quoted as saying in Chapter 3.

I have used the positive word *wealth* rather than the negative one *poverty* for the central column in Table 4.1 to indicate the ambition of all countries to grow their economy and increase the wealth of the country and its citizens.

**Table 4.1** Three levels for action on health

| Health | Wealth | Society |
|---|---|---|
| Increase immunisation | Anti-corruption measures | Promotion of civil society |
| More health workers with better education, regulation and legislative framework | Regulation of business and accounting | Agricultural reform and food security |
| Universal Health Coverage with funding scheme to enable access for the poorest | Tax reforms | Access to clean water |
| | Investment in infrastructure – electrification, water, transport and ICT | Develop education for all, including disabled children, and develop educational institutions |
| Strengthen primary care and public health | Promote local private sector and partnerships with the public and not-for-profit sectors | Promote sustainability |
| Regulatory frameworks for private healthcare providers, medicines and health products | | Health and safety at work |
| | Invest in science and health R&D | Free and fair elections and greater transparency |

The first level, tackling disease and ill health directly, is the most straightforward. At this level, practically every government in the world recognises health as one of its priorities alongside economic development, education and security. Most governments have established a national health system and have plans to improve the health of their populations. Most draw on learning and advice from elsewhere in doing so.

The second level, creating wealth and tackling poverty in a country and dealing with its wider impacts, is more complex. At this level, national governments take on all the aspects of poverty, often through wide-ranging national poverty action plans, and work to promote economic growth among poorer communities.

The third level of action, tackling the status quo internationally and nationally, is much more complex and problematic. It might seem as if this is purely a political matter with a need for the redistribution of power and wealth to create a fairer world and a level playing field. It is much more than this, however, involving as it does social, technological and economic changes that would not just flow from political change. It is not just government that needs to take the lead. Social leadership and advocacy of the sort necessary to change attitudes towards disabled people, to promote their education and potential, and to change the way women are allowed to receive help at childbirth are necessary.

Economic and technological changes are vital, including access to trade and other markets, and new technologies enabling people to participate in them and extend their potential. Mobile phones and computing bring social change as well as opportunity. The communications and internet pioneers have enabled reform and the levelling of the playing field in ways that social reformers and development workers could not dream of, although these also bring their dangers.

This table is a reminder of the upward and downward spirals shown earlier in Figure 4.2 and of how multiple actions can work together to bring improvement or make matters much worse. Francis Omaswa described how this worked in countries like his own Uganda. Economies have been growing fast in these countries in recent years, often 6% a year or more, and faster than in the West. But there has also been population growth of 3% with 70% of his country now under 30. Because of the way the economy is structured, he told me, the young people simply don't see opportunities for themselves and they migrate.

## LEADERSHIP

National and local leadership and political will are crucially important to making any such improvements. The implementation of these plans and long-term sustainable growth depend on local leadership and ownership.

In the research for *Scaling up, Saving Lives*, a report on how to improve and increase the training and education of health workers in low-income countries that I co-chaired with Bience Gawanas of the African Union, we looked at the evidence of what had worked in successful scale-ups around the world. The evidence was unequivocal: the most significant factor in every case was long-term sustained local political leadership.[31]

Foreigners can and do draw up excellent theoretical plans for improving health and health systems, but they won't work unless national and local leaders embrace them and implement them. Technological improvements can be significant, but they can only work to their full extent where countries and leaders accept and adapt them to their own cultures and environments.

International organisations from donor countries to the World Bank and the WHO and international NGOs all have a part to play in support of the local leadership, wherever this exists. As we shall see in Chapter 7, there is a great deal of controversy about exactly what role these external organisations have played and can and should play, and a great deal of questioning about the value of aid and international development.

This international dimension also needs to recognise our increasing interdependence in the face of spreading disease, the movement of populations, climate change and economic interconnectedness. The health of the world depends now more than ever on the strength of every country. As we all now know, diseases will find the most vulnerable places to incubate and multiply before they spread. We are in this together. The health of poorer populations concerns us all.

## SELF-DETERMINATION

It can be very easy in writing about health and poverty to discuss the actions of governments and business and international agencies and to ignore completely the experience and the potential of people who are themselves poor. As people from Georgia and Pakistan have said: *'Poverty is humiliation, the sense of being dependent on them, and of being forced to accept rudeness, insults, and indifference when we seek help'* and *'We poor people are invisible to others – just as blind people cannot see, they cannot see us.'*[1]

> Poverty is humiliation, the sense of being dependent on them, and of being forced to accept rudeness, insults, and indifference when we seek help.
>
> We poor people are invisible to others – just as blind people cannot see, they cannot see us.
>
> *Citizens of Georgia and Pakistan* in Narayan D, Patel R, Schafft K et al.
> *Voices of the Poor: Can anyone hear us?*[1]

In India I met the members of Urmul, a remarkable weavers' cooperative in the Thar Desert in western Rajasthan, who have set up health and education programmes as well as providing income and employment for local people. The cooperative members want to be self-determining, in control of their lives and able to design their own route out of poverty. Urmul has a very powerful vision: *'to lead the poor towards self-reliance by making available to them a package of development services that they themselves decide on, design, implement and eventually finance'*.

This example and others I describe later show groups and communities taking the future into their own hands. People, whoever they are, whether they are rich or poor, sick or well, disabled or able-bodied, want to be heard and listened to, they want to be involved in decision making and they want to be seen for who they are and not for who we imagine they are. They also want justice and fair treatment.

These same themes about self-determination or being in control, potential and possibilities, and justice are also very evident in the examples of health creation in the UK which I describe in Chapter 9. They apply as much to poorer and less powerful communities within even the richest countries of the world. These themes run throughout the entire book and are essential for the creation of a better future where no one is left behind.

## CONCLUSIONS

This chapter has provided an overview of health in poor countries as background and a starting point for the arguments that come later in *Turning the World Upside Down Again*. It offers a glimpse of the richness and variety of different experiences in different countries.

Each country is different and so is each community within it. There is good and bad. There are wonderful achievements and appalling crimes, great leaders and awful politicians. There are similarities and contradictions. There is great enterprise and there are appalling systems. High-income countries do good in lower-income countries, and they do harm. There are no simple answers.

This chapter has argued that efforts to improve health need to tackle problems at all three levels simultaneously – dealing clinically with disease, tackling poverty and disadvantage, and confronting the social, economic and political structures that get in the way of the solutions. Doing one without the others will have only limited impact.

Our search for understanding continues in the next chapter by looking at the current and past experience of high-income countries: health and wealth.

I have used several quotations from *Voices of the Poor: Can anyone hear us?* in this chapter. They come from a massive survey of people across three continents.[1] I finish with an observation based on another study, *Portfolios of the Poor: How the World's poor live on $2 a day*, which describes how poor people use an enormous number of different tactics to manage their money – far more than most of us do in our daily lives.[45] More generally, life on the edge is precarious and requires great ingenuity and tenacity. Most of us would probably not survive.

## REFERENCES

1. Narayan D, Patel R, Schafft K *et al*. *Voices of the Poor: Can anyone hear us?* World Bank. New York: Oxford University Press, 2000.
2. https://www.unicef.org/health/maternal-newborn-and-child-survival (Accessed 15 November 2021).
3. https://censusindia.gov.in/vital_statistics/SRS_Bulletins/MMR%20Bulletin%202016-18.pdf (Accessed 15 November 2021).
4. https://www.who.int/news-room/fact-sheets/detail/maternal-mortality (Accessed 15 November 2021).
5. https://www.brookings.edu/blog/future-development/2019/03/01/closing-africas-health-financing-gap/ (Accessed 15 November 2021).
6. https://www.who.int/news/item/13-12-2017-world-bank-and-who-half-the-world-lacks-access-to-essential-health-services-100-million-still-pushed-into-extreme-poverty-because-of-health-expenses (Accessed 15 November 2021).

7. Dowden R. *Africa: Altered states, ordinary miracles.* London: Portobello Books Ltd, 2008.
8. McArthur JW, Rasmussen K. *Change of Pace – Accelerations and advances during the Millennium Development Goal era.* Washington DC: Brookings, 2017. https://www.brookings.edu/wp-content/uploads/2017/01/global_20170111_change_of_pace.pdf (Accessed 15 November 2021).
9. UN. The Sustainable Development Goals. Washington DC: United Nations, 2015. https://sdgs.un.org/goals (Accessed 15 November 2021).
10. https://ourworldindata.org/grapher/life-expectancy-at-birth-total-years?tab=table (Accessed 15 November 2021).
11. Levine R. and the What Works Working Group. *Millions saved – Proven successes in global health.* Washington DC: Center for Global Development, 2004.
12. Andrasfay T, Goldman N. Reductions in 2020 US life expectancy due to COVID-19 and the disproportionate impact on the Black and Latino populations. *PNAS*, February 2021; **118**(5): e2014746118. https://doi.org/10.1073/pnas.2014746118 (Accessed 15 November 2021).
13. http://www.healthdata.org/ (Accessed 15 November 2021).
14. The Global Burden of Diseases report 2019. *The Lancet*, October 2019. http://www.healthdata.org/gbd/2019 (Accessed 15 November 2021).
15. https://www.who.int/teams/global-malaria-programme/reports/world-malaria-report-2020 (Accessed 15 November 2021).
16. https://www.who.int/news-room/fact-sheets/detail/tuberculosis (Accessed 15 November 2021).
17. WHO. World Health Statistics 2009. https://www.who.int/gho/publications/world_health_statistics/EN_WHS09_Full.pdf (Accessed 6 February 2022)
18. https://www.unaids.org/en/regionscountries/countries/southafrica (Accessed 15 November 2021).
19. https://unitingtocombatntds.org/progress/ (Accessed 15 November 2021).
20. Ezzati M, Vander Hoorn S, Lawes CMM *et al.* Rethinking the 'diseases of affluence' paradigm: global patterns of nutritional risks in relation to economic development. *PLoS Med*, 2005; **2**: e133. doi: 10.1371/journal.pmed.0020133.
21. https://www.diabetes.co.uk/diabetes-prevalence.html (Accessed 15 November 2021).
22. https://ourworldindata.org/causes-of-death#what-do-people-die-from (Accessed 15 November 2021).
23. Parry E, Godfrey R, Mabey D, Gill G. *Principles of Medicine in Africa.* 3rd edn. Cambridge: Cambridge University Press, 2004.
24. https://www.weforum.org/agenda/2015/10/where-are-all-the-women/ (Accessed 15 November 2021).
25. https://www.who.int/evidence/sure/frimprovingskilledbirthattendancethiopia.pdf (Accessed 15 November 2021).
26. De Silva M, Roland J. *Mental Health for Sustainable Development.* London: All-Party Parliamentary Group on Global Health and All-Party Parliamentary Group on Mental Health, 2014. https://globalhealth.inparliament.uk/sites/globalhealth.inparliament.uk/files/2020-12/APPG_Mental-Health_Report.pdf (Accessed 15 November 2021).
27. *New Directions for the Mental Health Workforce Globally.* London: All-Party Parliamentary Group on Global Health, July 2021. https://globalhealth.inparliament.uk/sites/

globalhealth.inparliament.uk/files/2021-07/New%20Directions%20for%20the%20 mental%20health%20workforce%20globally%20-%20full%20report.pdf (Accessed 15 November 2021).

28. https://hi.org/en/news/no-more-children-with-disabilities-out-of-school (Accessed 15 November 2021).

29. Harwood RH, Sayer AA, Hirschfield M. Current and future worldwide prevalence of dependency, its relationship to total population, and dependency ratios. *Bull World Health Organ*, 2004; **82**(4), 251–8. https://www.who.int/bulletin/volumes/82/4/251.pdf (Accessed 15 November 2021).

30. https://www.indexmundi.com/facts/world/age-dependency-ratio (Accessed 15 November 2021).

31. WHO. Declaration of Alma Ata. International Conference on Primary Health Care, Alma-Ata, USSR, 6–12 September 1978. The International Conference on Primary Health Care, 1978. https://www.who.int/publications/almaata_declaration_en.pdf (Accessed 15 November 2021).

32. WHO. *Macroeconomics and Health: Investing in health for economic development.* Report of the Commission on Macroeconomics and Health, 2001. https://apps.who.int/iris/ handle/10665/42463 (Accessed 15 November 2021).

33. Update on the International Health Partnership and related initiatives (IHP+). Prepared for the Health 8 Meeting, 28 January 2008, Geneva. https://www.who.int/healthsystems/ strategy/IHP_update5_30Jan.pdf (Accessed 15 November 2021).

34. WHO. *Global Strategy on Human Resources for Health: Workforce 2030.* Geneva: WHO, 2016, p. 44. http://apps.who.int/iris/bitstream/handle/10665/250368/9789241511131-eng. pdf;jsessionid=6C7B6635E6A568008E8CA0A0CA203311?sequence=1 (Accessed 15 November 2021).

35. https://www.who.int/health_financing/documents/health-expenditure-report-2019.pdf (Accessed 6 February 2021)

36. https://www.thelancet.com/journals/langlo/article/PIIS2214-109X(17)30263-2/fulltext (Accessed 15 November 2021).

37. https://data.worldbank.org/indicator/SH.XPD.OOPC.CH.ZS?locations=XM (Accessed 15 November 2021).

38. https://www.worldbank.org/en/topic/food-security (Accessed 6 February 2022)

39. https://www.who.int/data/gho/data/indicators (Accessed 15 November 2021).

40. https://www.who.int/teams/social-determinants-of-health/equity-and-health/commission-on-social-determinants-of-health (Accessed 15 November 2021).

41. Quoted by the Earl of Sandwich in the House of Lords. *Hansard*, 5 March 2009.

42. Collier P. More coups please. *Prospect*, 26 April 2009; 157.

43. https://mo.ibrahim.foundation/sites/default/files/2020-11/2020-index-report.pdf (Accessed 15 November 2021).

44. https://core.ac.uk/download/pdf/234690056.pdf (Accessed 15 November 2021).

45. Collins D, Morduch J, Rutherford S, Ruthven O. *Portfolios of the Poor: How the world's poor live on $2 a day.* Princeton: Princeton University Press, 2010.

# Health, wealth and power

**5**

She was 19 and dying.

A healthy young woman, she had caught a virus which, by a one in a million chance, had attacked the heart muscle cells and she was now close to death from heart failure.

The situation was dire. Although drugs could damp down the inflammation, there wasn't enough time for them to work. The doctors treating her knew that if she could only survive for 48 hours, the infection would be brought under control and her heart would start to recover. In a last attempt to save her, they turned to a surgeon who had developed the use of artificial heart pumps for patients with heart failure.

Soon after midnight she was transferred to Oxford. Professor Steven Westaby acted quickly to implant a small battery-powered centrifugal pump into the base of her heart. About the size of an orange and with the appearance of a miniature aeroplane engine, the pump's spinning turbine took over the function of her own failing heart.

The operation worked. The pump was removed 1 week later and the woman's own heart took back the task of keeping her alive. Twelve years later she is a healthy woman with a normal heart.

Professor Westaby has been pioneering the use of heart pumps in Oxford since the mid-1990s, when I was the Chief Executive of the Oxford Radcliffe Hospital, where he worked. His most successful patient to date has lived for 7 years with a pump in his heart, a pack of batteries strapped to his waist and a battery charger close to hand. Some of these devices had been used to keep patients alive while they waited for a transplant; but this was the first time that one had been used in this way in the UK as an interim 'bridge' to recovery in a young and otherwise fit patient.

In earlier operations, Professor Westaby had noticed that some of the hearts taken out of patients when they received their transplants showed signs of recovery. Resting them, while a mechanical pump did the work, appeared to help them to recover some of their old resilience and muscular strength. He wondered whether blood pumps might perhaps have a wider role in helping hearts to recover. He has subsequently set up a research programme to try to understand more about what is happening within the metabolism of the heart muscle and what role genetics may play.

DOI: 10.1201/9781003267706-5

This is a story made for journalism or the big screen and is a wonderful example of what modern medicine can do. It shows off the skill of doctors and other clinical staff, describes pioneering methods and illustrates very effectively the link between conventional surgery, new technology and genetics. It shows us that medicine and healthcare are still improving and allows us to believe that, given enough resources, even the most impossible-sounding challenges may yet be met. Not every new development is as dramatic or as expensive of course, and we will look in later chapters at innovations that can save thousands of lives relatively inexpensively.

These developments are not the whole story, however. This chapter describes some of the great successes of the last century but also shows how some very deep-seated problems have developed alongside them over the years.

## THE THREE LEVELS FOR ACTION ON HEALTH

There have been extraordinary improvements in health in western countries over the last century. In the last chapter I described how lower-income countries needed to take action at three levels in a combination of improvements in health services, measures to tackle poverty and social change if they were going to improve their health. Richer countries have benefited from just such a combination of action on health, action on poverty and social change.

In the UK, for example, life expectancy at birth has risen by 30 years over the last century and quality of life has changed dramatically. There are more and better treatments for our many ailments and we can have our hips replaced, our cataracts removed and our arteries re-vascularized as a matter of routine. Most cancers are now long-term conditions rather than quick killers, with dramatic improvements, for example, in childhood cancers. Roads and workplaces are far safer, housing and drains are better, and smoking is, at last, reducing. Health promotion and healthcare have added years to life and life to years.

It would be difficult to overstate these changes. When the Royal College of Obstetrics and Gynaecology was founded in 1929, a mother in the UK had about a 1 in 250 chance of dying with each child born, higher than the current figures for India but lower than that for Nigeria. Her great granddaughter's risk now is about 1 in 15 000.[1]

We are now mostly more affluent, fitter and healthier and have easier and more comfortable lives than our parents and grandparents. There is still poverty today although its impact is, in absolute terms at least, far less extreme. Before the National Assistance Acts of 1911 and 1946 and the establishment of the NHS in 1948, many people couldn't afford any kind of healthcare and the illness or disability of a breadwinner was often catastrophic for a family, just as it is today in so many poor countries. The NHS was aptly described by Anuerin Bevan, the minister responsible for establishing the NHS, as being 'in place of fear'.

> The NHS was aptly described . . . as being 'in place of fear'.

Social change in the UK has also been profound: we have far greater access to education, much better employment conditions and a range of benefits available to people to provide for disability, old age and unemployment. When the retirement age for men in the UK was set at

65 in 1925, pensioners expected only a few more years of life at most. Today, less than a century later, we can expect a healthy 'third age' to take us up to and into our 80s.

Table 5.1, which is by no means comprehensive, illustrates some of the different actions that between them have contributed in some way to health. Some are legislative, some purely medical and some are the result of popular campaigns or private sector or individual action. This, too, reflects the way that improving health in poorer countries needs to involve the public, not-for-profit and private sectors, and civil society as well as the professionals and public bodies.

**Table 5.1** The three levels for action on health – applied to the UK (1900–2021)

| | Health | Wealth | Social change |
|---|---|---|---|
| 2010–2021 | COVID-19 and impacts on other health issues Developments in AI, genomics, big data – and, later, vaccines Declining life expectancy | Economic impact of COVID-19 Policies of austerity 2010–2019 – cuts to welfare and services Financial crisis after 2009 | New priority for climate change and tackling inequalities Social movements on racism, gender, misogyny and cultural appropriation Brexit and widening divisions in country – north/south, leave/remain, and others |
| 1976–2009 | Genome decoded Control of tobacco Keyhole surgery New drug development Some cancers alleviated Hip, knee and cataract surgical replacements Seatbelt and drink-driving legislation | Minimum wage Childhood poverty programmes Equal pay legislation Deregulation of employment | Rapid expansion of use of information and communications technology into social networking and elsewhere Sure Start and nursery education Expansion of universities Antidiscrimination legislation Rise in school-leaving age |
| 1951–1975 | Open heart surgery Clean Air Act 156 to reduce air pollution | Rising standards of living and availability of consumer goods and technology | Health and Safety legislation Contraception and family planning Expansion of universities and Education Act 1962 – university students' grant scheme |
| 1926–1950 | Creation of the welfare state with the launch of the National Health Service in 1948, the Education Act 1944 creating free universal secondary education, the Family Allowance Act 1945, the National Insurance Act 1946, the National Assistance Act 1948 and the Children Act 1948 | | |
| | Penicillin (1928) and the start of modern antibiotics | Development of campaigns for better working conditions and equal pay for women | Votes for women |

(*Continued*)

**Table 5.1** (Continued)

|  | Health | Wealth | Social change |
|---|---|---|---|
| 1900–1925 | Safer anaesthetics (intravenous) 1920 Improved medical education, expansion of the medical Royal Colleges | National Insurance Act 1911 covering health and unemployment First old-age pensions introduced in 1908 | Education Act 1906 offering free school meals and the School Medical Service |

The events shown in Table 5.1 do not make up a coherent whole or link together in any direct way. Indeed, some may have moved the country in opposite directions from others. Some are the result of a particular political project or movement, but some aren't. Perhaps controversially, I have suggested here that both the earlier campaigns for better working conditions and the later deregulation of employment contributed in their time to reducing poverty and therefore improving health.

Readers will undoubtedly identify different candidates for inclusion here and feel that I have left out key players and key events. I have. The purpose is to illustrate in very broad terms one country's route to health improvement.

A table like this for a Scandinavian country would contain even more social and economic legislation and regulation; one for the USA would contain far less public activity and far more private enterprise. The Scandinavians have created a more equal society with higher average life expectancy, the Americans one with greater inequalities in everything including life expectancy, where the overall average is lower than in western European countries. There is no single route to take and countries will live with the consequences good and bad of the one they choose.

The most influential series of events in social policy in the UK in the twentieth century was the publication of the Beveridge report in 1942 and the subsequent creation of the welfare state in the middle and late 1940s, when the establishment of the NHS was accompanied by the reform and expansion of social security assistance and education. We are living with the consequences, good and bad, today and any political and social reformer needs to take account of them.

Equally, we are living with the history described in the 'Health' column where the Royal Colleges and other institutions consolidated their power in the early part of the century, negotiated a central position for themselves in the new NHS in 1948 and are now part of an explosion of invention and activity in the last quarter-century. Similarly, commercial companies have contributed enormously to improvement and have also grown in power. The power of the professions, commerce and the great health institutions has bred its own problems.

The most recent period, 2010 to 2021, shows that progress can be reversed. Austerity in the UK from 2010 to 2018 was extremely damaging to health and the social environment and COVID-19, of course, has affected all three areas of this table. Meanwhile, science and technology have continued to move on, with advances in AI, genomics, engineering and of course, vaccines and virology.

## THE WOMAN FROM READING

There are many good reasons to expect this remarkable progress to continue. Populations are getting wealthier and becoming better educated, scientific discovery continues and clinical expertise, aided by new technologies, is constantly improving.

However, all is not well even today and we can hear many stories about patients' experiences that are very different from the experience of the young woman in Oxford. Just as the UK 'health, wealth and social change' figure mirrors events in other countries, these stories can be found in any country with a developed western-style health system.

As Chief Executive of the NHS, I saw some of the very best of the NHS, where people received extraordinary treatment and excellent care. I also saw some of the worst complaints from patients and met some of the people worst affected by poor-quality treatment. Reading those accounts and meeting these people were depressing and salutary experiences.

Shocked by one such case, I asked each Chief Executive and Chair of an NHS hospital, health authority and primary care organisation personally to shadow a patient who had a chronic disease and to discuss what they had learned with their Board at the next meeting. I wanted all of us to gain a better understanding of what it was like to have a long-term condition and to need to keep coming back to the NHS for care and treatment. I did the same myself and spent time with a woman in Reading who had experienced a whole series of health problems over 30 years. She suffered or had suffered from many different ailments and had been investigated, operated on and cared for by many different NHS organisations.

I sat in her front room and listened with growing astonishment as she and her husband, now her full-time carer, told me stories about her cancers, her heart attack, the time she was in renal failure and no one had realised, and the different time when a quick-thinking doctor had saved her life. Now she needed long-term care for a number of conditions and made use of NHS services every week.

She, like Professor Westaby's patient, was an exception. Her experience, however, threw light on what it was like to be a patient with some of the more common problems that the NHS has to deal with on a regular basis. She was different simply because she had had a lot of them and had therefore tested the system out very thoroughly. She was very grateful for all the help she had received but told me, ticking off the examples on her hands as she spoke, that there were four things we could definitely do better.

The first was that she wanted whichever health professional she was seeing at any given time to be aware of all her health problems and to be able to talk with her about them all and help coordinate her care. She knew very well that she would need different specialists for her heart and her diabetes, but she did want to know how the different treatments related and, at the most practical level, that her hospital and family practitioner appointments would be coordinated wherever possible.

She wanted, in the words of Don Berwick, the leading expert on quality improvement and founder of the Institute for Healthcare Improvement (IHI), to know that the system remembered her and knew who she was.

She wanted to know that the system remembered her and knew who she was.

Warming to the task, she went on to describe, secondly, how badly referrals from one NHS organisation to another were sometimes managed and how, even within an organisation, the different departments were frequently not good at communicating with each other. Her experiences echoed what other people had told me. It also reminded me that some people had even worse problems. Users of mental health services, in particular, often have great difficulty in receiving physical care, while patients with physical illnesses frequently find it very hard to obtain mental health treatment.

Her third complaint was also one I had heard before: '*Something almost always goes wrong.*' She had endured major problems with the service on a few occasions but found that minor problems occurred on almost every occasion. This was almost always true of her times in hospital where there may be 100 or more interactions between staff and patients in an average stay, covering everything from mealtimes to drug rounds and from diagnosis to treatment. There was a lot to go wrong, and something almost always did. Some of these problems appeared to her to be important, like the name of a medicine spelled wrongly or an X-ray missing; most were irritating problems like being kept waiting, being given contradictory information about an appointment or not having messages passed on to her.

Various studies have suggested that her experience is not particularly unusual. One study estimated that such deficits in care cost about US$1.3 trillion annually in the US alone.[2] There is no reason to think it would be particularly different in other high-income countries.

Her final complaint was about communication and about whether people listened to her or kept her informed. She gave me several examples where, if someone had explained things better or more fully, she would have been able to head off problems herself. '*And, of course,*' she pointed out to me, '*things would have gone better if they had listened to me.*' This may or may not always have been true, but she certainly knew a lot about her own problems and her treatments.

> And, of course, things would have gone better if they had listened to me.
>
> *NHS patient*

None of these problems is unique to the UK. Reviews of patients' experiences and their complaints from around the world reveal very similar patterns, with some countries scoring better on some aspects and worse on others. The Commonwealth Fund conducted a review of patients' reported experiences in six of the richest countries in the world at about the same time as I was listening to the woman from Reading. Among other things, it looked at whether patients felt that they had been given a good enough explanation of their condition and treatment. No country received better than a 66% good rating. The UK was in the middle of the pack.[3]

These two stories, from Oxford and Reading, come from my own personal experience and observation but it would be very easy to replicate them with other observers in other countries. They illustrate how health services are better at dealing with some sorts of patient than others and that, typically, it is patients with multiple conditions and more complex needs who miss out.

The NHS is an integrated system with everyone working to the same basic procedures and protocols, yet even we didn't get it right. Countries with large numbers of independent providers, each of which may well focus on their particular role and boundaries, have a more difficult problem. A patient visiting different hospitals or physicians may receive very different care in the different places, may have no way of joining them up and, as a result, their care may be poorer and the risk of something going wrong may be higher.

The woman from Reading raised profound issues about the way the NHS operated in practice. It was a pretty devastating account even if, as she told me, these things didn't happen all the time and, she said, sweetening the pill, she had experienced wonderful care most of the time.

## COSTS AND VARIATION

The NHS Chairs and Chief Executives I asked to look at quality also had other things to think about. Top of the list for most of them was the rising expenditure and anxiety that services couldn't be sustained in the future, let alone improved. There was a good basis for this fear. All these new treatments and technologies are expensive, ageing populations need more care and the public's expectations of good health and good services continue to rise and they become more demanding.

At the global level, we can see these pressures reflected in a very well-established trend across countries whereby, as each gets richer, it spends a higher proportion of its income on health. Although there is variation between countries, a rough average is that every 1% growth in gross domestic product (GDP) is accompanied by 1.1% growth in health expenditure. Health costs are eating up more and more of our national wealth and it is not clear how long this trend can be sustained. Western European countries spent a range of between 8% and 12% of their GDP on health in 2018, with the USA spending 16.8%.[4]

The public in almost all high-income countries recognise these problems and, pre-COVID, saw health as one of their top worries, alongside the economy and security. Their concern is reflected in the way politicians have given healthcare reform increasing priority. Speaking to the American Medical Association in June 2009, US President Obama said that *'Reform is not a luxury; it is a necessity,'* and went on to say dramatically that *'If we do not fix our healthcare system, the US may go the way of General Motors – paying more, getting less and going broke.'*[5] Healthcare costs and delivery have continued to be one of the most prominent and polarising issues in US politics ever since.

> Reform is not a luxury; it is a necessity.
>
> *US President Obama*

While President Obama may have been speaking about the costs of health services, it is worth noting that ill health is an enormous cost to the whole economy. It is estimated that ill health cost the UK economy about £91 billion in working days lost in 2019, with no account taken of the costs of treatment or lost production or the number of people unable to work at all.[6]

The Chairs and Chief Executives would also have been worried about clinical outcomes and standards and about making sure that their hospital or service was using evidence and best practice in caring for their patients and was not failing them or, worse, damaging the people in their care. They would have known that there is enormous variation in standards of care and in its cost – and that higher costs didn't mean better care.

The Dartmouth Institute has over the last 20 years documented these variations in the USA, describing in many articles how some hospitals and some States spend twice as much as others yet achieve the same or lower levels of quality. In a commentary on a study of variations, an article in the *New England Journal of Medicine* read: *'Patients in high-cost regions have access to the same technology as those in low-cost regions, and those in low-cost regions are not deprived of needed care. On the contrary, the researchers note that care is often better in low-cost areas.'* The authors argue that *'the differences in growth are largely due to discretionary decisions by physicians that are influenced by the local availability of hospital beds, imaging centers and other resources – and a payment system that rewards growth and higher utilization.'*[7]

> . . . those in low-cost regions are not deprived of needed care. On the contrary, the researchers note that care is often better in low-cost areas.
>
> *Sutherland, Fisher and Skinner*[7]

In these few words, the commentary explodes any complacency that people in high-income countries might have about their health systems. It exposes problems of variation in quality, waste of resources and a system and professionals driven by what appear to be very perverse incentives. These are fundamental problems and, in the last few years, quality, safety and variation have at last become central to all healthcare planning.

The Chairs and Chief Executives would also have been aware that, even in the NHS, founded on the ideal of equality of access to care, the poorer and people from many minority groups get a poorer deal. There are serious inequalities in health and healthcare. We are all becoming fitter, consuming more healthcare and living longer but in some areas inequalities in health and life expectancy are growing.[8]

The findings of the Commission on the Social Determinants of Health, discussed in the last chapter, are just as relevant in these countries as in low- and middle-income ones. The inverse care law, whereby those most in need within any population get least and those least in need get most, applies everywhere.

An observer may feel that most of these problems are simply management and leadership problems and that the Chairs and Chief Executives themselves need simply to do better or to make way for others who can do so. These are, of course, in part, at least, leadership and management problems. Some systems and some countries do better on these issues than others, however, all struggle.

Why is it so difficult in the UK to provide a joined-up service to the woman from Reading while containing costs, offering evidence-based care and making sure it is available to everyone? Why does some care cost twice as much as others in the USA and may be of poorer quality?

At the heart of the problem, I believe, lie three issues that concern management and leadership as well as service design and clinical practice. They also take us into the realms of politics, social and economic structures, and values.

## THREE SIMPLE HEADLINES

As with health in poor countries, there are three very simple headlines. The first is that the nature of the diseases we suffer from is changing. The major health problems of the early twenty-first century are not the same as those in the early and middle parts of the twentieth century, when our healthcare systems were formed.

The second, and closely linked, headline is that we need new approaches and new services to deal with the new needs of the twenty-first century. Success in avoiding these risks or treating these diseases depends as much on our actions as individuals and as societies as it does on new drugs and technologies, although both are vitally important.

The third headline is very simply that all the incentives of the current system are geared towards maintaining the status quo and keeping things as they are. They are proving a very powerful and resistant barrier to creating new approaches and new services.

To put it at its simplest, the current system can't deal with the new problems and is actually getting in the way of our doing so. Many of the very things that helped us make such excellent progress in the twentieth century have, paradoxically, now become a major part of the problem.

The first two headlines, that the diseases we have to deal with have changed and that we need new approaches and services, are relatively straightforward and will be described fairly briefly here. The third headline, that the current system can't deal with the problems and is actually getting in the way, is more complex and will be dealt with at greater length.

## THE FIRST HEADLINE – THE CHANGING PATTERN OF DISEASE IN THE TWENTY-FIRST CENTURY

Life has moved on. Looking back over the last century it is easy to see the changes in the patterns of deaths and illness. Many infectious diseases have been brought under control, deaths of mothers and newborn children have been dramatically reduced, antibiotics have contained infection and there are far fewer industrial injuries and diseases than there were.

Causes of death have changed over the last century: where infectious diseases once dominated, cancer and heart disease now overshadow all other causes, except for what the statisticians call 'external causes' (drug misuse, suicide and self-harm) in younger adults.[9]

The biggest impact on health services over the 100 years has been in the increased morbidity associated with the growth of conditions where patients require long-term care and which give rise to long-term costs. Cancers and heart and vascular disease may be the ultimate cause of death, but where they once killed swiftly, they are now managed over many years as chronic or long-term conditions. At the same time, we have seen a big rise in other long-term conditions, often associated with age, such as diabetes, arthritis and dementia, which may not themselves kill people but which require care and attention over years.

There has also been a significant increase in long-term mental health problems, partly due to better diagnosis. One in four of us will experience some degree of mental illness in our life and for some people it will have a major impact on their health in the long term. Mental illness now accounts for about 12% of NHS costs. Greater affluence has not made us less susceptible to mental illness or happier but, rather, appears to have revealed high levels of mental illness and unhappiness.[10] COVID-19, as noted before, has made this worse.

These longer-term conditions are, perhaps not surprisingly, more common in older people where in the UK about 58% of the over 60s have one or more condition compared to only 14% in people under 40. There is also a steep social gradient with the lowest socioeconomic group in the UK having a 60% higher prevalence and 30% greater severity of disease than those in the highest group.[11]

Taken together, it is now these groups with long-term illnesses and long-term needs that account for much the greatest part of healthcare expenditure. Other problems haven't gone away. People still need emergency care, contract infections and require operations for one-off problems, but, except during a pandemic, infections are not the things making the biggest demands on people and resources.

People with long-term conditions now account for about 50% of all GP appointments, 64% of all outpatient appointments and over 70% of all inpatient bed days. Treatment and care for people with long-term conditions is estimated to take up around £7 in every £10 of total health and social care expenditure. This means that 30% of the population account for 70% of the spend.[11]

> This means that 30% of the population account for 70% of the spend.

An analysis from the US describes the different groups of patients that are admitted to hospital from those who are healthy to those whose condition is described as being on a 'long, dwindling course' and gives a calculation of the percentage of hospital costs that can be attributed to each group. The single largest cost is attributed to people with a 'chronic condition, normal function'.[12] This analysis is summarised in Table 5.2.

The final part of the new mix of diseases and conditions that health systems have to deal with is, of course, the new infections and diseases, the genuinely new and those like multiple drug-resistant TB that mutated from old ones, which can sweep around the world so easily under twenty-first-century conditions – as we have seen with COVID-19.

**Table 5.2** US healthcare percentage of costs for different groups in the population

| Group | % of costs |
|---|---|
| Healthy | 6.5 |
| Maternal and infant health | 3 |
| Acutely ill, mostly curable | 15 |
| Chronic condition, normal function | 40 |
| Stable, significant disability | 14.5 |
| Short period of decline near death | 2.5 |
| Organ system failure | 5 |
| Long, dwindling course | 13 |

The incidence of these non-communicable long-term conditions, sometimes called diseases of affluence, has been growing strongly in recent years in lower-income countries as their economies have grown. They are already a significant problem in South Asia and are giving Africa a double burden of communicable and non-communicable disease. At the same time, with the movement of populations from lower-income to higher-income countries, there have been some changes in disease patterns locally. In London, for example, many of the people with communicable diseases are found among these groups.

## THE SECOND HEADLINE – THE NEED FOR NEW APPROACHES AND NEW SERVICES

These new diseases and threats require different approaches and different solutions. We need new services, but we also need a much greater emphasis on prevention and health education, getting in early to stop the incipient problems of alcoholism and obesity before and as they start. We also, as I will argue later, need to develop a new multisector approach to health creation and promoting the causes of health – not just tackling the causes of disease.

To put this in economic terms, as demand changes, the supply side also needs to change. At the risk of oversimplification, the normal model of hospital care for the last century has been an episodic and linear one. A patient in the UK is referred by their GP (or family doctor) to a specialist for treatment, they have outpatient appointments and diagnostic tests, are treated in hospital or elsewhere and their problem is dealt with, whether successfully or not.

This, very crudely, resembles a production line where the healthcare system produces a product, in this case an operation or a treatment. The patient is carried along by the flow from one point to the next with relatively little discretion or choice. There may be diversions off the main route for a series of diagnostic tests or further consultations with other specialists, but the general structure of the process looks like that in Figure 5.1.

While not all patients are actually handled in this way, the important point here is that this is how the system has been conceived and set up and, crucially, what people are paid for. Even family practitioners and the UK's GPs practise quite largely in this way with episodic interventions, although they are increasingly adopting more innovative models. In the UK, for example, hospitals are paid for 'episodes of care' and most American and other insurance companies still largely pay for services on this model. To a considerable extent, it is these payment systems that determine the model of care.

It is easy to see how anyone whose needs don't fit this pattern – perhaps because, like the woman from Reading, they have more than one disease or need a mix of care from different

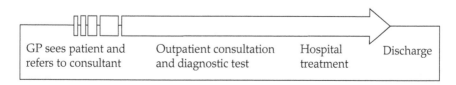

| GP sees patient and refers to consultant | Outpatient consultation and diagnostic test | Hospital treatment | Discharge |

**Figure 5.1** The production line.

people – is going to have problems. Their carers have to bend the system and probably the rules to provide care. It is no wonder it so often goes wrong.

I have heard complaints from doctors and managers in both the UK and the USA that 'the system' doesn't allow them to give the best treatment or, if they do, they don't get paid for it. The diagram in Figure 5.1 illustrates the sort of problem they are encountering. Administrative and payment systems reinforce the production line approach.

I have listened to doctors in the UK complain that they can't set up a particular service in the community, where they think it would be better sited than in a hospital, because they can only get paid through the hospital. In the USA I have also heard a former medical director of the Johns Hopkins Hospital, one of the most prestigious in the USA, complaining that he couldn't set up a service the way that was best for his patients because legislation dating from 1964 specified what he could be reimbursed for and what it was legal for him to do. The largely private sector healthcare industry of the USA has, perhaps surprisingly, more regulation in this regard than state systems like the NHS.

In practice, humane nurses, doctors and managers very often find ways round these restrictions and get things done, despite the system. These problems do, however, illustrate why so many of them are so critical of administration and the administrators bound by the system.

> In practice, humane nurses, doctors and managers very often find ways round these restrictions and get things done, despite the system.

A more appropriate model of care for patients with long-term problems would look something like the 'life belt' illustrated in Figure 5.2, where the patient, at the centre, is able to receive services from any of these sources in turn and in any order. Our health systems need

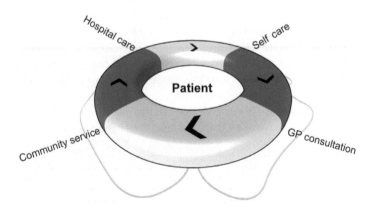

**Figure 5.2** The life belt of care.

to be able to deliver services based on this sort of model as well as on the episodic 'production line' model – both are needed – and doctors and hospitals need to be able to be paid to do so.

These issues are well understood among clinicians, health planners and policymakers. They also well understand that many of the most significant diseases and problems we are facing relate to our behaviours and our society, whether we are talking about smoking, alcohol consumption, sexual behaviour and diet or the impact of unemployment, poverty, education and the environment. To oversimplify for greater effect: where we once faced diseases that were simply parasitic on our physical bodies, we now face diseases that are also parasitic on our behaviours and on our society.

Service planners and system designers need to take account of this whole wide range of issues for the future and plan for different services that will deal with accidents and emergencies, urgent care, the management of chronic diseases or long-term conditions, acute care, palliative care, primary and community care, and self-care. They also need to work both with individuals and with all the major forces in society that influence health from employers to schools, and manufacturers to designers and architects, every one of which has a role to play in enhancing care, preventing disease and contributing to creating health and a health-creating society.

There has been a wave of innovation in service design in recent years. Carers have become more recognised as have *expert patients* and peer supporters and experts by experience, particularly in mental health. 'Case managers', often nurses, have been employed to guide and look after a patient throughout the system. Navigation aids have been provided for patients faced with daunting choices and apparent confusion. Effort has gone into designing 'patient pathways' so that patients travel through the system in ways that are appropriate to their condition – and, also importantly, are able to see what is happening to them.

There have also been reforms of payment systems, and business thinkers, such as Clayton Christensen of Harvard Business School, for example, have proposed new 'disruptive' service, organisational and business models.[13] He shows that, in principle at least, it would be possible to create a high-quality and lower-cost system that offers people the services they need if health is treated purely as a commodity, professionals were simply employees and healthcare was subject to all the normal give and take of the market. It doesn't attempt to deal with the wider social, economic and political aspects of health, which would need to be handled separately.

Elsewhere in the US and in other countries we can see the development of more person- (as opposed to consumer-) based approaches which ask people *'What matters to you?'* and design care accordingly. There is a new emphasis on compassion and kindness as well as on safety, quality and variation. Social prescribing has taken off in the UK where GPs can prescribe singing, exercise or gardening rather than drugs or treatments. And I have been personally involved in global and national campaigns on strengthening the role of nurses and promoting health creation. All of these developments can be supported and enhanced by improved technology.

These will all be discussed in the chapters on practical knowledge for the twenty-first century, Chapters 10 and 11, which bring together learning from all parts of the world.

There is a danger, of course, with some of these innovations that they just add tasks and make matters more complicated. Health systems are already fiendishly complex and wrapped in jargon and processes that are often impenetrable to outsiders. I have seen too many innovations over the years, worthwhile in themselves, that have added complexity and been reduced to 'tick box' exercises by exhausted staff. We need transformation not more transactional processes.

We may well ask why, if the problems are so well understood and all this brainpower has been applied to them, is it proving so difficult to tackle them? Why can't we just change the service and business models? Why can't we have 'life belts' as well as 'production lines'? Why can't we change the system?

This takes us on to the third simple headline in which I asserted that the current system itself was a major obstacle to progress.

## THE THIRD HEADLINE – THE POWER OF THE SYSTEM

The problems here are twofold. Firstly, so many institutions and so many people from the health professions, science, commerce and government have so much invested in the current system, and therefore have so much to lose by change. Secondly, the public, politicians and patients are almost all conditioned by history to think about health and healthcare in particular ways. It is for these reasons that we are not just dealing with leadership and management problems but need to address political, economic and social issues.

It should be stressed at the outset of this discussion, of course, that we are indebted to many of these institutions and individuals, singly and in combination, for so much progress over the last century and longer. It is the very lack of them in poorer countries, as we saw in the last chapter, which means so many people suffer and die. However, their very success, translated into power and influence, is now causing problems.

Before looking at this in greater detail we need to sidetrack briefly to consider an important distinction between public or population health on the one hand and clinical medicine on the other. It helps to explain the problem and point the way towards solutions.

I am using 'public health' here in the British tradition to mean everything that affects the health of the public or the population in an area or country. It includes such things as the provision of clean air and water, good nutrition and safe roads. It seeks to improve the health of the whole population; health services are just a part of this overall effort.

The story of how public health has developed in the UK has many similarities with the situation in poorer countries today. Many of the great gains of the nineteenth and early twentieth centuries were due to matters as seemingly simple as clean water, safer working environments and public education. It is a story of scientific observation and research from the time of John Snow in the mid-nineteenth century, who memorably identified a water pump in Soho as the source of a cholera outbreak and removed its handle so it could no longer be used, to the work of current researchers on topics as diverse as the impacts of climate change and of family structures.[14]

Engineering and technology have also played their part. The nineteenth-century engineer Sir Joseph Bazalgette built the sewers of London and thereby eliminated the 'great stink' arising from the open sewer of the River Thames, with all its accompanying diseases. Modern-day engineers tackle pollution and ensure we have clean air and safe working environments.

> Sir Joseph Bazalgette built the sewers of London and thereby eliminated the 'great stink' arising from the open sewer of the Thames, with all its accompanying diseases.

Florence Nightingale was a public health pioneer who used her mathematical ability to analyse deaths in the Crimea and show that infection was a greater killer than battle. In later life, she was very conscious of the impact of 'poisonous air' and wanted her new hospital built in the fresh air of the countryside and far from the dangerous banks of the Thames. On what must have been a very rare occasion for this remarkable and remarkably persistent reformer, she didn't get her way and the new development of St Thomas's was built facing Parliament across the river in the heart of London.[15]

It is also a story of public campaigns and public education. Today, we are very familiar with all the efforts to stop us from smoking and to encourage us to eat healthily, exercise and have safe sex lives. Looking back on earlier generations in the UK we can see that there were campaigns for people to register with the family doctors available through the new NHS and for mass screening for TB and a very strong emphasis on teaching girls about health and how to look after their families. All of these might seem very familiar to a public health worker in Africa or India today.

Public health can lay claim to creating the foundation for all the improvement in health we have seen over the last century or longer. Its impact has been profound. Looking forward, the discipline has much more to offer. Analysis from the WHO shows that all the most cost-effective health interventions are public health rather than clinical ones. They are about immunisation, clean water and the education of girls in poorer countries and about lifestyle changes in richer ones.[16]

> All the most cost-effective health interventions are public health rather than clinical ones.

Despite both the successes of the past and its potential for the future, public health has become, in effect, the junior partner to clinical medicine and been less powerful and less well funded. COVID-19 will do something to redress the balance but underlying it all is a story of money and power.

Medicine has ancient roots, going back thousands of years, with the western scientific tradition starting in the last 500 years as universities became more active in medicine and the first standard setting body, the Royal College of Physicians, was established in London in 1518. It was only in the nineteenth century and at the beginning of the twentieth, however, that the practice of clinical medicine was at last put onto a regulated and unassailable scientific basis thanks to the Medical Act 1858 in the UK and the work of pioneers such as Abraham Flexner in

1910 in the USA. Previously, 'quacks' of all types flourished in a society that permitted 'doctors' to practise largely at will.[17]

These European and American developments have been hugely influential internationally and helped ensure the development of western scientific medicine as a distinctive body of knowledge and practice throughout the world. Over the past century it has become the dominant model globally, carried around the world with colonisation and trade. It has, as we shall see, allied itself with scientific research and commerce and secured the backing and funding of governments.

At around the same time, the discipline of public health, which has its own long and distinguished history, became largely separated from clinical medicine. In the USA, the Rockefeller Foundation's Welch-Rose Report of 1915 set barriers between the two that last to this day and, while the separation was less rigid in the UK and Europe, clinical medicine has continually become more powerful and influential, eclipsing its near relative.

Public health has had revivals and reinvented itself over the years, experiencing brief periods when its importance was recognised. It has never quite managed, however, to link itself sufficiently closely to the scientific establishment and commercial interests to challenge the hegemony of clinical medicine.

Clinical medicine, meanwhile, has gone from strength to strength. Its great institutions, its Royal Colleges and Medical Associations, have become very grand and powerful. They have influenced the way populations think about health and largely determined the shape of health services and the whole health industry. Flexner and others not only sorted out the quacks from the professionals, they consolidated the power of the clinical medical profession.

> Flexner and others not only sorted out the quacks from the professionals, they consolidated the power of the clinical medical profession.

The last century has seen science and medicine advancing together, as a few simple examples remind us. The first antibiotics ended the grip of pneumonia, the 'old man's friend' and a major cause of postoperative mortality, in the 1940s. While he was Prime Minister and at war with Germany, Winston Churchill was successfully treated for pneumonia with the new drug, a sulphonamide, colloquially called M and B after its manufacturers, in 1943 in what seems to be a clear case of science changing the course of history or, perhaps more accurately, making sure that it didn't change.[18]

Medical imaging has developed enormously with scanners using X-rays, magnetic resonance, positron emissions and sound waves able to assist diagnosis and reduce the need for investigative surgery or for time-consuming biological and chemical tests. As the capability of these grows, scientists and clinicians are able to discover more and more about how our bodies work and interact with the environment. Functional magnetic resonance imaging (fMRI) scanners now allow us to see what brain activity corresponds with our moods and feelings and offers the promise of better understanding of the physical aspects of mental illness.

Genetics, AI, Bluetooth, the development of new computer-controlled and -designed technology and the power of connection and analysis available to every scientist in a high-income country drives scientific advance apace. We are entering a world of genetic engineering and personal medicine where we have no idea of the limits to discovery and invention and where all things seem possible.

Commerce and industry have worked alongside the scientists and the professions in the development of new treatments and technologies. While public and private universities and research institutes have undertaken most of the basic research, private enterprise and the search for profit have generally driven the development of the new drugs and therapies, the imaging and the creation of new diagnostic tools. In many other cases, it is the commercial businesses that have invested the very large sums needed for development. New drugs have depended on private sector funding, as have many new technologies such as the heart pump used by Professor Westaby in Oxford.

Government is also linked in closely with these other partners of the professions, the scientists and the businesses. Health is big business. Pharma and health-related technology companies are among the largest companies in the world, while health insurers and private healthcare companies are a significant and powerful part of some national economies. In Massachusetts, home to a vast medical industry, healthcare represents more than 20% of the economy and pays the wages of more than 1 in 7 of the working population. Bioscience and biomedicine are now the largest contributors to the UK economy, other than the financial services, and the fastest growing of them all.

> Bioscience and biomedicine are now the largest contributors to the UK economy, other than the financial services, and the fastest growing of them all.

This economic profile means that health is a significant political and governmental issue and makes for a complicated relationship between business and government. In the UK, the Department of Health set up the Pharmaceutical Industry Competitiveness Task Force to support the development of the industry while at the same time negotiating reduced prices for the NHS for their products.

This juxtaposition makes explicit something that may be hidden in other countries where the health system is not so directly the responsibility of government. In virtually every rich country, however, government will have an interest both in protecting its industry, whether it is pharmaceuticals or anything else, and in controlling the costs to its population through regulation, subsidy or other means.

Government has proved to be a very generous funder of healthcare, as Figure 5.3 shows. In 1920 the Government of the UK spent less than 1% of its GDP on health. By 2010 it was spending about 7.5% of GDP.[19] The USA spent very little public money on health in the first half of the century and only reached 1% of GDP by 1964. Thereafter, spending accelerated and public expenditure in the USA, too, reached about 7.5% of GDP in 2010.[20]

Both countries subsidise health from government to a remarkably similar degree. The big difference between the two countries, of course, is that the USA spends a further 9% of GDP from private sources, mainly insurance, bringing its total to 16.5%, while the UK spends only about 2.0% of private money, bringing its total spend to about 9.5% of GDP. This was much higher in 2021 due to expenditure on the pandemic.

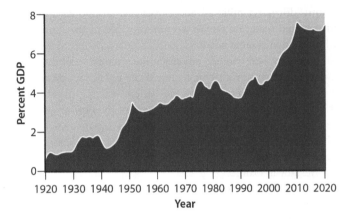

**Figure 5.3** UK growth in government expenditure on health as a percentage of GDP from 1920 to 2020.

Politicians and policymakers are responding to public opinion with increased spending. Greater wealth has raised the priority richer populations give to health or, to put it another way, greater affluence and leisure have given people more time to worry about the quality of their health and their lives rather than simply struggle for survival.

## DIFFERENT HEALTH SYSTEMS BUT COMMON ASSUMPTIONS

This account has brought out the close relationship between all the big players in health and healthcare. This has been enormously beneficial, but it has also created problems. You don't have to be a conspiracy theorist to see that there is a medico–academic–commercial–governmental alignment of interests that could work to the benefit of patients, but which may not.

These powerful linkages have, inevitably, also driven self-interest, created hierarchy and elites and, over time, become self-referring, closed and resistant to change. This has created conflicts of interest and, in some cases, promoted the insider interests of its practitioners, whether they are scientists, doctors, businessmen or government officials, and neglected the changing interests of its beneficiaries, its patients and its customers.

The way the system works reinforces this. In looking at why the US costs were so much higher than those of any other country, the McKinsey Foundation concluded that there were two main factors. The first was a far higher rate of investigation and of hospitalisation. The second was the almost complete absence of anyone in the system who had an incentive to reduce expenditure. The Foundation found that hospitals, physicians and suppliers alike had strong incentives to provide more treatment, even if patient benefits were very small or non-existent.[21]

In particular, it is the triad of the professions, commerce and technology that has driven costs. Commerce has marketed the products of technology with the active involvement of the professions. All three parties are strongly incentivised to do more, treat more patients and increase overall costs. None is incentivised to manage costs or control waste.

We, as the public, are also active participants in this process with our apparent belief that greater expenditure is always a good thing and should always bring greater benefit. This interaction is well illustrated by the account given in *The New York Times* of a doctor being asked by fellow doctors to join them in purchasing the latest computed tomography (CT) scanner.[22]

> We, as the public, are also active participants in this process with our apparent belief that greater expenditure is always a good thing and should always bring greater benefit.

The doctor is tempted and you can understand why. It will be a new service he can offer patients. He will be popular with his colleagues, and it will probably be a good investment. Altogether it sounds like a win–win situation. He resists, however, because he is worried that he and the other doctors in the clinic would feel pressure to give scans to people who might not need them in order to pay for the equipment. Yet, the article goes on to say, more than 1000 other cardiologists and hospitals have installed CT scanners on this basis. Not everyone resists the temptation.

These pressures play out differently in different countries. Countries have their own ways of defining and organising their role in health and have created very different systems. In very broad terms, there are typically European-style systems based on an idea of social solidarity, funded through tax or social insurance, and American-style private systems funded through private or employment-based insurance schemes although, as noted earlier, the US system is subsidised by the Government from public funds to the same level as the UK's NHS. There are some other very significant variations in how this works in practice. Singapore, for example, has created its own distinctive and successful hybrid, where individuals have their own budgets in part funded by the state but they can top them up privately.

For Europeans, again very broadly, the health of individuals and the population as a whole is seen as something of public concern and governments have a proper role in making sure people have access to healthcare and are protected from disease. Health, in economists' terms, is a public good. In the USA, very broadly, people are expected and expecting to look after themselves with the state providing a safety net and protecting the interests of the country as a whole. Health is largely considered a private good, which citizens should seek and provide for themselves in a healthcare marketplace.

In reality, while these broad generalisations accurately reflect the prevailing politics and the rhetoric, they gloss over the fact that there is a great deal of similarity in what happens in practice. The social solidarity systems mostly allow people to opt out and 'go private' and to use elements of the different public and private systems at different times, depending on nationally or locally determined rules and procedures. Similarly, the private systems operate safety nets and private philanthropy plays a more substantial role. Moreover, as we have already noted in this chapter, the USA and UK subsidise healthcare to about the same extent.

These differences do matter, however, because while American systems, as the McKinsey Foundation report shows, incentivise more activity and treatment, European systems, with resources pooled, will incentivise action to promote the health of whole populations and be more likely to seek cheaper solutions and weigh treatments against each other. If the risk in the private system may be overtreatment or no treatment (if you can't pay), the risk in the public system is more likely to be undertreatment. One rations access by cost, the other through explicit decision making.

> If the risk in the private system may be overtreatment or no treatment, the risk in the public system is more likely to be undertreatment. One rations access by cost, the other through explicit decision making.

The differences between the systems appear clearly in the attitudes and opinions of citizens of the different countries. Many Americans are appalled at the thought of what they see as European 'socialised medicine', which would limit their choices over healthcare. Similarly, many Europeans are appalled by what they conceive as a totally private system that gives no attention to the poorest and sickest in the population and where 'the devil takes the hindmost'.

The spectre of 'socialised medicine' is one that opponents of US healthcare reform are keen to use. Michael Moore's film *Sicko* goes in the opposite direction and applauds European systems while ridiculing the US system, or lack of it. The differences between the European and American approaches are a major cause for conflict and, as always with conflict, people lose sight of the reality.

These examples are rich in cultural and political differences. They serve to show the very different assumptions that people bring to their thinking about health and healthcare and to their approaches to technology. As we shall see in Chapter 7, where we discuss the current race for influence in Africa, these different cultural attitudes also underpin the thinking that informs the different approaches to international development and can lead to unhelpful conflict.

Whilst rich countries make different assumptions about the balance of the role of the state and the individual and about solidarity versus personal responsibility, their institutions and systems nevertheless share a very similar range of assumptions in other areas. These are assumptions about the position and responsibilities of the professions, the importance of science and technology, about governance and accountability, and about the roles ascribed to patients and citizens, and, as important as any of the others, an assumption that greater spending means greater improvement. They are implicit and sometimes explicit in our healthcare systems and institutions.

These assumptions, with only a degree of exaggeration, cast the individual as someone who needs to be educated and persuaded to adopt the right course of action, accepts without question the outcomes of science and research, is a largely passive and patient recipient of care from the professionals, is a consumer who is sold services and who, of course, is paying an increasingly large proportion of their personal income and taxes to support health improvement and, with it, a whole healthcare industry.

Strong professional groups, for example, which led such improvement in the twentieth century, tend to disempower their patients and restrict their ability to make decisions about their own health. Patients who have long-term chronic diseases, like the woman from Reading, often know a great deal about their own health yet can find it very difficult to get doctors and nurses to listen to them. Many people still can't see or own a copy of their own medical record; doctors have to act on their behalf.

It is ironic that many individuals in high-income countries, patients and the public, share a sense of powerlessness about their health with people in lower-income countries. The context is very different in the two cases. People in lower-income countries need more resources and strengthened health systems. In high-income countries, however, the system itself is so strong and so well resourced that it takes the power away from its citizens.

> People in lower-income countries need more resources and strengthened health systems. In high-income countries, however, the system itself is so strong and so well resourced that it takes the power away from its citizens.

As the public, we have played our part in creating this dependence. We have learned constantly to want more from our scientists and professionals. The professions and the professionals have become over-mighty and the drug companies over-strong. We have become dependent on ever-growing amounts of money being spent in healthcare and, often, demanded it from our politicians. Sir Sam Everington, an experienced London GP, talks of the danger of a mutual dependence between doctor and patient – the patient wants to depend on the doctor and the doctor wants to be needed.[23]

These assumptions, which may have seemed unexceptional to many people only 30 years ago, are now, however, coming under increasing individual and collective scrutiny. It is evident that many people are not satisfied with the roles ascribed to them as patients and consumers of health and they are beginning to break away from the assumptions and biases of the institutions and systems.

Increasingly, patients and the public want to see the system turned upside down so that the burden and weight of the whole system does not bear down on the patients, making them conform, but rather the patients sit above the system, drawing on it as they need to. Many doctors as well as patients want to see change and are making it happen wherever they can.

## CONCLUSIONS

The problems described here are enormous and their solutions both difficult and very long term. We need to look in a great deal more detail at what is happening around the world, to understand better some of the social trends that are affecting us all and to learn from the pioneers and innovators, wherever they are to be found.

We will come back to these issues in Chapter 11 where we consider how health systems need to change and discuss some of the latest technological and other innovations, including the development of virtual hospitals in China.

Our search for understanding continues in the next chapter by beginning our exploration of the relationships between richer and poorer countries.

## REFERENCES

1. Loudon I. Maternal mortality in the past and its relevance to developing countries today. *Am J Clin Nutr* [Online] 2000; **72**: 241S–6S. doi: https://doi.org/10.1093/ajcn/72.1.241S (Accessed 16 November 2021).
2. Pronovost P, Urwin J W, Beck E *et al*. Making a dent in the trillion-dollar problem: toward zero defects. *NEJM Catalyst Innovations in Care Delivery*, January 2021; **2**(1). doi: https://doi.org/10.1056/CAT.19.1064 (Accessed 16 November 2021).
3. Schoen C, Osborn R, Huynh PT *et al*. Taking the pulse of healthcare systems experiences of patients with health problems in six countries. The Commonwealth Fund, 2005. https://www.commonwealthfund.org/publications/journal-article/2005/nov/taking-pulse-health-care-systems-experiences-patients-health (Accessed 16 November 2021).
4. https://www.commonwealthfund.org/publications/issue-briefs/2020/jan/us-health-care-global-perspective-2019 (Accessed 16 November 2021).
5. Remarks made by the President at the Annual Conference of the American Medical Association. Washington DC: The White House, 15 June 2009.
6. https://www.uk.mercer.com/newsroom/britains-92-billion-pounds-productivity-loss-nations-first-productive-day-is-now-21st-february.html (Accessed 16 November 2021).
7. Sutherland JM, Fisher ES, Skinner JS. Getting past denial: the high cost of health care in the United States. *N Engl J Med* 2009; **361**: 1227–30. doi: 10.1056/NEJMp0907172.
8. https://www.health.org.uk/sites/default/files/2020-03/Health%20Equity%20in%20England_The%20Marmot%20Review%2010%20Years%20On_executive%20summary_web.pdf (Accessed 16 November 2021).
9. https://www.ons.gov.uk/peoplepopulationandcommunity/birthsdeathsandmarriages/deaths/articles/causesofdeathover100years/2017-09-18 (Accessed 16 November 2021).
10. Layard R. *Happiness: Lessons from a new science*. London: Penguin, 2005.
11. https://assets.publishing.service.gov.uk/government/uploads/system/uploads/attachment_data/file/216528/dh_134486.pdf (Accessed 16 November 2021).
12. Lynn J, Straube B, Bell KM *et al*. Using population segmentation to provide better health care for all: the 'Bridges to Health' model. *Milbank Q*, 2007; **85**: 185–208. https://pubmed.ncbi.nlm.nih.gov/17517112/ (Accessed 16 November 2021).
13. Christensen CM, Grossman JH, Hwang J. *The Innovator's Prescription: A disruption solution for healthcare*. New York: McGraw-Hill, 2009.
14. Vinten-Johansen P, Brody H, Paneth N *et al. Cholera, Chloroform, and the Science of Medicine: A life of John Snow*. New York: Oxford University Press, 2003.
15. Nightingale F. *Notes on Nursing: What it is and what it is not*. New York: D Appleton & Company, 1859.
16. WHO. Primary Health Care: Now more than ever. The world health report, 2008. www.who.int/whr/2008/whr08_en.pdf (Accessed 16 November 2021).
17. http://archive.carnegiefoundation.org/publications/pdfs/elibrary/Carnegie_Flexner_Report.pdf (Accessed 16 November 2021).
18. https://www.rcpe.ac.uk/sites/default/files/jrcpe_47_4_vale.pdf (Accessed 16 November 2021).

19. https://www.ukpublicspending.co.uk/healthcare_spending (Accessed 22 November 2021).
20. http://www.usgovernmentspending.com/year_download_2010USpn_22ps2n#usgs302 (Accessed 16 November 2021).
21. McKinsey Global Institute. Accounting for the cost of healthcare in the United States. 2007. https://www.mckinsey.com/industries/healthcare-systems-and-services/our-insights/accounting-for-the-cost-of-health-care-in-the-united-states (Accessed 16 November 2021).
22. Berenson A, Abelson R. Weighing the cost of a CT scan's look inside the heart. *The New York Times* [Online] 29 June 2008. www.nytimes.com/2008/06/29/business/29scan.html (Accessed 16 November 2021).
23. Sir Sam Everington. Personal communication 2020.

# 6 Unfair trade (1) – exporting health workers

The facts are plain. Many thousands of health workers who were trained in their own countries have migrated to other countries to work and the receiving countries have benefited as a result. This is part of a far wider pattern of migration from low- and middle-income countries by workers in different sectors seeking employment and opportunity.

This pattern of economic migration is, in turn, part of a much larger movement of people seeking opportunity or escaping war, persecution and famine. It is a sad fact that there are 26.4 million refugees today, more than have ever been recorded before. There are also 48.0 million internally displaced people; 4.1 million asylum-seekers; and 3.9 million Venezuelans displaced abroad – together making a total 82.4 million people.[1] The destructive consequences of climate change will add millions more.

Not all reasons for migrating, of course, are negative. Many people move from one country to another for positive reasons – opportunities, retirement, a better climate, joining a partner, adventure and more. Many of the people described in this book and many people reading it will have migrated or their parents or grandparents did. It is simply a part of modern life for many people.

This chapter describes one half of the unfair import–export business in which lower-income countries export, mostly unintentionally and unwillingly, many of their health workers whilst at the same time receiving, often inappropriate and sometimes discredited, ideas and ideologies from high-income countries. There are exceptions, as we will see, where countries such as Cuba and the Philippines have deliberately chosen to send health workers abroad, albeit for very different reasons in the cases of these two countries.

The chapter provides an insight into the many and varied ways in which health workers migrate around the world, with ultimately a net health and economic benefit to high-income countries and a net loss to lower-income ones. It also describes how emigration is part of a wider set of issues, including poor pay and employment practices, bad working conditions, shortfalls in training and lack of resources, which combine to create a desperate shortage of health workers in many low- and middle-income countries.

There is a global shortage of health workers which affects every country in the world and which is likely to get worse as a result of the pandemic, with countries everywhere strengthening

DOI: 10.1201/9781003267706-6

their health systems. This can only be resolved through more creative use of technology, changing job roles and a new appreciation of the role that wider society plays in health.

## MIGRATING HEALTH WORKERS

It is impossible to calculate with any accuracy how many health workers who were first trained in the countries of sub-Saharan Africa, for example, are now living in other countries. Moreover, the position varies enormously from one country to another and from one region of the world to another. However, the underlying pattern is clear: there is now a global labour market in trained health workers and a flow of talent and skill, which goes very largely, but not entirely, from lower-income countries to higher-income ones.

> There is now a global labour market in trained health workers and a flow of talent and skill, which goes very largely, but not entirely, from lower-income countries to higher-income ones.

It is equally clear that this export of trained people costs their home countries dearly and that it benefits the countries where they now live and work. It is not just countries, of course, that gain and lose from this export and import business. The individuals who leave their own countries mostly gain and those left behind, coping with staff shortages as well as everything else, lose significantly. It is not surprising that this causes rancour and some returning migrants report being abused and made unwelcome in their home country.

Estimates suggest that the loss of skilled professionals from the health sector alone costs the African continent around US$2 billion a year.[2] This is part of a much greater export of wealth from Africa, where the costs of the wider brain drain across all the educated sectors of society as well as the extraction of natural resources and wider 'capital flight' are greater than the flows of inward investment and aid money. Remittances sent home from migrant workers, as we shall see later, help offset this to a considerable extent.

Richer countries undoubtedly benefit from this migration, whether this is a result of a deliberate policy of undertraining or not, because of the enormous cost in training medical staff as the following two examples show. It cost about US$333 000 to train a general medical graduate in Australia in 2015.[3] The cost of a fully trained medical specialist in the USA was estimated at US$1.1 million in 2014.[4] Bringing in a migrant doctor provides an enormous saving to the national budget.

Although the exact figures can be argued over, we can see that we are dealing with very large sums of money here. These calculations must be pretty compelling if you are only concerned about how to ensure the country has enough doctors and about how to do so within the constraints of your own Australian or American health budget. They are deeply worrying if you are concerned about how to staff your own health service in a low-income country.

This chapter is concerned with migration between countries, but we should not forget the migration within countries, particularly between rural and urban areas and from poorer communities to richer. It is always more difficult to access services in remote areas and, even in high-income countries, most professionals base themselves in affluent areas.

## THE WIDER PICTURE

These figures don't tell us the whole story. The underlying and most significant problem, in terms of numbers, is that not enough health workers are being trained globally in countries around the world.

Migration is not the biggest staffing problem in most lower-income countries. It is vitally important, but even if we don't know the exact figures, we can safely say that, if every trained health worker who had left Africa were to return to their country of origin, they would make a relatively small contribution to the numbers needed. The numbers who have left are the smaller part of the projected shortage of the more than 6 million additional health workers that the WHO projects will be needed in the African region by 2030, as described later in this chapter.

The bigger problem is that many more health workers need to be trained globally, and we mustn't let a focus on the 'brain drain' obscure this fact. As one senior African told me, attacking the West about migration lets African governments off the hook. Only two governments, Rwanda and South Africa, had met the Abuja Declaration made by African Heads of State to spend 15% of government income on health.[5] They could do more, particularly to address the issues which lead to many workers wanting to migrate in the first place.

> The bigger problem is that many more health workers need to be trained globally, and we mustn't let a focus on the 'brain drain' obscure this fact.

The issue of health worker migration is one of the most emotive in health globally and, as the former Chief Executive of the NHS, I have often been challenged about the UK role in this. Personally, I have no doubt at all that the UK has benefited enormously from waves of health workers coming from the Caribbean, South East Asia and Africa and that many of these workers have represented a real loss to their homelands. I also believe – and have argued strongly – that the UK has an obligation to help solve the problem of the lack of health workers in countries from which we have received trained health workers.

The patterns of migration are complex and ever-changing, with many health workers moving, for example, between African countries, others returning home from abroad with new skills, and health workers from high-income countries working for a period in low- and middle-income countries. In some countries, there are many trained workers who are unemployed because there are no funded posts available.

The way forward will undoubtedly involve a wide mix of factors. These must include improved working conditions and better pay, training more health workers – in all countries – ensuring there are funded employment opportunities, encouraging circular migration and partnership working, and developing country to country protocols supported by the implementation of strong codes of ethical practice in international recruitment.

The starting point is to understand the position better.

## PATTERNS OF MIGRATION

There have been large flows of people from former colonies to the former colonial powers where the language, culture and health systems are similar. People have moved from lower-income to higher-income countries within their own region with South Africa, for example, benefiting from trained health workers from elsewhere in sub-Saharan Africa. The USA has received people from around the world, with particularly large numbers from Latin and South America and from India, and with many others coming as 'secondary migrants', after a spell in another country first.

Doctors present much the largest problem in terms of the percentage of trained health workers who have emigrated, with in some cases one-third or more of medical students in a country migrating after graduation. More nurses migrate in total, but they represent a much smaller percentage of the numbers trained. The numbers involved are very large, as Figure 6.1 shows, with some countries, most notably the UK, the USA, Australia, Canada, Israel, Norway, Switzerland and New Zealand, benefiting from having very large numbers of doctors and nurses who had their initial training abroad. About a quarter of doctors working in the UK and the US in 2017 first trained abroad.

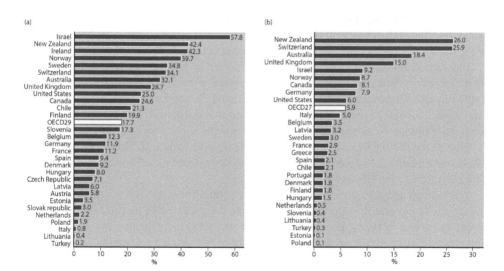

**Figure 6.1** Shares of foreign-trained doctors **(a)** and nurses **(b)** in OECD countries in 2017.
Source: OECD.[7]

The flow of migrants is increasing. The number of foreign-trained doctors working in Organisation for Economic Co-operation and Development (OECD) countries increased by 50% between 2006 and 2016 (to nearly 500 000 in 2016), while the number of foreign-trained nurses increased by 20% over the 5-year period from 2011 to 2016 (to nearly 550 000). These migrants are not all from low- and middle-income countries – there is a great deal of movement between OECD countries – but they do show an upward trend in mobility and illustrate both how fast the global marketplace for health workers is developing and the international nature of many country's health workforce.[6]

The UK provides a good example of the complexity of the situation. There were around 1.9 million people employed in the healthcare workforce in the UK in 2018 across the public and private sectors. Of these, British nationals made up 88% of the workforce and non-British nationals made up 12% – 6% EU nationals and 6% non-EU nationals.

The proportion of non-British nationals in the healthcare workforce has remained broadly stable since 2012, but at the same time the numbers have increased from 155 000 to 227 000, with EU nationals accounting for the majority of the increase – until, of course, Brexit took effect.[8]

Migrants from lower-income countries will mainly be included in the 6% of the UK health workforce from outside the EU. This is a small percentage of a large workforce but the numbers migrating are a very large percentage of the much smaller workforce in their countries of origin.

A recent report from THET describes the situation in Uganda.[9] According to the country's medical regulator, 209 Ugandans asked for certificates of good standing in the year to June 2019. These are needed for migrating doctors to practise in another country. In the same period, 664 foreign practitioners were registered to practise in Uganda.

At first sight, this suggests a net inflow to Uganda, but these figures are not like for like. Some Ugandan doctors emigrated to countries which don't require these certificates, and many of the foreign doctors were almost certainly practising in Uganda for very short periods.

The authors noted that 169 UK doctors volunteered in Uganda between 2016 and 2018 for a total of over 3000 days between them – on average, around 3 weeks each – as part of the THET-run UK Aid-funded Health Partnership Scheme. Temporary doctors, however skilled, can't replace the role of permanent doctors working in a stable and effective health system – which is, of course, the aim of the Ugandan government.

Most of the doctors leaving Uganda in that period were early and mid-career, aged up to 40. Almost a quarter (24%) went to Canada, 21% to Kenya (a total of 27% went to East African countries), 17% to the UK, and 10% to South Africa.

This example provides some insights into the position. The world is not a single place and the circumstances and the opportunities as well as the perils facing its citizens are rich and varied. There is a wealth of personal stories and anecdotes that illustrate this diversity well and present a much more complicated and even confusing picture of migration.

> The world is not a single place and the circumstances and the opportunities as well as the perils facing its citizens are rich and varied.

There is also a great deal of temporary migration. The USA and the UK have been and still are the great medical educators of the world, although China, Russia and Cuba have all developed their capacity in recent years. Many people have travelled to these countries for training at all levels, including the more specialist training that they would not have been able to get at home.

Migration is often not a single event in someone's life or, indeed, a once-and-for-all one-way process. Migrants may move from one country to another and on to a third or a fourth. They may acquire new training and skills and they may return home after a few years or retire. Their children may grow up in a foreign country and, at some point in their lives, return to their parents' country of origin.

Individual examples bring these points to life. The Honourable Socco Kabia became the Health Minister for Sierra Leone in 2008. As a young man, he left his country to become a medical student in Germany but returned home as a graduate because he was unable, as a foreigner, to progress on to clinical training. He later migrated to the USA for training and worked there for many years.

He returned to Sierra Leone in 2005, following the ending of conflict in his country. Determined to help improve the health of the population, he entered politics and took over one of the most difficult jobs in the world. How, one might ask, does one work to improve health in a population where women at the time had a 1 in 7 lifetime chance of dying in childbirth, 75% of the health workers died in the country's internal conflict or fled the country and you have less than US$5 a year per head of the population to spend on health?

Many other health ministers in Africa have trained and worked abroad. I have talked about their personal experience with an Ethiopian Minister with higher degrees from the UK, a Ugandan Minister who trained and worked in Chicago for many years as an obstetrician, and a Zambian Minister who trained and worked as an orthopaedic surgeon in London, UK. There are many other leading doctors in Africa who can tell similar tales.

There are, of course, migrants who have risen to the top of the profession in their new country, refugees who have found the freedom to live and work without constant fear and poverty, and we all know of the grandson of a Kenyan goatherder who became President of the USA.

These personal stories are part of much wider patterns in many countries that go far beyond healthcare. Ben Male fled from his schoolroom in Uganda when Idi Amin's soldiers killed his father. Arriving in Tanzania he was mistaken for a spy by the rebel Ugandans preparing to invade the country and once again had to flee for his life. Physically disabled from birth, Ben was penniless and unable to speak the language when he finally reached safety in Rwanda, where missionaries took him in and cared for the bewildered 17-year-old.

By a remarkable chance, the missionaries introduced him to a British schoolteacher who recognised his intelligence and abilities and, raising money from the students at Rugby School, arranged for him to complete his schooling at that archetypal English public school. Ben graduated from Sheffield University and, after some years working for NGOs in Europe, returned to Uganda, where he was the country representative for Sightsavers and active in the developing civil society.

Ben is, of course, an exception because of his luck and his talent. However, there are many people whose life stories should be recorded both as inspiring in themselves and as being so descriptive of the lives of millions – the lucky and the unlucky – in Africa and in many other poor countries.

Not all migrants are as lucky or as capable as Ben or any of these ministers. Many come to grief on their travels. Unscrupulous traffickers and employers exploit many. Others simply find that their skills are not utilised, their expectations are not met and their hopes are destroyed. London and Washington contain many migrants and refugees whose skills can't be used because of regulations about medical and other practice. Their numbers, of course, are growing and their impact on host countries can be enormous. Uganda has the biggest refugee camp in the world with 1 million people on site.

Not everyone lives the uneventful lives of many people in long-settled countries in Western Europe. These mobile lives are becoming even more common. We need to understand this mobility if we are to have a positive impact on managing the damaging effects of migration from poor to rich countries and the effects on the migrants themselves.

On the other side of the equation, people from high-income countries choose to work abroad for a whole range of personal reasons. This mobility, with people choosing to work in different countries at different points in their lives, is undoubtedly on the increase.

> This mobility, with people choosing to work in different countries at different points in their lives, is undoubtedly on the increase.

The success of organizations such as Médecins Sans Frontières, Médecins du Monde, and others that recruit volunteers to work in poor countries shows just how attractive this lifestyle can be, at least at certain stages in life.

Individuals, too, have found their own ways to work in their own country and abroad. Chris Lavy, for example, worked for many years as a surgeon in Malawi before returning home when his children were at an age when he and his wife wanted them to have English schooling. He is now a Professor in the Department of Orthopaedic Surgery at Oxford and manages to combine his work in the UK with continuing involvement in Africa, helping create, for example, the East African College of Surgeons as a means of driving up standards and improving practice.

Sir Eldryd Parry is an inspiration to many British people working in health globally. He has been dean of medical schools in Ghana and Ethiopia and served on the faculty in Ibadan in Nigeria during a long career spent mostly in Africa. He founded THET with the aim of working in partnership to support health workers across the world more than 30 years ago and, aged 90, is still active in promoting its aims.

Many middle-aged health professionals from all disciplines and backgrounds, after a career in their own countries, want to do something to help improve health in poorer countries. Even more significantly, very many young people in the UK and the USA see their whole lives differently from older generations and aspire to careers in 'global health'. They are helping to create a new way of looking at the world and their profession, a new collaborative and compassionate global outlook which is so vital for the future.

## WHY PEOPLE MIGRATE

There are many reasons why health workers migrate; some are directly related to health services, some are not. There are many factors 'pushing' people to leave their own country: from the fear of persecution and the lack of personal and economic security to the sheer frustration of working in awful conditions with no drugs and no equipment and no hope. A survey carried out in the four African countries of Cameroon, South Africa, Uganda and Zimbabwe showed that the four main reasons people emigrated were to achieve better remuneration, a safer environment, better living conditions and better facilities.[10]

Feedback from nurses to the International Council of Nurses was that the main reasons for nurses emigrating or leaving the profession in poor countries are the working environment and the facts that they can't get adequate housing, access to services or schools for their children. A lack of jobs is another important factor in many countries. The President of the Ugandan Nurses and Midwives Union estimated that there were 29 000 nurses unemployed in the country in 2019.[9]

Families also influence the decision to leave. In many parts of the world, university graduates are expected to earn a high income to benefit both themselves and their, often very extended, families. Many of these families understand very well that there is much more money to be made abroad. In one survey, a remarkable 77% of final-year university students in Zimbabwe said they faced family pressure to emigrate. Elsewhere, there is evidence that medical faculty advise students to migrate in search of better training and to achieve their personal goals.[11] A 2015 survey of 146 medical schools in Africa indicated that about 25% of their alumni emigrate within 5 years of graduation.[12]

> In one survey, a remarkable 77% of final-year university students in Zimbabwe said they faced family pressure to emigrate.

Many people go abroad for training that may not be available in their own country, and many return home afterwards. Sri Lanka, as a matter of good practice, has traditionally encouraged its higher trainees to spend 2 years abroad learning their speciality. Other governments send trainees who do not have local facilities to specialist centres. UK qualifications are in high demand in India and UK institutions still provide much of the educational infrastructure in former British Colonies. The Royal College of General Practice, for example, accredits family doctor training in many parts of South East Asia in association with local bodies. Half the membership of the Royal College of Obstetricians and Gynaecologists is from outside the UK.

A Chinese doctor gave me a personal slant on this: *'We learn our trades abroad and are now putting them to good use at home. When I returned home 5 years ago, there were chicken coops, now there are multinationals.'*

These educational links provide some counterbalance to the damage done by migration and could, as I will argue, be built on much more strongly than at present to help increase the health workforce in many countries.

Table 6.1 summarises some of the main push and pull factors for individuals.

There are many outside forces 'pulling' people. Some rich countries actively encourage the import of health workers; others have, knowingly or unknowingly, allowed it to happen. In the UK, the establishment of the NHS in 1948 was accompanied in the following years by a big increase in demand for services and a big increase in costs. Looking at the circumstances of the time, I don't think it was the costs of training that drove the government of the day to support such large-scale immigration of health workers, but rather the shortage of trained health workers for the NHS.

**Table 6.1** Push and pull factors

| Push | Pull |
| --- | --- |
| No jobs | Greater opportunities |
| Low pay | Higher pay, can send money home |
| Poor housing, schools, etc. | Better opportunities for families |
| Poor work environment | Professional fulfilment |
| Family pressure | Active recruitment |
| Unsafe environment | |

The UK Government wanted to deliver on its promise of a universal health service for all its people. This promise drew in health workers from what were then its colonies, with the Caribbean providing many nurses and South Asia many doctors. It is clear that the NHS could not have prospered without this immigration.[13]

It is clear that the NHS could not have prospered without this immigration.

Other countries may not always have made such explicit promises. Even without promises, rich countries need to keep meeting the rising demands for healthcare, which come from their increasingly older and more prosperous electorate.

The NHS looked towards international recruitment again in 2000 during my time as Chief Executive to help implement the ambitious NHS Plan. Over the following years we developed new policies of ethical recruitment, as described later in the chapter. In 2021, a new UK Government once again saw international recruitment as part of its strategy to improve the NHS.

Some governments that want valuable hard currency sent home by their citizens working abroad actively encourage this migration. Of Ghana's GDP, 7.4% came from such remittances in 2018, so I was not surprised that the former Minister of Health advocated the approach to me, suggesting that the UK might want to set up a planning agreement to do so. Overall, remittances from migrant workers in all sectors to developing countries stood at US$540 billion in 2020 – down US$8 billion due to COVID-19 from the 2019 figure – and were much higher than Foreign Direct Investment (FDI) of US$259 billion and overseas development assistance of US$179 billion.[14]

The story of the Philippines is often quoted. It is a remarkable example of a country that has taken the initiative. It has very deliberately chosen to export its labour and, as Patricia Santo Tomas, formerly Minister of Labour and Chair of the Philippines Development Bank explains, to *'manage the potential damage to our country from the migration of health workers'*. Several countries, including Japan, the Netherlands, Norway and Denmark, have established training schools in the country and the Philippines has agreements on recruitment with more than 80 countries.

Cuba is very much an exception. It has a long history of exporting doctors which started immediately after Castro took power in 1959. It has supported other countries, for example, by supplying doctors to assist in the aftermath of the Chilean earthquake in 1960; to Algeria requesting assistance in 1963; and, more recently, to Haiti's earthquake and subsequent cholera outbreak in 2010. This is all done in pursuit of internationalism and solidarity with the peoples of the world.

It has also exported doctors for economic reasons: for example, in 2000 Cuba agreed a trade of 'doctors for oil' with Venezuela. A further agreement in 2005 provided for the training of 50000 medical personnel in Venezuela and the creation of 1000 free medical centres. Oil shipments to Cuba increased to 90000 barrels a day. Many in Venezuela have welcomed this, although it is reported that Venezuelan doctors protested strongly that these incomers were taking their work away. The powerful trades unionism of the profession is as evident in poorer countries as in richer.

Cuba established the Latin American Medical School in Havana. It opened its doors to its first students in 1999 with the aim of educating doctors from countries around the world. They have since come in their thousands. By 2015, it had graduated over 30000 physicians from 121 countries. South Africa alone has more than 3000 current or past students. As I write, 1000 students from all over the world are studying medicine in Cuba.

The School was designed to train physicians for the people who need them the most – the poor, the isolated and the excluded. It does so by training people from those very backgrounds because its evidence shows that they are much more likely to go back to their own people rather than, as many doctors do, migrate to the cities and find better opportunities in richer parts of the country or abroad. In order to do this, it has established a system of Medical Scholarships to provide opportunities and support for people from the poorest and most remote backgrounds.

> The School was designed to train physicians for the people who need them the most – the poor, the isolated and the excluded.

As Dr Margaret Chan, the former Director General of the WHO, said on a visit to the School in 2009, '*For once, if you are poor, female, or from an indigenous population, you have a distinct advantage, an ethic that makes this medical school unique.*'

## THE NEW PATTERNS EMERGING

The patterns of migration are, however, not standing still and there is plenty of evidence that the global movement of trained health workers will increase as the newly rich countries of the Gulf, South Asia and, increasingly, India and China demand a greater share of this scarce resource. They will draw health workers from high-income countries as well as elsewhere, which in turn will put more pressure on low-income countries.

Singapore, for example, only recognises the qualifications of doctors trained in a relatively small list of registered universities and actively recruits abroad.[15] Singapore and other South Asian countries such as India and Thailand cater for the growing demand for high-quality healthcare from people who are willing to travel to obtain international standards and can afford to do so. Singapore is within 7 hours' flying time of 40% of the world's population, 2.5 billion people. It and its competitors have planned for a growing market and need the staff to deliver. The COVID-19 pandemic has curtailed such travel at least temporarily and there are now concerns about the long-term viability of this approach.

The Gulf States, too, are hungry for people. In 2009, Dr Elsheik Badr from the Sudan described to me what he saw happening in the Gulf States and its likely longer-term impact. He told me that in these six countries, with a population then of about 35 million, around three-quarters of both doctors and nurses already came from abroad and the proportions as well as the actual numbers were set to grow further.

Dr Badr was understandably concerned about the impact on his own country. The Gulf States have a preference for Arab-speaking Muslims. Of Sudanese doctors who match these preferences, 10% were already there. There were many 'pull' factors – geographical proximity; language, social and cultural similarities; a suitable environment for families; policies promoting expatriate labour; good remuneration and active recruitment. Sudan, sadly, has in recent years provided more 'push' factors than 'pull', with internal conflict, lack of stability and a weak economy continuing to push people away.

The latest figures for the region show that, despite big increases in training in Saudi Arabia, still around 75% of doctors and nurses are from abroad.[16]

> The latest figures for the region show that, despite big increases in training in Saudi Arabia, still around 75% of doctors and nurses are from abroad.

Francis Omaswa has also pointed me recently towards the growing number of young Ugandan women who are travelling to work as domestic servants in the Arab states, illustrating another facet of the wider patterns of emigration.

This discussion has largely concentrated on doctors, primarily because there is better information available on their numbers and their movements. There are overlapping patterns for other groups of health workers. Many nurses have migrated from their homelands. I was told by government officials in India that they expect to lose about two-thirds of the nurses trained there within 2 years of graduation.

There may, however, be a changing pattern here as well. Dr Badr has noticed that the Gulf States have recently wanted more nurses than before as their health services develop and more care can be given. As more sophisticated services develop in other countries and as nursing itself raises its profile and status, we can expect this new pattern to develop. It is far harder to analyse migration patterns for other disciplines because of the lack of information and, frequently, the lack of common definitions of roles and professional boundaries.

These new patterns and increased movement are aided enormously by improved communications and technology. A significant part of this is due to the internet and its 24-hour-a-day capability to roam the world. Like everything else, health worker migration has speeded up as a result.

## ETHICAL POLICIES FOR INTERNATIONAL RECRUITMENT

The increased demand from the newly prosperous and rapidly growing parts of the world adds to growing demand from the already prosperous parts with their ageing populations.

Migration has also continued apace along the old routes as pressures to increase health staffing are continuing. Some estimates suggest that the USA will require 1 million more nurses in the next 10 years.

In 2000, the UK, once again as in 1948, set out on an ambitious plan to improve the NHS and, once again, required a massive increase in staffing. As Chief Executive, I oversaw a planned growth in staffing in the NHS by 250 000 from 1.1 million to 1.35 million in a 5-year period to 2005. Our strategy this time was threefold: to train more health workers ourselves, to bring people – mainly women who had left to have children – back into nursing, and to recruit internationally for staff who would fill some of the gaps while we trained our own. Our aim over time was to be self-sufficient in staffing. We also brought into healthcare for the first time many more people as helpers, assistants and technicians to support the work of professionally trained staff.

Our strategy was very successful. The NHS was able to deliver on almost all its planned improvement targets, thanks in part to these new staff. And, by 2007, the increased number of UK graduates whom we had trained was coming into service and the UK came nearer to being self-sustaining in terms of education and training.

The UK had come under serious criticism from African countries, led by South Africa, in the late 1990s and had developed both an ethical international recruitment policy and, later, a code of practice. It subsequently signed an agreement with South Africa to support each other's health systems through the exchange of information and personnel for mutual benefit. As a result of this agreement, around 330 doctors and other health professionals from the UK went to work in South Africa for periods between 2002 and 2005.

Almost 30 000 of the UK 250 000 increase in staffing came from international recruitment, with the rest generated internally. The ethical policy and code of practice meant that we tried very hard to take health workers only from countries with a surplus and where their governments supported the recruitment. To this end, we signed agreements with the Philippines, Spain and countries in Eastern Europe and saw a large increase in staff from some of these countries. Most of the 30 000 who we recruited abroad came from these countries, but not all.

While the ethical policies had a significant impact, some people found ways around the rules. Some recruiters working for private sector health companies continued to recruit from other countries. Once in the UK, it was comparatively easy for health workers to switch to the NHS. Additionally, some health workers came to the UK for family or other reasons and found jobs in the care sector or other industries.

> While the ethical policies had a significant impact, some people found ways around the rules.

There were also many sad cases of foreign doctors, particularly from South Asia, who had heard via the media or family members that jobs were plentiful in the UK and spent all their savings to come to the UK in search of their fortunes. Many more than were needed came and the vast majority never found jobs. In the end, we posted advertisements in a number of Indian cities to discourage health workers from coming to the UK in order to try to halt this flow.

When the increased output from training at home started to come through, the UK tightened its immigration rules and made nursing no longer a 'shortage speciality' in 2006, a designation which had brought with it relatively easy entry to the country in earlier years. This made immigration to the UK very difficult for health workers from outside the European Community for the next few years, although, as already noted, the position has changed again. The flow of nurses from South Africa, for example, fell from its height of 2114 in 2002 to 39 in 2007.

However, other doors were open in other countries for would-be migrants and, crucially, any global recruitment policy and code of practice must aim to address the 'push' factors as well as the 'pull'. High workloads, poor conditions and low pay can be very powerful incentives.

The UK ethical policy and code of practice was seen as a milestone by many and much of the African criticism of the 1990s turned into the desire to see this as a forerunner of more such policies and codes in the 2000s. At the same time, ethical policies and codes were developing in different parts of the world, such as in the South Pacific and Latin America, while the Commonwealth, with its large African membership, created a code of practice in 2004.

The pressure from low- and middle-income countries, which were generally the source of all this migration, continued to grow, and in 2004 the World Health Assembly passed resolution 57.9 that, among other things, called for the development of a global code of practice on the international recruitment of health personnel.

As a result, the Health Worker Migration Global Policy Advisory Council, chaired by the former President of Ireland, the Honourable Mary Robinson, and Professor Francis Omaswa from Uganda, was established to review existing practice, collect ideas for implementation and propose a global policy and code. The Council, of which I am a member, supported the WHO in designing a Code of Practice that was approved by the World Health Assembly in May 2010.[17]

This Code, for the first time, aims to bring together all aspects of international recruitment and seeks to address the roles and responsibilities of all parties, i.e. the source and destination countries, the recruitment agencies, the employers and the health workers themselves. It is very deliberately two-way. It addresses both the damaging drain of skills and talent from poor to rich countries and the rights and well-being of migrants who all too often face abuse and exploitation.

> [The Code] addresses both the damaging drain of skills and talent from poor to rich countries and the rights and well-being of migrants who all too often face abuse and exploitation.

The Code is not binding on member states and can't by itself deal with all the problems. It does, however, set out the clear expectations of the world health community and has the moral authority and standing to help all those who in their own countries are struggling to manage the effects of migration and improve the lives of migrants. A report is given to the World Health Assembly every 3 years and a review is held every 5 years.

A report from an expert group covering the first 10 years of the Code is expected to be published in early 2022. It is likely to call its overall effectiveness into question – it has no sanctions to use against countries which contravene it – but to point to how some countries have used it very effectively to reform their own practice.[18]

The Code does not directly address the issue of whether 'sending' countries could and should be compensated by the 'receiving' ones for training health workers who subsequently migrated. There have been many demands for this. The simple notion that a country should compensate another for every health worker that moved from one to the other fails to come to terms with the practical difficulties as well as the political difficulties of implementing such a scheme.

At the practical level, all sorts of questions arise, from how to trace a worker through the complex patterns of migration to the question of who should compensate whom for the postgraduate training received abroad by a migrant who brings their new skills home to serve their native country. The political issues are also complex, with some recipient countries simply not willing to discuss compensation and others wondering why they should compensate countries that fail to provide health workers with good working conditions or, worse still, persecute their citizens.

My view, as I recommended in *Global Health Partnerships*, a report to the UK Prime Minister published in 2007, is that the UK should recognise that it has responsibilities as a global employer because so many of its doctors and nurses were first trained abroad. I argue that, as part of that responsibility, it should support a massive scaling-up of training, education and employment of health workers in developing countries. The UK Government did not accept this in its formal response to my report but instead said that it would support international efforts to strengthen health worker training and employment.[19]

These efforts, as the next section shows, have not yet had a major impact on workforce numbers in low- and middle-income countries. Meanwhile, the UK, Norway and other countries have published their own new or revised codes of practice on international recruitment.[20]

## THE WORKFORCE CRISIS

There is a critical shortage of health workers worldwide. It is not a local problem for poor countries but a global crisis that affects us all.

It is not just a health worker crisis. It is a health crisis. There are about 1 billion people in the world without healthcare. Around another billion have minimal access to help and support. This means that, in the absence of sometimes quite simple help and advice, thousands die or are disabled from preventable and treatable causes. These thousands of individual tragedies are a tragedy for us all.

It is not just a health worker crisis. It is a health crisis.

It is worth asking whether trained health workers make a great deal of difference. Intuitively, one would expect that having health workers able to give advice and even simple treatments would help improve health and save lives. The evidence shows they do. Trained health workers with the right skills in the right place at the right time reduce levels of maternal mortality and increase child and infant survival, as Figure 6.2 shows.

There are many other factors, of course, that contribute to improving health such as the education of women, improvements in the environment and the availability of drugs and equipment. Our health is determined by much more than health systems and health workers, as earlier chapters have shown. More health workers will not be sufficient by themselves to

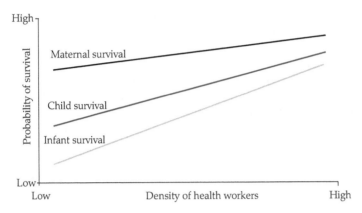

**Figure 6.2** Health workers matter. From *World Health Report 2006: Working together for health*.[21]

improve the health of a population, but they will certainly be a significant and necessary part of any wholesale improvement.

The WHO's Global Strategy on Human Resources for Health: Workforce 2030 showed that the global health workforce was over 43 million, based on the latest data from 2013.[22] This included 9.8 million doctors, 20.7 million nurses/midwives, and approximately 13 million other health workers. It made projections, based on current trends in training and funding, that there would be 55% growth in the total by 2030 to 67.3 million health workers. This would be made up of approximately 13.8 million doctors, 32.3 million nurses/midwives and 21.2 million other health workers.

The Strategy also estimated the need for health workers in 2030 based on 12 indicators that covered the SDGs and referred specifically to non-communicable diseases, maternal, newborn and child health, and infectious disease priorities. These were weighted in importance based on their contribution to tackling the global burden of disease. This was used to create an SDG index threshold of 4.45 physicians, nurses and midwives per 1000 population.

In order to achieve this level of health workers in every country, the shortage of health workers is projected to be more than 14 million in 2030. This means that current trends of health worker production will not be sufficient to meet the shortage of healthcare workers by 2030. Table 6.2 shows the actual shortfall in health workers in 2013 and the projected shortfall in 2030. In all regions bar one, the shortage will have stayed the same or reduced in this period, but it will increase in the African region where population numbers and need are increasing.

It is clear that the wonderful ambitions of the SDGs will not be achieved without large increases in trained health workers. A report on workforce numbers will be presented to the World Health Assembly in May 2022 at the halfway point in the delivery of the SDGs, 7.5 years into the 15-year period. It is likely to show that progress on health worker numbers overall is on target due to very big increases in China and elsewhere but that most low- and

**Table 6.2** Estimates of health worker needs based shortages (in millions)* in countries below the SDG index threshold by region, 2013 and 2030.[23]

| Region | 2013 | | | | 2030 | | | | % change |
|---|---|---|---|---|---|---|---|---|---|
| | Physicians | Nurses/ midwives | Other cadres | Total | Physicians | Nurses/ midwives | Other cadres | Total | |
| Africa | 0.9 | 1.8 | 1.5 | **4.2** | 1.1 | 2.8 | 2.2 | **6.1** | 45 |
| Americas | 0.0 | 0.5 | 0.2 | **0.8** | 0.1 | 0.5 | 0.1 | **0.6** | –17 |
| Eastern Mediterranean | 0.2 | 0.9 | 0.6 | **1.7** | 0.2 | 1.2 | 0.3 | **1.7** | –1 |
| Europe | 0.0 | 0.1 | 0.0 | **0.1** | 0.0 | 0.0 | 0.0 | **0.1** | –33 |
| South East Asia | 1.3 | 3.2 | 2.5 | **6.9** | 1.0 | 1.9 | 1.9 | **4.7** | –32 |
| Western Pacific | 0.1 | 2.6 | 1.1 | **3.7** | 0.0 | 1.2 | 0.1 | **1.4** | –64 |
| **Grand total** | **2.6** | **9.0** | **5.9** | **17.4** | **2.3** | **7.6** | **4.6** | **14.5** | **–17** |

* Since all values are rounded to the nearest 100000, totals may not precisely add up.

middle-income countries have made little improvement. In other words, inequality is growing and many of the lower-income and less powerful countries are falling further behind.

> It is clear that the wonderful ambitions of the Sustainable Development Goals will not be achieved without large increases in trained health workers.

While migration is a major factor, it is only one of many problems in ensuring that there are sufficient health workers to deliver improved health and improved services in poor countries. As noted earlier, even if every African health worker who has emigrated were to return home, Africa's health workforce problems would not be solved. They would make up only part of the extra 6 million needed in the continent.

The biggest single factor is that not enough health workers of all kinds are being trained. This applies in almost every country in the world, as the following few examples show.

Many countries have increased training levels but not yet to high enough levels. The UK in 2019 graduated 8730 medical students for a population of 67 million, the US had 21 622 medical graduations, a smaller proportion in a population of 328 million. Both had increased levels by around 30% since the start of the century. India, where many doctors migrate, trained about 100 000 new doctors in 2019, an even lower proportion than the US for a population of about 1.37 billion.

It is difficult to calculate the number of doctors currently trained in Africa. The best estimate I have seen is from a 2012 baseline study which showed there were 169 medical schools in sub-Saharan Africa and that they train about 10 000 a year.[24,25] This is a significant increase from the past. Until 2007, Ethiopia trained between 150 and 200 doctors a year. If all these doctors had stayed in the country, they would now have to look after a population of about 80 million. A 2009 review of 12 sub-Saharan African countries showed that, at present rates of training, it would take 36 years to reach the WHO's then target of 2.28 health professionals per 1000 population and that some countries would never reach it.[26] Today's requirement to meet the SDG goal of 4.45 per 1000 is even further out of reach.

It is interesting to note from the WHO Strategy document that the global nurse/midwife to doctor ratio was 2:1 in 2013. In many high-income countries, it is around 3 or 3.5 to 1. There is considerable scope for the well-trained nurses of today to play an even bigger and more significant role in health and healthcare in the future as service providers and leaders. This is one of the reasons I started the Nursing Now campaign in 2018, as described in Chapter 10.

> There is considerable scope for the well-trained nurses of today to play an even bigger and more significant role in health and healthcare in the future as service providers and leaders.

The pattern with nurses is also hugely variable. India has the capacity to train about 120 000 per year for a population of 1.37 billion (1 to 11 400 in the population), compared to the UK's training of 20 500 for 67 million (1 to 3350 in the population).[27]

Training is not enough by itself. Health systems and health employers also need employment and operational policies that counter the 'push' factors described earlier. Poor working conditions, poor pay and employment conditions, the lack of drugs and equipment all need to be confronted. They not only push many health workers to emigrate, but they also persuade others to leave the health sector altogether.

This push to other sectors also applies, if less dramatically, in high-income countries. When we in the UK wanted to encourage more women to return to nursing after having children, we found that the biggest factors were often that the working conditions didn't match their needs. We had to become very flexible and offer daytime and even term-time-only contracts, part-time jobs and crèche facilities.

Poor working conditions, employment and pay all contribute to health workers leaving government employment in the general health services of a low- and middle-income country and moving internally to work for the NGOs, the not-for-profit and the for-profit healthcare providers and suppliers. This movement, often bitterly resented by health ministries, contributes to the fragmentation of services and a concentration on the priorities that NGOs and outside donors see as important. The general health of the population may suffer as a result.

Underpinning many of these problems is the lack of money. Funding restricts the numbers of health workers that can be employed, their pay and conditions and the quality of their working environment. Shifting and short-term funding promotes the sort of 'churn' we see as health workers move from one organisation to another or from one country to another in pursuit of jobs and higher wages.

A further financial constraint in several poor countries has been the role previously played by the World Bank and IMF, as described in Chapter 7. Their policies of structural adjustment in the 80s and 90s led to cuts in public spending, including health and education. This short-sighted and narrow policy has been very damaging in some countries and has left a legacy of destruction and bitterness. In many African countries, there were and still are unemployed health workers unable to find jobs in healthcare as a continuing legacy of these policies.

These human resources issues – of too few people being trained, concerns about pay and employment conditions as well as the working environment and the lack of money for health – affect people in some way in almost all countries of the world. In higher-income countries, there are added complications arising from inbuilt rigidities in the way health workers are trained, employed and regulated.

There has been a continuing trend towards ever greater specialisation in the USA in particular but also in many other rich countries. This specialisation combined with greater regulation has led to peaks and troughs in the demand and supply of highly trained health workers. We have seen, for example, specialists in these countries becoming redundant as the demand for their skills shifts. A particular example in recent years has been in cardiac surgery, where many more patients who might previously have required surgery are being treated medically by cardiologists.

Specialisation and regulation also tend to increase costs and, in a world with shortages in crucial groups of health workers, there is rapid wage inflation. Dr Badr reports how the Sudan has doubled the pay of doctors but, given the huge differences in what they can earn abroad, it has made little if any difference to the retention of doctors. Other countries in Africa, too, are thinking of or have doubled doctors' pay, thereby using up significant sums from the nation's health budget.

> The Sudan has doubled the pay of doctors but, given the huge differences in what they can earn abroad, it has made little if any difference to the retention of doctors.

This is a global labour market and it is helpful to look for the insights of economists in order to understand some of the dynamics. This chapter has shown how demographic, political and economic factors have driven up the demand for trained health workers in high-income and rapidly growing countries. It has painted a picture of massive flows in many different directions as 'pull' and 'push' factors tug or thrust people into movement.

These sorts of discussions are often couched in the language of what is needed in a country with little reference to what can be afforded. Richard Scheffler brought just such an economist's insight to bear by generating a new model of the supply and demand for doctors globally, where he uses demand to mean what can be and is afforded in a country.

Scheffler's model generates some different patterns with oversupply in some countries – where they can't afford to employ their own medical graduates – and undersupply in others – where actual economic demand is unmet. Interestingly, it shows an oversupply in some richer countries. He uses this analysis to challenge conventional thinking.[28]

Scheffler argues, for example, that the USA is not suffering from a shortage of doctors. Rather, we are seeing the results of decades of misguided public policies. These policies have created a healthcare marketplace that often fails to deliver the right number of doctors, of the right specialty, in the right locations. Healthcare reform, Scheffler argues, is not just a matter of training more doctors. What the USA needs is a reform of healthcare policy that will spur the development of an efficient, cost-effective and high-quality healthcare system. Few would argue with this conclusion.

These arguments take us on to the questions of what sort of health workers we need and want. This is a very live discussion, as we shall see in later chapters.

## CONCLUSIONS – A GLOBAL VISION

This chapter has shown that the supply of trained health workers is truly a global issue and needs global attention and some global regulation if the lowest-income countries in the world are not to suffer. Individual countries will not solve it by themselves. Three things stand out clearly amid all this complexity. Firstly, there is now a very largely free and unregulated labour market in trained health workers that is creating instability in countries everywhere. Secondly, it is the lower-income countries and poorer or more remote parts of countries that suffer from the migration of health workers. Thirdly, the current situation is unsustainable.

The key question is very simple: how can low-income countries in Africa staff themselves and how can high-income Norway staff itself if we stick to the traditional approaches we know and understand? To answer this, we need to create a new vision of what the world could be like if we didn't have this global instability and the accompanying and highly damaging export of valuable people, with all their skills and talent, from poor countries to rich. This vision would be based on three foundations:

- We must understand that, in terms of our health, we are interdependent – our national success or failure in combating disease and improving health affects us all internationally. COVID-19 has reinforced this point massively.
- The free movement of ideas and people – and the opportunities to train and work abroad – will help us all in our shared quest for better health. Circular migration should be encouraged.
- We need a shared commitment that each and every country must have a safe minimum level of health workers to meet the needs of its population.

The Health Worker Migration Global Policy Advisory Council set out just such a vision in its submission to the WHO on the code of practice.[29] This vision – of interdependence, free movement and universal minimum standards – sets out the direction we must travel. We also need to know how to get there.

We have already seen some of the steps we must take. We need international codes of behaviour to provide a shared framework of rules and expectations, whether they be about international recruitment or, as we will discuss in the next chapter, intellectual property. We need massive increases in the education and training of health workers, with rich countries supporting the poor. We need improvements in both employment and working conditions.

Underneath it all there is a global problem of resources. More Overseas Development Aid and philanthropic funding need to be directed at developing the workforce. However, it is not just about funding. We need to go further and redesign the whole way we conceive of health and deliver healthcare. We need to change the design of our healthcare systems and of our health workforce.

We also need to understand what technology can do for us when trained human time will be at ever more of a premium. In conversation, Ruth Levine, of the Centre for Global Development, has taken this insight further and suggested to me that we really need to measure productivity in health services in terms of labour used not money expended. Human time is the real measure of expenditure in a service that is dependent on human skills and human caring.

> Human time is the real measure of expenditure in a service that is dependent on human skills and human caring.

We are already seeing change in countries around the world and learning from low-and middle-income countries. Chapter 8 will describe an example of a community health worker scheme based on the Brazilian model being piloted in the UK. Many countries and many planners have adopted an approach generally called 'task shifting'– the transfer of tasks from a more expensive staff group to another less expensive one – as a means of making scarce skills and resources go further. This has often been done with some reluctance and the expressed opinion that this is a second-class way of doing things that will be abandoned when more money is available.

I will argue, however, that this very profession-centric view of the world misses the point. We need to train people to do the work that needs doing in any country and not just to meet the needs of the professions. Nurses may well do some things currently done by doctors better than they do them, as well as less expensively. Technology can help improve both quality and cost. Perhaps most importantly, the patient and community also have very important roles to play – in health creation, disease prevention and care.

A radical redesign of health worker roles is needed with, as I will argue, the professional playing a much bigger role as agents of change, facilitating, supporting and influencing improvements in all aspects of health.

We need different ways to educate and train health workers, support the public in their roles and deliver services. As part of this, I believe that there is enormous scope for more joint ventures and partnership schemes in education and service provision that will benefit richer and poorer countries alike.

This redesign will bring profound changes for the professions and for their education and training. It will be an important part of moving on from the existing conception of western scientific medicine and helping make it fit for the twenty-first century. However, before we explore these changes, we need to look at the other side of the unsustainable import–export business, the import of ideas to lower-income countries from high-income ones.

The next chapter describes the modern *Race for Africa*. It concentrates on the actions of the western world and the impacts of its ideas and activities in lower-income countries. It also begins to show, however, that these countries are perfectly able to create their own ideas and to create their own new designs to deal with the health problems that they so well understand.

## REFERENCES

1. https://www.unrefugees.org/refugee-facts/statistics/ (Accessed 17 November 2021).
2. https://mo.ibrahim.foundation/news/2018/brain-drain-bane-africas-potential (Accessed 17 November 2021).
3. https://www.ncbi.nlm.nih.gov/pmc/articles/PMC5347354/ (Accessed 17 November 2021).
4. https://hospitalmedicaldirector.com/the-total-cost-to-train-a-physician/ (Accessed 17 November 2021).
5. https://www.who.int/healthsystems/publications/Abuja10.pdf (Accessed 17 November 2021).
6. https://www.oecd-ilibrary.org/social-issues-migration-health/recent-trends-in-international-migration-of-doctors-nurses-and-medical-students_5ee49d97-en (Accessed 17 November 2021).
7. https://www.oecd-ilibrary.org/docserver/4dd50c09-en.pdf?expires=1630318640&id=id&accname=guest&checksum=D558160D694ECEA47E796C5A5838DA20 (Accessed 17 November 2021).
8. Office for National Statistics (ONS). International migration and the healthcare workforce. London: ONS, 2019. https://www.ons.gov.uk/peoplepopulationandcommunity/populationandmigration/internationalmigration/articles/internationalmigrationandthehealthcareworkforce/2019-08-15 (Accessed 17 November 2021).
9. https://www.thet.org/our-work/policy-work/from-competition-to-collaboration/ (Accessed 17 November 2021).

10. WHO. *The World Health Report 2006: Working together for health.* 2006. https://www.who. int/workforcealliance/knowledge/resources/whreport_2006/en/ (Accessed 17 November 2021).

11. Hagopian A, Ofosu A, Fatusi A *et al.* The flight of physicians from West Africa: views of African physicians and implications for policy. *Soc Sci Med*, 2005; **61**: 1750–60.

12. Chen C., Buch E, Wassermann T *et al.* A survey of sub-Saharan African medical schools. *Hum Resour Health*, 2012; **10**: 4. https://doi.org/10.1186/1478-4491-10-4 (Accessed 17 November 2021).

13. Department of Health. *Many Rivers to Cross – The history of Caribbean contributions to the NHS.* London: The Stationery Office, 2006. https://www.tsoshop.co.uk/bookstore. asp?FO=1159966&Action=Book&From=SearchResults&ProductID=0113227213&trackid= 000009 (Accessed 17 November 2021).

14. https://www.worldbank.org/en/news/press-release/2021/05/12/defying-predictions-remittance-flows-remain-strong-during-covid-19-crisis (Accessed 17 November 2021).

15. https://www.healthprofessionals.gov.sg/docs/librariesprovider2/default-document-library/list-of-registrable-basic-(1-jan-2020)-medical-qualifications---effective-from-1-jan-2020.pdf (Accessed 17 November 2021).

16. https://www.aspeninstitute.org/wp-content/uploads/files/content/images/GCC%20 and%20HWM%20Policy%20Brief.pdf (Accessed 17 November 2021).

17. https://www.who.int/hrh/migration/code/WHO_global_code_of_practice_EN.pdf (Accessed 17 November 2021).

18. The WHO Workforce Department's draft evidence for the 10-year review is available at https://www.who.int/docs/default-source/health-workforce/eag2/2nd-review-of-code-relevance-and-effectiveness-evidence-brief-2-code-effectiveness.pdf?sfvrsn=8f250b55_2 (Accessed 17 November 2021).

19. Crisp N. *Global Health Partnerships: The UK contribution to health in developing countries.* 2007. https://www.who.int/workforcealliance/knowledge/resources/ globalhealthpartnerships/en/ (Accessed 17 November 2021).

20. https://www.gov.uk/government/publications/code-of-practice-for-the-international-recruitment-of-health-and-social-care-personnel/code-of-practice-for-the-international-recruitment-of-health-and-social-care-personnel-in-england (Accessed 17 November 2021).

21. WHO. *The World Health Report 2006: Working together for health.* Figure 1: Health workers save lives, p. xvi. https://www.who.int/workforcealliance/knowledge/resources/ whreport_2006/en/ (Accessed 17 November 2021).

22. WHO. *Global Strategy on Human Resources for Health: Workforce 2030.* Geneva: WHO, 2016. http://apps.who.int/iris/bitstream/handle/10665/250368/9789241511131-eng. pdf;jsessionid=6C7B6635E6A568008E8CA0A0CA203311?sequence=1 (Accessed 17 November 2021).

23. WHO. *Global Strategy on Human Resources for Health: Workforce 2030.* Geneva: WHO, 2016, p. 44. http://apps.who.int/iris/bitstream/handle/10665/250368/9789241511131-eng. pdf;jsessionid=6C7B6635E6A568008E8CA0A0CA203311?sequence=1 (Accessed 17 November 2021).

24. https://smhs.gwu.edu/medicine/sites/medicine/files/125.pdf (Accessed 17 November 2021).

25. https://human-resources-health.biomedcentral.com/articles/10.1186/1478-4491-10-4 (Accessed 17 November 2021).

26. Kinfu Y, Dal Poz MR, Mercer H, Evans DB. The health worker shortage in Africa: are enough physicians and nurses being trained? *Bull World Health Organ*, 2009; **87**(3): 225–30. doi: 10.2471/blt.08.051599.

27. https://www.statista.com/statistics/318922/number-of-nurses-in-the-uk/ (Accessed 17 November 2021).

28. Scheffler RM. *Is There a Doctor in the House? Market signals and tomorrow's supply of doctors.* Stanford, CA: Stanford University Press, 2008.

29. Health Worker Migration Global Policy Advisory Council Meeting: Conference Proceedings 18–19 September 2008, Marlborough House, Commonwealth Secretariat, London, UK.

# Unfair trade (2) – importing ideas and ideology

**7**

I was the wrong person with the wrong question at the wrong time. As the Mozambique Minister of Health entered the small committee room with his officials in tow, I could see immediately that he was cross, very cross. We were at the World Health Assembly in Geneva – the annual meeting of the WHO's member states – and I had requested an interview in order to ask him what more the UK should be doing to help improve health in Africa.

I don't know where he had just come from. I now wonder if he had been sitting all morning in meetings where he and his African colleagues had felt patronised by people from rich donor countries telling them what they should be doing; perhaps he was merely suffering from too many hours of long speeches and the interminable time-wasting of that great Assembly.

Upright, smartly dressed and very articulate, he let me know from the outset that he was fed up with being told what to do by foreigners. He understood his own country very well, thank you. He knew what his priorities were. Did I understand that the international agencies providing pills for immunisation were only doing part of the job? What use was a pill if a child didn't have any clean water to swallow it with? He didn't care if immunisation was their priority. He wanted help with infrastructure, water, roads, schooling and employment. He didn't want to be told what he should be doing.

This, my first meeting with Minister Paulo Ivo Garrido, reminded me of the story I had heard about one of his predecessors as Health Minister for Mozambique, who had naturally assumed that on taking office he would be responsible for the health of his population. He discovered, however, that he was really the Minister for health projects which, he paused for effect, were run by foreigners.

It also underscored very clearly what it felt like to be a recipient of foreign aid. Mozambique, in common with other countries, received aid from many individual countries, including the UK, from international agencies and from many NGOs, small and large. All of them gave aid on their own terms and all of them wanted it monitored against their own criteria. It is only a small step from here to telling people what to do.

Minister Garrido knew what needed doing. Why did donor countries think they knew better? Why didn't they support him with his plans?

DOI: 10.1201/9781003267706-7

Minister Garrido knew what needed doing. Why did donor countries think they knew better? Why didn't they support him with his plans?

This problem is not unique to sub-Saharan Africa. Many countries receive more than 100 separate monitoring visits a year, two or more per week, and have to write reports for all their donors. Many countries need to devote significant amounts of their precious time to dealing with foreigners and 'projects run by foreigners'.

It must have been very galling for the Minister. I learned, as I got to know and respect him at later meetings, about the passion and energy he brought to the role. Unlike many, he was in the post for the long term and, as a surgeon, understood healthcare well.

For my part, I got more from the interview with the Minister than I had expected by being forcefully reminded that aid and development are also about power and about who sets the agenda and, of course, about who is accountable to whom.

This story sets the scene for a chapter in which I describe some of the ways in which ideas and ideologies are imported from richer to poorer countries alongside aid, trade and other relationships. It is very important to stress at the outset that very many of these ideas are extremely beneficial: scientific knowledge, technical know-how, commercial and governmental understanding are all immensely valuable. However, like all good things, they bring their own problems, some of which get in the way of progress. This chapter concentrates on this darker side.

Power is at the heart of this since it gives richer countries and institutions the ability to impose their ideas, intentionally or unintentionally. It has as its social and psychological accompaniment what I call here an 'unconscious superiority', which affects the way people think and behave.

The chapter looks first at how power influences economic relationships – aid, trade and investment – and also shapes the way healthcare can be delivered by influencing what problems can be addressed and how this will be done. It goes on to look at some of the psychological aspects that have led, among other things, to undervaluing local knowledge and neglecting context and circumstance.

The chapter concludes by arguing that accountability needs to be reversed if aid and international development are going to have lasting impact. I think that, in general, people need to ask Minister Garrido for permission to work in his country and for his approval for what they are doing, not the other way round. There are obvious exceptions, of course, such as Myanmar, discussed in Chapter 3, where tyrannical, corrupt or vicious governments pursue their own ends and not the benefit of their people.

Life has moved on since I wrote about this in *Turning the World Upside Down* in 2009. Some attitudes have changed but much of the practice hasn't. People I have talked with have suggested to me that the biggest change is on the side of people from low- and middle-income countries who have become more confident, less deferential to the people arriving in their country with money to spend and advice to dispense, and more willing to implement their own solutions. There is a great deal of discussion of country-led planning but development partners are still very largely in control of what happens.

## THE NEW RACE FOR AFRICA

There is a new 'Scramble for Africa' underway that is in some ways reminiscent of the way seven western European powers rushed to colonise Africa between 1870 and 1914 – a period when European control of the continent rose from 10% to 90% with only Ethiopia and Libya remaining independent. Today's scramble is for trade, resources and influence.

We start by looking at how aid, trade and investment are being used in the global competition for influence and access to natural resources.

In the eighteenth and nineteenth centuries, the European great powers competed for territory and resources around the world, from India and South Asia to the Americas, Africa and Australia. They wanted the best harbours and the best marketplaces from which to control the trade routes and secure the diamonds, gold and other metals waiting to be unearthed in the vast interior of these continents.

They divided Africa up between them, leaving a legacy of language, religion and law and a continent of nation states constructed around the boundaries of their conquests and treaties rather than on Africa's own heritage of peoples, empires and kingdoms.

The contest sprang to life again in the twentieth century, but this time it was much more about influence, with the communist and non-communist worlds buying the favours of the 'non-aligned' newly independent states of Africa with investment and aid, arms and hospitals. Marxist–Leninist philosophy flourished in a variety of local forms, far distant in every sense from its northern birthplace, while right-wing dictators, hardly distinguishable from their communist neighbours, lived in luxury under western protection.

Today, the new great powers of China and India use different weapons to compete with the Europeans, Americans and Russians for natural resources as well as influence. Both these countries, once themselves recipients of development aid, provide aid and investment in their turn to other countries. China, in particular, through its Belt and Road Initiative has been very heavily involved in major infrastructure projects – roads, airports, telecommunications, hotels and much more. This has given it access to mineral deposits, seaports, and open markets for its vast manufacturing output.

Western countries tie development assistance to conditions about monitoring, outputs and methodologies, seeking to shape the outcomes and, to some extent, the way health systems and even government operate in a country. The Chinese, as one African put it to me, are more respectful and behave as one developing country to another. They don't impose conditions of these sorts but operate commercially, offering loans and contracts. This, of course, means that ownership of assets reverts to them if a country defaults on payments.

A number of important assets in several African countries have transferred to the ownership of Chinese state-owned organisations in this way. Francis Omaswa told me that a significant part of Uganda's public spending now went on debt interest, and that the country suffered from 'capital flight' as earnings from foreign-owned enterprises including mines and tourism as well as infrastructure left the country. He reported that Uganda was now trying to buy back important state assets including the airline and some banks and reassert national control over its economy.

> A number of important assets in several African countries have transferred to the ownership of Chinese state-owned organisations in this way.

Many Africans have an ambiguous attitude towards Chinese investment. On the one hand, they want the assets that are created, and which potentially hold the key to future prosperity, but on the other hand, they are concerned about increasing Chinese ownership and loss of control of their economy. There is a parallel ambiguity about their attitude to western development assistance.

In this century, the total amount of investment into Africa has overtaken international aid for the first time, with China playing a major role. It is no wonder, therefore, that there was such a good response from African countries when they were first invited to Beijing in November 2006 to discuss friendship and development. Forty-one African heads of state out of a total of 53 in the continent attended. Almost all now attend similar summit meetings.

Francis Omaswa makes the telling point that China has a strategy for Africa, but Africa doesn't have a strategy for China. Countries with stronger economies such as Kenya can negotiate terms from a stronger position than those with weaker ones like Uganda or Zambia or Malawi. As we noted in Chapter 4, growth in African economies hasn't trickled down or led to significant opportunities improvements for the whole population. There is a need for a more radical economic strategy than an overdependence on infrastructure funding from foreigners. It is an echo of the point made by the Mozambique minister talking about his dependence on health projects run by foreigners.

Africa doesn't have a strategy for the West either. All this aid and investment has not yet made the recipient countries rich and is unlikely to do so at the present rate of progress. The common thread throughout all this discussion is power and the way that international relationships are almost always skewed in favour of the rich and powerful. International treaties, international organisations, infrastructure projects, trade deals and the way aid is given all reflect power relationships. They all help to maintain the status quo.

> All this aid and investment has not yet made the recipient countries rich and is unlikely to do so at the present rate of progress.

Aid itself provides a good example. It is still often linked with trade so that a good part of the money given in aid returns to the donor in payment for goods and services. This happens in three main ways. The first, which we have already touched on, is that the aid given is tied, directly or indirectly, to a trade deal or to access to resources of some sort. Money may be given, for example, for a dam or a hospital on condition that a company based in the donor country builds it or perhaps that permission is given for mining.

The UK had a rigid separation between trade and aid for about 20 years from 1997. More recently, its Department for International Development has been integrated into the Foreign, Commonwealth and Development Office in a move that replicates what has happened in other countries and is designed to ensure that development assistance is part of UK foreign policy and soft power. At the same time, UK development policy has shifted to focus more on supporting local economies, in part to tackle the issues described earlier, and to address areas of importance to foreign policy.

The second link between aid and trade is that aid money itself may be returned directly to the donor country to buy services. Research by the NGO Action Aid showed that one-quarter of the aid provided by rich countries in 2006, or US$20 billion a year, funded expensive external technical assistance such as consultants, research and training instead of going directly to the countries concerned.[1] Expatriate consultants typically cost around US$200 000 per year; more than one-third of this is spent on school fees and child allowances.

Life has moved on to some extent, with many more international NGOs and development partners employing local people, but large contracts are still awarded to foreign firms rather than local ones. The argument is made that local companies lack the necessary capacity and capability to deliver them. Why, one might ask, is development assistance not used to build the local capacity rather than maintaining this dependence on outside expertise and capability?

The third link is the servicing and repayment of loans. These three links mean that the value of aid flows is reduced by giving concessions on trade, debt servicing and repayment, and buying services from donor countries.

> *The value of aid flows is reduced by giving concessions on trade, debt servicing and repayment, and buying services from donor countries.*

A large part of the historic loans by the multinational organisations such as the IMF, the World Bank and the African Development Fund has been paid off. To date, 37 of 40 eligible countries have between them received £76 billion in debt relief from the Highly Indebted Poor Countries (HIPC) Initiative and 19 countries through the Multilateral Debt Relief Initiative (MDRI).[2,3]

These schemes have been controversial because countries must adopt adjustment and reform programmes suggested by the IMF and World Bank in order to qualify for the relief. However, as the IMF points out, *'before the HIPC Initiative, eligible countries were, on average, spending slightly more on debt service than on health and education combined. Now, they have increased markedly their expenditures on health, education, and other social services. On average, such spending is about five times the amount of debt-service payments.'*[2]

Debt has, however, built up again in many countries and from many sources and remains an acute problem. Organisations such as the European Network on Debt and Development continue to monitor the situation and press for change, most recently in relation to the impact of COVID-19 on debt and development.[4]

Figure 7.1 shows how the value of aid flows is reduced by giving concessions on trade, debt servicing and re-payment and buying services from donor countries.

Today, trade, aid and investment may have replaced colonialism and shared ideology as the main basis for the relationship between countries but the imbalance in power remains the same.

High-income countries are better able to lobby and influence others in international negotiations and have the financial resources to sit out disagreements. The Doha Round of Free Trade negotiations set up in 2001 and subsequent global trade efforts at reform have failed to deliver any benefits for low- and middle-income countries due to disputes between high-income countries. The European Common Agricultural Policy, which protects small farmers in

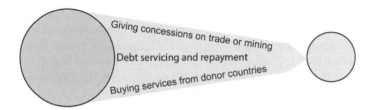

**Figure 7.1** Shrinking aid – the costs of receiving aid reduces its value.

European countries, remains largely unreformed and low- and middle-income countries still face many tariff and non-tariff barriers. High-income countries can find many different ways of being protectionist.

Many low-income countries have relatively little bargaining power because they produce very few goods for export; some have only one crop or product. They are very vulnerable to global price swings in copper, tobacco or coffee, or whatever their particular product is, as well as to mood swings among rich consumers over tastes and concerns about 'food miles'.

Aid for Trade was established to *'improve developing countries' standing through financing trade-related infrastructure, institutions, and regulatory and policy reforms, which are believed to facilitate trade and ameliorate the effects of suspected trade roadblocks.'*[5] The evidence suggests that flows of OECD aid from OECD countries to all sectors and to economic infrastructure have increased both Africa's imports from and exports to OECD countries. Some progress is being made.

However, despite this and other international commitments to make trade work for Africa, there has been little change and the whole continent still has only 3% of world trade.[6] It is a very similar picture with regard to inward foreign investment. Higher-income countries get the bigger share.

> *Despite . . . international commitments to make trade work for Africa, there has been little change and the whole continent still has only 3% of world trade.*

The short-term outlook makes the picture even gloomier. The World Trade Organization has predicted that global trade volumes will decline by 9% during 2021 as a consequence of the pandemic with low-income countries worst affected as richer countries contract their commitments, aim for greater self-sufficiency and become more protectionist.

Figure 7.2 illustrates the relative size of aid, foreign direct investment (which is more than eight times greater) and trade (which is more than 124 times greater than the total of aid).[7,8,9] It also shows how important aid is to the 46 least-developed countries in the world where in total aid amounts to US$33 billion and trade to US$51.7 billion. It also suggests, however, that the greatest prize for them and other developing countries will be to increase their share of foreign investment and of trade and thereby grow their economies. They need bigger slices of the two bigger cakes.

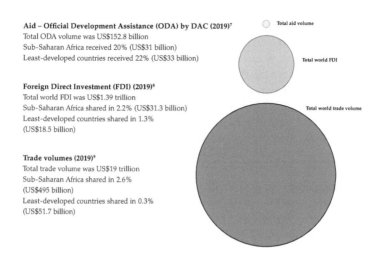

Aid – Official Development Assistance (ODA) by DAC (2019)[7]
Total ODA volume was US$152.8 billion
Sub-Saharan Africa received 20% (US$31 billion)
Least-developed countries received 22% (US$33 billion)

Foreign Direct Investment (FDI) (2019)[8]
Total world FDI was US$1.39 trillion
Sub-Saharan Africa shared in 2.2% (US$31.3 billion)
Least-developed countries shared in 1.3%
(US$18.5 billion)

Trade volumes (2019)[9]
Total trade volume was US$19 trillion
Sub-Saharan Africa shared in 2.6%
(US$495 billion)
Least-developed countries shared in 0.3%
(US$51.7 billion)

Total aid volume

Total world FDI

Total world trade volume

**Figure 7.2** Aid, investment and trade – some key figures for 2019.
Source: OECD Development Assistance Committee (DAC),[7] World Bank.[8,9]

African countries are, however, trying to redress the situation for themselves. The African Continental Free Trade Area (AfCFTA), which was launched on 1 January 2021, could be transformational.[10] It will bring down tariffs and trade barriers across Africa and create the largest free trade area in the world measured by the number of countries involved. The scope for growth is enormous: only 17% of African country exports are within the continent compared to 68% for Europe and 59% for Asia.

The World Economic Forum says: '*Connecting 1.3 billion people across 55 countries with a combined gross domestic product (GDP) valued at $3.4 trillion, the pact comes at a time when much of the world is turning away from cooperation and free trade.*'[11] It estimates that the agreement will increase Africa's exports by US$560 billion, exports within Africa would increase by 81%, and those externally by 19%, while the increase to non-African countries would be 19%. Markets and economies across the region will develop, new industries will be created, and African countries will become more competitive.

None of this will be easy, barriers won't come down easily, millions of people will need to change how they do things and there will be every sort of implementation problem. However, the first steps are being taken which, with sustained political will, will start to change Africa and the prospects of its citizens from within. It could be a model for other developments.

## IMPORTING IDEAS AND IDEOLOGY

The international financial and economic institutions have faithfully reflected these power relationships and adopted the ideas and ideologies of the powerful countries that created and continue to control them. For the best part of three decades from the 1970s, the Bretton Woods Institutions, led by the IMF, required countries that sought their help to introduce 'structural adjustment' policies.[12]

These policies, derived from the Washington Consensus, a liberal free-market view of the world, were designed to ensure that developing countries had sound financial systems that would encourage private sector investment and the development of commercial activity. One consequence of this was very often a requirement to cut government expenditure. This, in turn, led to reduced spending on health, education and social development, which was seen as non-productive and, in the short term at least, not a priority for economic development.

There is continuing controversy as to the precise impact of these policies. The main point here is that they undervalued the importance of investing in health and education and the consequences of not doing so. One direct result was damage to the retention and recruitment of health workers as salaries were frozen or decreased and investment in tertiary institutions was reduced.

Nursing schools were closed and many health workers left unemployed – contributing to migration abroad – and there is still a hangover from these policies today that can be seen in the lack of development of institutions and staffing shortfalls.

In southern Africa, in particular, the resulting damage to health and social development was enormous at a time when AIDS was already beginning to kill a generation of productive workers and throw millions into destitution. The authoritative Commission for Africa recognised these problems and recommended renewed investment in higher education and universities in order to rebuild the infrastructure that was needed.

> The authoritative Commission for Africa recommended . . . renewed investment in higher education and universities in order to rebuild the infrastructure.

The IMF has the responsibility, with the World Bank, to help stabilise economies in difficulties and to work with countries to achieve sustainable growth. This means it must continually balance social expenditure with growth and affordability. Too often it was seen to get the balance wrong and, most tellingly, to ignore the contribution that health and education make economically through building what economists call 'human capital'. This is the very human capital made up of healthy productive workers that, coupled with financial capital, is needed to drive the engine of the economy.

Much more radical reforms are needed today to tackle COVID-19 and climate change and get countries back on track with the SDGs. The old economic and financial institutions created after the Second World War have not served us well in these crises. The time has come to turn the world upside down, get rid of the old orthodoxy and think afresh about what we are trying to achieve and find new and imaginative ways to do so.

There is a sense, as I write, that we are still using the weapons of the last war to fight the next one.

## POWER SETS THE HEALTH AGENDA

In health, as Minister Garrido understands too well, power sets the agenda. Ideas and ideology come with the money. It is no surprise that donor countries impose explicit conditions on how money is spent. It shouldn't come as a surprise either to know that donor countries don't all want the same things.

In 2005, for example, the UK required Malawi to make basic health services free to all its citizens as a condition of a massive investment in staffing and health infrastructure. The USA, by contrast, promotes health insurance and, by implication, wants users to pay some of the cost of their own healthcare. Each country, it seems, exports its own beliefs about how health services should be run, apparently regardless of the success or failure of those policies in their home countries.

> Each country . . . exports its own beliefs about how health services should be run, apparently regardless of the success or failure of those policies in their home countries.

This is not in itself a new trend. Former British Colonies from Hong Kong to Jamaica have health services modelled on the British NHS and for a long period their medical and nursing schools had many expatriates on their staffs. This legacy lives on in the thousands of young professionals who have come to the UK for their training and who still aspire to membership of one of the UK Royal Colleges.

Medical staff from former French Colonies can tell a similar story and exhibit the same high level of pride in their graduation from a French University and their years of training in Paris or Lyon or Marseilles. They, just like the South Americans or Filipinos trained in the US system, take home with them a share in the experience and worldview of their teachers and mentors.

More problematically, we have seen the intrusion of current domestic politics into international development. Two linked issues, birth control and abortion, have heavily influenced American policy over the years, with positions changing depending on the politicians in power at the time. We have just seen how local issues affect policy in the UK where the current government has cut its commitment to Overseas Development Aid in response to ideological issues and a perception of what its voters wanted.

I have heard American friends saying that, with their new Administration, they will once again be able to rejoin the world community, sign up to the treaties and come to the table. Or, as Joe Biden has said, 'America is back.' Or so it had seemed until the retreat from Afghanistan revealed that the US was once again retreating into a more insular approach and has no intention to be the world's policeman.

Peter Sands, the Executive Director of the Global Fund for AIDS, Tuberculosis and Malaria (The Global Fund) makes the point very powerfully about who controls the global agenda on health. In a recent blog about the pandemic, he writes: '*For the rest of the world, though, this looks disturbingly like the repeat of a previous pattern: Once a pandemic stops being an acute threat to life in high-income countries, the urgency drops, the focus shifts, and resource flows dwindle. This is what's happened with earlier pandemics, such as HIV and AIDS, and tuberculosis: Decisive action was taken to contain the threat to life in rich countries, but it was then allowed to linger in poorer, more vulnerable countries, killing millions.'[13]*

> Once a pandemic stops being an acute threat to life in high-income countries, the urgency drops . . . it was then allowed to linger in poorer, more vulnerable countries, killing millions.
>
> Peter Sands

There is another pattern that keeps being repeated which shows how richer and more powerful countries are often very unreliable partners and dependent on their own internal politics. US development policy has shifted markedly with each new administration from Bush to Obama to Trump and to Biden.

More recently, the UK Government cut its aid budget by almost 30% at very short notice. It ignored the years of planning that had gone into developing some projects and the fact that its officials had entered into negotiations with many countries about the detail of spending. It continued with programmes and projects where contracts were signed and it had a legal obligation but cut others, even many where the deal was all but done. Only one minister – to her great credit – resigned. Happily, some other western countries increased their spending.

## VERTICAL POWER

Another significant development over the last three decades has been the way in which international organisations and donors have come together to tackle the major health problems. The Joint United Nations Programme on HIV/AIDS (UNAIDS), which brought together 10 UN agencies to confront HIV/AIDS, was set up in 1994. We have subsequently seen the introduction of several other global health initiatives: the big international funds set up in partnership by a consortium of donors to tackle one or a small number of diseases such as the Global Fund and Global Action on Vaccination and Immunisation (GAVI). The USA, under President Bush, presumably wishing to maintain its own identity as a donor and thereby emphasising its separation from the rest of the world, set up its own version in the President's Emergency Plan for AIDS Relief (PEPFAR).

These bodies have very large sums of money at their disposal. The Global Fund's budget for 2019 was US$4 billion;[14] GAVI's was US$777 million;[15] PEPFAR had US$6.9 billion to spend during the same year including a contribution of US$ 1.5 billion to the Global Fund.[15] These bodies, also known as 'vertical funds' because they take a single aim and pursue it down through the system making sure that everything is aligned to achieve the aim, have generally been very successful in their immediate aim. GAVI, for example, has helped to immunise a whole generation – over 760 million children – preventing more than 13 million deaths and helping halve child mortality in 73 countries.[16]

The Global Fund rightly claims great credit for ensuring that, in 2020 alone, 21.9 million people received antiretroviral therapy (ART), the treatment that keeps AIDS patients alive.

In addition, 4.7 million were treated for TB, and 188 million mosquito nets were distributed to help control malaria. It estimates that in aggregate 44 million lives have been saved by its activity.[17]

> The Global Fund rightly claims great credit for ensuring that, in 2020 alone, 21.9 million people received antiretroviral therapy. In addition, 4.7 million were treated for TB, and 188 million mosquito nets were distributed.

The organisation has, however, been criticised for its very vertical nature and the way in which it ignores and sometimes damages other services in pursuit of its aims. Like PEPFAR, it has been accused of ignoring the potential for working with other services, poaching their staff by paying higher wages, and dominating and distorting the whole health system in a country through the sheer amount of money that it is able to bring to bear.

The dominance of the global initiatives is shown by the example of Zambia, where in 2006 the PEPFAR spending of US$150 million was higher than the total government budget for all other health services of US$136 million. It is not surprising that many local health workers preferred to work for PEPFAR or other agencies with their cash and clear focus rather than for poorly funded government services which have to deal with a far wider range of diseases and pressures.

Vertical funds, whether these enormous global initiatives or the smaller versions often run by NGOs, undoubtedly have had some negative effects. If any issue or disease is given priority status, it will mean that others are given lower or no priority and treated accordingly. It is the nature of priority setting. I know from my own experience of running the NHS in England that it can be very difficult to keep a balance between the priority services and the rest and that it is not possible to have priorities and pretend that you can treat every service equally. The real criticism is that more could be done both to ameliorate the bad effects and to contribute to strengthening the local health system.

I went to see Mark Dybul, then the Head of PEPFAR, to discuss this early in 2008. He is a US Admiral and, because he was shortly to attend a state occasion with the President, met me dressed in his formal blue uniform complete with silver buttons and braid. We sat beside the large American flag in his office while, courteous and informal as ever, he talked me through the issues.

Mark was one of those people who work at the point where power meets practicality. He had to reconcile on a daily basis the demands of the politicians and the needs of patients. He was directly accountable to the President and dependent on Congress for every dollar he spent. His budget had been voted as an Emergency Fund for AIDS and at that time Congress expected every dollar to be spent on AIDS and on nothing else. As a doctor, experienced and knowledgeable about working with AIDS patients in poor countries, he had a deep understanding of the problem on the ground and of what needed to be done.

> His budget had been voted as an Emergency Fund for AIDS and Congress expected every dollar to be spent on AIDS and on nothing else.

He told me about what he was already doing to counteract any problems that PEPFAR might be causing and help strengthen health systems more generally. He had opened his supply chains to other organisations, so they could deliver other drugs and equipment. He paid for the training of health workers who did more than just work on HIV/AIDS. He funded shared facilities and clinics. He pointed out that his local staff did work with others, took account of local conditions and had a measure of flexibility within the overall framework set by the President and Congress.

We discussed what could be done about the fact that PEPFAR could pay health workers more than they would get from local organisations and that, as a result, existing health services lost people to PEPFAR and perhaps even had to close. It was obviously an important freedom for his organisation and meant that it could be confident about employing people to deliver the services his Congress required. Nevertheless, he was open to ideas to limit the freedom and to make some recompense by training more people locally.

Figure 7.3 gives a very simplified version of the dilemma that vertical funds have faced in trying to deliver their goals while supporting the local health system. On the positive side, their focus can lead to quick results; but on the negative side, it can inadvertently lead to damaging other services.

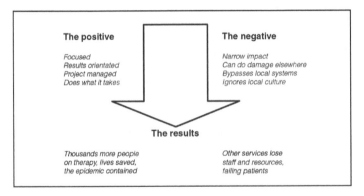

**Figure 7.3** The paradox of vertical power – how to maximise the positive impact whilst minimising the negative effects.

While the threat posed by the big communicable diseases dominated thinking at the turn of the century, attention, until the COVID-19 pandemic, switched to the need to strengthen health systems. Long-term success in tackling communicable diseases as well as non-communicable diseases and securing the safety of mothers and children depends on having a working health system in every country in the world.

The massive global vertical funds have adapted over the years, opening new 'windows' of funding for other elements of health services. The Global Fund and GAVI now explicitly fund health system strengthening. In the longer term, it has been suggested that the Global Fund and PEPFAR might widen their remits and, even, become general global funds for health.

They have become more horizontal, seeking to balance the horizontal strengthening of the whole system and the priority of the particular goal. More recently, of course, they have been accused of becoming less effective as a result. There is a constant communication job as well as a management task here.

This vertical approach is, however, also used by many much smaller NGOs. Less well resourced, they may, nevertheless, also do damage at the same time as they are doing good. They, too, need to tackle this paradox of vertical power and minimise the negative effects whilst maximising the positive impact.

## MULTIPLE REQUIREMENTS FROM MULTIPLE SOURCES

The vertical funds represent one source of the import of ideas to poor countries. Top-down and focused, they encapsulate a particular notion of how improvement can be delivered. In doing so, they make assumptions about how citizens and professionals alike behave and about how health systems need to be organised.

Over the same time period we have seen a spate of health reforms being introduced around the world that adopt a very different, and rather more horizontal, model of change. Often inspired by the World Bank or one of the big consulting firms, they take an economist's perspective and seek to influence behaviour. They concentrate on incentives for citizens and for providers, aim to generate more funds mainly through insurance and advocate mixed public and private systems of clinicians, clinics and hospitals.

Sometimes the vertical fund and the more horizontal incentives-based system are brought together as, for example, in Rwanda. Here, the Global Fund works closely with a developing insurance system in an effort to build a functioning health system whilst at the same time tackling the scourges of AIDS, TB and malaria.

Other factors and other players complicate the mix. New philanthropists, most notably The Bill and Melinda Gates Foundation in the last two decades, have joined the many existing bodies with proud records such as the Rockefeller Fund and China Medical Board. The Gates Foundation through its sheer scale – it spent about US$5 billion in 2019 – is able to influence other donors and help shape global priorities as well as implement huge programmes of its own.[18]

The problems of multiple donors with multiple priorities and multiple monitoring requirements have been recognised internationally for years. The SDGs, and the MDGs before them, were both statements of intent and powerful means for unifying priorities. From 2000 onwards, there has at least been agreement on the top priorities.

The Paris Declaration of 2005, signed by more than 100 countries, moved this forward by setting out principles for working together. These principles cover the importance of countries owning their own development plans, alignment of international efforts, harmonisation of processes, results orientation and mutual accountability.[19]

> *The Paris Declaration set out principles for working together . . . countries owning their own development plans, alignment of international efforts, harmonisation of processes, results orientation and mutual accountability.*

Over the years, there have been other attempts to bring greater order out of chaos, better coordination and less waste. COVAX, the body set up to distribute vaccines to low- and middle-income countries, is one such example. However, even it has been undercut by countries conducting their own 'vaccine diplomacy'.

All of the initiatives to improve the situation have made some progress. However, wording is open to interpretation, aid and investment overlap, governments change and, most importantly, many countries and organisations are not signed up to these processes. Moreover, there is reluctance by some of these long-term donors to collaborate with China, India, Brazil or the Middle Eastern countries that are now entering the arena, and vice versa. There is a tendency to keep each other at a distance rather than a willingness to share know-how and experience. Geopolitical manoeuvring is getting in the way of progress.

There is little evidence of accountability to the recipient country and its people when all the governments and organisations are looking homewards to their populations, parliaments and boards for direction and accountability. The power relationships are all one-way. It is clear who makes the decisions. Recipient governments can challenge the donors; some, the most powerful, do and a very few low- and middle-income countries, such as Cuba and Eritrea, choose to stand outside this whole framework of relationships. Most, however, need the money and accept the deal on offer.

Donor governments are, of course, accountable to their parliaments and people and will want to take credit for their work; however, they could find ways to be more accountable to the recipients. Most donors now talk in terms of country-led plans or budget support, whereby they do give aid directly to a government to support its plans. While this goes a long way towards recognising that countries 'own' their own plans, the reality is that the money still comes with strings and involves an enormous amount of negotiation and authorisation.

## UNCONSCIOUS SUPERIORITY

Power, as we have seen, influences global economic structures and relationships and the way healthcare is supported globally. There are also social and psychological aspects to be considered. The power relationship is embedded in behaviour and attitudes among donors and recipients alike.

It is easy to see continuity here with colonial times. The structure of health services and thinking about healthcare has been very much influenced by its origins. Healthcare was organised primarily for the colonialists and the local elite, with the majority of people looking to local healers and missionaries for help.

After independence, the new rulers continued broadly with the same institutions and structures and built central and regional hospitals, and very often continued to look towards the former colonial power for leadership. Outlying areas were still left to traditional healers and missionaries. Traditional medicine itself was ridiculed or ignored, observed but not studied, and certainly not really taken seriously until the last decade. The colonialists had left, but their ideas remained.

Professor Barbara Parfitt has written extensively about how western nurses unconsciously apply their own values and prejudices in their work in developing countries. I met her, perhaps appropriately for the topic, in the UK's House of Lords. In a richly decorated room with paintings of famous British sea victories on the wall, the atmosphere redolent of history, power and empire, we discussed how the attitudes and values of British nurses, formed over many years, were exported around the world.

Barbara had herself worked for long periods in low-income countries and, as she explains in *Working Across Cultures*, noticed how some nurses were able to achieve a great deal and others, apparently as well skilled and motivated, very little.[20] She noted the traps nurses could fall into in their unconscious assumptions about their patients and the power of western medicine and, most particularly, that they could set up an unhealthy dependency relationship with their patients and the whole local community.

The problem, put simply, was that the nurses with their western ways and skills became too powerful. They ignored and thereby disempowered traditional knowledge and skills and became the sole possessor of knowledge and the only one who could help.

> *The problem, put simply, was that the nurses with their western ways and skills became too powerful.*

This problem is, of course, familiar to clinicians and patients in high-income countries, where it is easy for a confident and capable nurse to become the expert on my health and, as it were, to own my problems and my solutions. This is, as we have seen in Chapter 5, a very powerful theme in western medicine whereby the professionals own the whole process and practice of healthcare with patients being not just patient, but totally passive. Commercial organisations reinforce this dependency with the often mysterious, to the layman, power of their potions and treatments.

The problem is far worse, however, where there is an in-built power relationship as there is between the trained western clinician and the much less educated local person, and where a culture of deference to graduates and professionals may enhance the effect.

The values, beliefs and knowledge of the clinician are potential barriers to care and independence in multicultural London, Paris, Toronto and New York just as they are in poor countries. They reflect the dominance of western scientific medicine and the power it lends its practitioners. Barbara has subsequently developed a model to show how nurses can understand and manage their own behaviour and help create a more collaborative and sustainable approach to health.

I discussed these issues with a psychologist friend, Penny Jones. She had been commissioned by Voluntary Service Overseas (VSO) to create a training and development programme for their volunteers before they took up their posts. She had interviewed and observed a number of VSO volunteers in Sierra Leone as part of her preparation for doing so and she described to me the three main ways that she had seen volunteers behave.

Some had adopted what was effectively a colonial approach: accepting the deference and dependency and perhaps even encouraging it, the attitude was similar to paternalism, sometimes creating a 'master/servant' relationship with local people as had been customary during colonial times. Others had identified strongly with the local people and tried to get alongside them. In extreme cases, this went as far as the volunteer marrying into the local tribe.

Both of these two groups, in attempting to deal with the anxiety about how to help, were creating different sorts of dependency relationships and projecting some of their own vulnerabilities and needs onto the local people. In both approaches, the response of the national people seemed to be acceptance. But Penny observed that neither led to the kind of development which promoted self-sufficiency and independence, which is what VSO wanted.

There was a third group who, in practice, seemed to work more successfully to enable a sort of 'collegial' relationship and who didn't build inappropriate dependency on either side. She described their approach as one of 'managing marginality', with the volunteers being able to stand alone as neither belonging to the home nation (the colonial approach) nor joining (the 'going native' response). They remained aware of their role being to develop/teach/enable/ pass on expertise by careful definition of roles in the work and the relationships they were establishing. They understood and held on to the recognition of the complexity of the situation they were dealing with.

As a result of her own observations, Penny Jones stressed to me the importance of good preparation for people working in these sorts of situations, self-awareness of their own instinctive approach, and offering people frameworks within which to think about what they were setting up, and continuous review of what was happening. You can't altogether avoid dependency – and some is necessary for a learning situation to be successful – but it is vital to understand the risks and what is happening in a relationship and to manage it as professionally as you can.

## COPYING THE RICH AND POWERFUL

So far in this chapter I have described the way ideas and ideologies are passed on from the dominant rich countries to the poorer and less powerful. It is a top-down process that reflects where power sits. However, it is equally apparent that many people want many of these imports. People want western medicine. They can see it works. People want to be doctors and to enjoy the income and status it brings. Their extended families want to share in their success. Equally, many countries have taken on those secondary characteristics of medicine as a profession, which, as I argued in Chapter 5, can be so useful but can also be so damaging to health.

They have embraced a far-reaching idea of professionalism and the need for regulation to the extent that doctors and their trade unions are even more powerful than they are in high-income countries and that strict regulation, for example in South Africa, India or Brazil, means that only doctors can carry out tasks that are done by other health workers in the UK, Australia or the USA. This is a closed shop.

Many have also wanted to show that they, too, can have facilities, services and expertise every bit as good as the West. There was a tendency, particularly at the time of independence, for African countries to invest in hospitals and prestige services within their capitals when, in reality, the biggest need was for primary care and public health spread throughout their country. It is worth noting that politicians in western countries are not immune to this tendency either, being just as keen on visible demonstrations of what they have achieved for their people and caring about their legacy. Today, in England, the Government is promoting its hospital plan rather than focusing on the needs of the community and primary care.

A variant of this, which has had long-lasting detrimental effects, was the way that Ethiopia changed its medical curriculum in the 1980s to an American model. Previously, its curriculum was based much more on primary care and public health and geared to the needs of the country. Now it turns out graduates who understand the specialities and the needs of western environments and who are, therefore of course, ideally suited to emigrate to Washington, take their Board exams and add to the 'brain drain'. It is only in the last few years, with inspired local leadership, such as in Jimma as described in Chapter 2, that they have reversed this process and created a local curriculum again.

This desire to keep up with the West and copy its activities is still very evident in some places today. I remember visiting a large hospital in Africa where the chief executive, himself a doctor, and his senior doctors showed me round some of its facilities. It was a large site with ward blocks and departments spread throughout the grounds. Each block had two wards, one on top of the other, each of which consisted of a large open area with around 30 beds, a small treatment area and open lavatories. At a rough count, I could see that there were about 60 patients in each ward, some on the floor and some on the beds, and about an equal number of relatives and friends. More were camped outside.

> This desire to keep up with the West and copy its activities is still very evident in some places today.

It was a dismal and depressing scene of the kind found too often in Africa. The blocks were discoloured concrete, the grounds full of rubbish. At one end there was a large tip of discarded equipment, much of it looking as if it had been donated from richer countries. There was surprisingly little noise given the number of people who sat and stood around, following our little group with their eyes. It wasn't a particularly hot or humid day, but the buildings stank.

The chief executive showed me where a new emergency department was being constructed with US$50 million provided by the government. He said it would have a helicopter landing pad and be equipped to international standards. He also told me proudly of the new cancer centre they had just opened and of his plans to increase the range of specialities.

In the cancer centre, new and not yet in use by patients, the lead doctor gave us a horrifying slide show made up of pictures of his patients. All of them had enormous tumours on different parts of their bodies; one with a tumour growing from his shoulders almost the size of a second head. It was sad, depressing and, I thought, unnecessary. Only later did I understand why he had done it.

My wife had been following at the back of the group and talking to the doctors there, just out of earshot of the chief executive. The cancer director told her that he had an impossible task. There was so much to do in cancer in his country, but he couldn't do it in the cancer centre. He wanted to be working more closely with local services in the town and the countryside, tackling prevention, diet and, where possible, early diagnosis. Here, in his new centre, he would only get the hopeless cases, the people he could do nothing for, the people with the enormous tumours, the people in the slide show.

The obstetrician told her a similar story. He desperately wanted the funding to train and support workers in the countryside, who could help look after mothers, identify problems early and get them to his hospital. Instead, he felt stranded where he was, receiving too many patients who were too late to save, already too far gone in bleeding to death when they arrived in his care. The precious money was all going into the prestige of the hospital and not the services that were needed.

Later, we saw the cancer doctor in a bar in town. He asked me to try to change the government's plans and help set up a locally based service that would address the real needs of the population. Back in the capital my comments were clearly unwelcome. It was too late; the money was committed.

This simple story helps illustrate the complicated nature of the problem. Here was a country taking a western model and applying it inappropriately to its own circumstances. It was both ironic and tragic.

> Here was a country taking a western model and applying it inappropriately to its own circumstances. It was both ironic and tragic.

The irony was that western planners faced with anything like this position would almost certainly have tried to develop a community-based solution. The tragedy was, as already noted, that almost 30 years earlier an international consensus was established at Alma Ata that the most effective way to improve health in poor countries was to invest in community-based services and primary care. It simply didn't need to be like this.

## LEARNING TO LISTEN

This chapter presents a fairly depressing picture. The powerful western world still exerts a huge influence on its former colonies. It still controls the levers of power. It still gets the better part of the deal in trade negotiations and still finds ways to exploit the natural resources, human and physical, of the poor countries in the world.

Turning to health, we export our ideas and ideologies to poor countries alongside our aid. We introduce our beliefs about how to organise health services and how to get things done. We accompany them with our values about life and society and freedom. We reinforce them with our behaviour and our attitudes. We exercise an unconscious superiority. We explain and educate. We make demands about structures and organisation. We tell people what needs to be done. We set the agenda.

The effect of all this is to overpower other ideas and beliefs and to encourage people to copy the things that have made us so successful in the past and to adopt our winning strategies. These things are so powerful precisely because they have been so successful. Western medicine with all its accompanying science, professionalism, commerce and vast expenditure has, as I have argued earlier, been astonishingly successful. However, as I have also argued, it is now beginning to fail us because it is unable to handle the complications of context and society and the complexities of human behaviour.

> The effect of all this is to overpower other ideas and beliefs and to encourage people to copy the things that have made us so successful in the past.

The power is so overwhelming that it can stop us even thinking about context and society. We can, if we are not careful, discount the differences between societies, ignoring how women and children are treated, ignoring the corruption, and forgetting that the very poor live lives of such fragility that any setback become a catastrophe. We can simply fail to realise that an idea that works so well at home may become completely irrelevant elsewhere. The force of our ideas is, in effect, so noisy that it can stop us listening to other perspectives.

This can quite literally be the case. Over the last 3 years I have been in many meetings discussing health in poor countries and planning action for improvement. In many cases, there has been a majority present from the rich world and, although I have not done the analysis, I am quite sure that the minutes would reveal that many more words were spoken from that perspective.

This can be very uncomfortable for all concerned as the lonely African or Asian finds themselves by turn expected to speak for all developing countries or simply ignored. It is very easy, if you are looking for it, to catch the exchange of glances between people from low- and middle-income countries as others are speaking and, just occasionally, to see them group together to press a point.

I remember one meeting with 15 of us present, two of whom were from Asia and two from Africa, when my Pakistani neighbour, a very distinguished clinical academic, turned to me and said, 'Go on, Nigel, back the developing countries on this one.' He was making explicit a hidden split that is there in many meetings.

It is very easy to see how this has happened in the recent past. Organisers have an extraordinarily difficult job in setting up international meetings and making sure that they get good people to attend. They can always find another well-educated and articulate North American or European and, because there are so many of them and they are richer, they are more likely to be available and able to travel. It makes it even easier, of course, if the meeting can be held in North America or Europe.

Times are changing now, and technology is helping. There are growing numbers of well-educated young people in countries around the world who are more assertive than their elders and have ideas of their own – and don't need people from the rich West to make them happen. Technology, virtual meetings and conferences mean that now almost nobody has to be excluded from key meetings and events. It is helping rebalance the debate.

Listening is two-way, of course. There needs to be dialogue between all parties, with the points of view and knowledge of people from richer or poorer countries listened to and evaluated on their merits.

## IS IT ALL A WASTE OF TIME?

It is little wonder that some people have looked at all this and concluded that aid doesn't work, that international development is a waste of time and that western interference in the affairs of poor countries is just that, interference.

There is a considerable charge sheet to answer. This chapter has exposed three of the main charges: that what really matters is economic growth and not aid, that aid is wasteful and bureaucratic, and that aid builds dependency. We will examine each in turn but will start with the most damning claims of all: that governments haven't kept their promises and that aid doesn't work anyway.

The various organisations that monitor progress as official or unofficial watchdogs present a bleak picture of the ways in which the international community has failed to deliver on its promises to provide more money and describes how, where money has been provided, it has failed to use it to make the necessary impact. The ONE's *DATA Report* similarly demonstrates that many governments simply haven't done what they promised and rates countries on their performance: some do slightly more than they promised but most are struggling to meet targets or falling far behind.[21]

These analyses serve the very useful purpose of publicising performance and thereby holding governments to account to public opinion. Many such analyses also draw out the importance of the underlying power and economic relationship between donors and recipients and argue that the existing model for international development, which doesn't address this imbalance, is flawed. Aid, as I show in this chapter, won't help if at the same time trade deals systematically undermine a country's ability to grow its economy and raise its people out of poverty.

It is worth at this point returning to the discussion in Chapter 4, where I argued that, to improve health, it was necessary to do three things at the same time: (1) tackle the health problems directly; (2) alleviate poverty and its associated problems; and (3) change the way that national and international social, economic and political structures, between and within countries, get in the way of improvements. They keep the rich rich and the poor poor. They maintain the status quo.

Using this framework and the discussion in this and earlier chapters, it is possible to put together a rough score card for the impact of aid and international development on health, as shown in Figure 7.4. I believe there has been progress on the purely health aspects, some improvement on poverty but little on changing global structures.

There are problems in holding governments to their promises and failures in delivery, but there has been undeniable progress in tackling the specific health issues and in dealing with

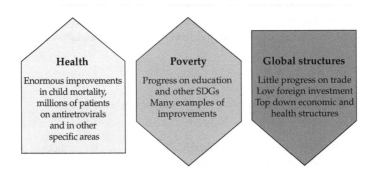

**Figure 7.4** Aid and development – a rough scorecard.

some of the problems associated with poverty. However, as I said at the outset, the criticisms in this chapter should not make us lose sight of the remarkable progress that has been gained by using the knowledge, the science and the economic strength of richer countries. Moreover, it has been very impressive to see the way in which many world leaders continued to press this agenda, even at a time of financial crisis.

People may disagree with the particular assessments I have made in Figure 7.4, but no one, surely, will disagree with the fact that it is the social, economic and political structures and imbalances that are now the biggest obstacles to progress.

> *It is the social, economic and political structures and imbalances that are now the biggest obstacles to progress.*

Looking at the charges on the charge sheet in turn, they all have some validity. The first is the very simple assertion that all you need for development is economic growth. People who take this view point out that the astonishing rise of several countries in South East Asia was not due to aid and development support. China, they add, has taken more people out of poverty through economic growth in the last 10 years than all the development activity in the rest of the world put together.

Dambisa Moyo, herself an economist from Zambia, has argued that aid and development create dependency and give support to poor national leadership and government and that other countries should stop interfering altogether in local affairs. They should be allowed to stand on their own feet and develop themselves in their own way within a global free market.[22]

These arguments are very important in emphasising the role that economic growth can play in development, promoting the idea that countries have to take responsibility for themselves and countering any notion that external aid and international development support is sufficient. However, in their simplest form they misinterpret both history and the current environment.

Any analysis of the successful growth of these economies shows that there were many factors responsible for the growth including government activity, protectionism and foreign investment. Many too, including China, have been the beneficiaries of aid. Other commentators critique the argument that free trade and open markets are enough by pointing to the fact that today's rich nations built their economic empires on very different and much more protectionist approaches. Rich countries that advocate a simple free market approach are in effect 'kicking away the ladder'.[23]

The picture that is presented is too simple. It also ignores the present reality that growing protectionism and reducing global trade are now making the position harder for lower-income countries to grow and that, even if growth comes eventually, their populations have health needs today. Their health needs, as we have seen elsewhere, are important to us all.

Nevertheless, economic development must surely take centre stage. Figure 7.2 earlier in the chapter, which shows the relative sizes of aid, foreign direct investment and global trade, clearly demonstrates how important it is for developing countries to get access to the investment and the trade flows they need to grow.

## THE INVENTION OF INTERNATIONAL DEVELOPMENT

The earlier description of the multiplicity of donors is pretty damning and lends credence to the assertions of some critics that aid is wasteful and bureaucratic and serves only to create an industry that benefits thousands of people from the richer countries. This chapter has hinted at something of the extraordinary amount of activity that goes on internationally around development and aid.

There are meetings, conferences, assemblies, planning sessions, reviews, monitoring visits and liaison between donors and recipients, between donors and donors and between regional and national groupings. It is the domain of economists and policymakers who mix politics with their professional analysis as they dispense vast sums of public money.

There is waste, there is bureaucracy, and both must be tackled; but there is also a wider problem embedded in the very notion of international development. This is the implication it so often carries of people doing things for other people, of knowing better, and of there being somehow a clear distinction between developed and developing countries.

We have invented this massive infrastructure – or perhaps more accurately superstructure – of international development and used it to capture everything to do with the development of a country. It now deals with everything from the global economic issues of trade and financial stability to the detail of education, agriculture, health and transport.

They are, of course, all connected and it is very important that someone has the overview and the whole picture. Moreover, I have constantly been impressed by the quality of the people working in this field. However, in bringing together all these topics there is a danger of losing focus on the important detail of each one and of the things we share.

Taking health as just one example, it is clear that development agencies and the associated think-tanks and universities have become the experts on international development and health. Agencies and government departments employ many such individual experts. However, they are not necessarily the experts on all aspects of health, who, as one would expect, generally work in health services and in other parts of universities.

Governmental and organisational structures reinforce this separation. Departments for international development find it very hard, in my observation of a number of western countries, to draw on the expertise in their own country. They have their own internal experts and it is only occasionally, as with the threat of pandemics, when the country itself feels threatened that the whole government structure – from Health Department to International Development, Foreign Affairs Ministry and Treasury – pulls together around a global health problem. More often than not it is the development experts who talk about health systems and health worker training from a theoretical point of view, without having been involved recently with these issues in their own country.

Our structures continue to treat the health issues of other countries as if they were quite distinct from health issues in our own. It is the old world where academics talked of international health and meant the health of other people, rather than the new world, often characterised as being about global health, where we are beginning to understand just how connected and interdependent we all are.

In practice, this separation can be problematic and Dr Paul Farmer rails against development experts in Africa, whom he has seen using sensitivity to local culture as a reason for not giving a child a medicine.[24] A sick child is still a sick child. They need to be treated by a health expert, not an international development one.

> A sick child is still a sick child. They need to be treated by a health expert, not an international development one.
>
> Dr Paul Farmer

He illustrates the wider point. Health issues are still health issues even if they are in low-income and faraway countries. We risk a great deal if we separate these countries off from the global mainstream. We will both be the poorer for it.

The recent critiques of global health discussed in Chapter 1 reinforce these points. We must unfreeze our minds and think more clearly about international development and what it has become. The very success of inventing a new professional discipline may now be part of the problem. Putting it at its simplest and perhaps rather unfairly, do we need a model where development experts do all aspects of development or one where a far wider group of people – teachers, farmers, engineers and nurses – use an understanding of development in their work?

This echoes my own criticism of 'so-called' reverse innovation in the Preface of this book. Innovation is innovation, health is health.

We need to go beyond top-down international development and think instead about how we need to develop together or not at all. The idea of co-development needs to replace the outdated concept of international development.

## AID CREATES DEPENDENCY

There is a very real risk of aid creating dependency; however, crucially, if we understand this better we can do something to mitigate its effects. This is by no means a hopeless task, particularly if we learn to listen better.

We could start by listening to individuals. We could invite more people from lower-income countries to our meetings. We could listen better. We could find better ways to listen to the voices of the poor and try to understand why so many poor people *'define poverty as the inability to exercise control over their lives'*.[25]

We must also recognise the long-lasting impact of colonisation and the impact it has on people's behaviour, thinking and attitudes. It affects so much that has been discussed here from the shaping of trade routes to the 'unconscious superiority' to the attitudes of aid workers and the neglect of local and traditional knowledge. Understanding and addressing the impact of colonisation is not the whole story but it is an important part of creating a better future.

We could also try to listen out for and understand better the implications of the far-reaching changes underway in many countries. I have concentrated in this chapter on sub-Saharan Africa and the lowest-income countries in the world and presented a relatively simple picture of the relationship between countries. The reality is much more complex and far messier.

Power and influence are shifting and what, even 10 years ago, looked to the West like a fairly simple picture of high-, low- and middle-income countries with a one-way flow of aid and development is now much more differentiated and complex. There are different power groupings, different flows of aid, different influences and different identities being forged.

A high-income country such as the UK's relationship with lower-income countries is not just about the people of those countries and their needs. It is also about us and our needs. We are at a point when many people in western countries are beginning to recognise the problems there are in sustaining and growing existing health systems. We are reaching the limit with our current model. It needs major attention. This is our crisis too.

> *We are reaching the limit with our current model. It needs major attention. This is our crisis too.*

Recognising our own weakness in this way should make us more open to new ideas. It should also help us to support the development of poor countries better. It could even break down some of the barriers between countries and help us as equal partners to learn and develop together.

We must also free our minds from some of the ingrained assumptions associated with western scientific medicine. These are very powerful, deep-seated and difficult to challenge. This is nowhere better illustrated than by the current debate about 'task shifting'. This expression is used to describe the way in which some tasks previously done by one group of professionals such as doctors is shifted to another group such as nurses. Similarly, some tasks done by nurses might be shifted to other less well-trained groups.

It is often argued that poor countries can't afford to have many doctors and nurses and therefore every effort should be made to find ways to shift as many tasks as safely as possible to cheaper groups. Many people seem to see this as a purely temporary solution to be used only until the countries can afford the desirable level of staff. Nevertheless, a great deal of effort is now going into devising training courses and protocols to put this in place.

I remember discussing this in a meeting in Kampala when, one by one, the Africans in the room ridiculed the notion. Their complaint was not about unskilled people taking on these tasks, but about seeing the world purely in terms of the established professions. Why were we starting with the professions and deciding what would be done? Shouldn't it be the other way up? Shouldn't we decide what needs to be done and then decide who is best placed to do it? Or as they put it rather more forcefully, who do they think has been doing these tasks all along? Let them send us some doctors and nurses and we will gladly shift some tasks to them.

> *Let them send us some doctors and nurses and we will gladly shift some tasks to them.*

In unfreezing our minds, we need to look at what is happening elsewhere and think about how it applies to the high-income world as well. BRAC, the massive Bangladesh NGO, is doing just that and is applying its learning in its home country to projects it is establishing in Africa, but also in the USA.

This chapter has been about the ideas, knowledge and ways of seeing the world that are exported from high-income to lower-income countries. What if we turned it upside down? What might we learn?

Ultimately, it is the coming together of ideas from countries all over the world that will have the most effect. In the next chapter, we look at the lessons from low-income countries, which, for the reasons we have discussed, go largely unnoticed or misunderstood, and with their wider significance unrecognised.

## REFERENCES

1. Action Aid International. *Real Aid: Making technical assistance work.* 2005. https://actionaid.org/pu-blications/2006/real-aid-2-making-technical-assistance-work (Accessed 18 November 2021).
2. IMF. Debt relief under the Heavily Indebted Poor Countries (HIPC) initiative. 23 March 2021. https://www.imf.org/en/About/Factsheets/Sheets/2016/08/01/16/11/Debt-Relief-Under-the-Heavily-Indebted-Poor-Countries-Initiative (Accessed 18 November 2021).
3. IMF. Multilateral debt relief. 28 July 2017. https://www.imf.org/external/np/exr/mdri/eng/index.htm (Accessed 18 November 2021).
4. https://www.eurodad.org/ (Accessed 18 November 2021).
5. Lemi A. Aid for trade and Africa's trade performance: evidence from bilateral trade flows with China and OECD countries. *J Afr Trade*, 2017; **4**(1–2): 37–60. https://www.sciencedirect.com/science/article/pii/S221485151730021X (Accessed 18 November 2021).
6. https://sdg.iisd.org/news/wto-report-highlights-programmes-to-strengthen-africas-trade-capacity/ (Accessed 18 November 2021).
7. https://www.oecd.org/dac/financing-sustainable-development/development-finance-data/ODA-2019-detailed-summary.pdf (Accessed 18 November 2021).
8. https://data.worldbank.org/indicator/BX.KLT.DINV.CD.WD?contextual=region&name_desc=true (Accessed 18 November 2021).
9. https://data.worldbank.org/indicator/NE.TRD.GNFS.ZS?locations=XL (Accessed 18 November 2021).
10. https://au.int/en/cfta (Accessed 18 November 2021).
11. https://www.weforum.org/agenda/2021/02/afcfta-africa-free-trade-global-game-changer/ (Accessed 18 November 2021).
12. Riddell JB. Things fall apart again: structural adjustment programmes in sub-Saharan Africa. *J Mod Afr Stud*, 1992; **30**(1): 53–68.
13. https://www.theglobalfund.org/en/blog/2021-07-07-whose-pandemic-is-it-anyway/ (Accessed 18 November 2021).
14. https://www.theglobalfund.org/en/financials/ (Accessed 18 November 2021).
15. https://www.gavi.org/sites/default/files/2020-08/GAVI-Alliance-2019-Annual-Financial-Report.pdf (Accessed 18 November 2021).

16. https://www.gavi.org/news/media-room/gavi-helps-immunise-65-million-children-2019-though-covid-19-puts-progress-under (Accessed 18 November 2021).
17. https://www.theglobalfund.org/en/ (Accessed 18 November 2021).
18. https://www.gatesfoundation.org/about/financials/annual-reports (Accessed 18 November 2021).
19. https://www.oecd.org/dac/effectiveness/parisdeclarationandaccraagendaforaction.htm (Accessed 18 November 2021).
20. Parfitt BA: Working Across Cultures: a study of expatriate nurses working in developing countries in primary health care; Farnham, UK; Ashgate Publishing, 1998.
21. https://www.one.org/international/ (Accessed 18 November 2021).
22. Moyo D. *Dead Aid*. New York: Farrar, Strauss & Giroux, 2009.
23. Chang HJ. *Kicking Away the Ladder: Development strategy in historical perspective.* Bel Air, CA: Anthem Press, 2002.
24. Farmer P. *Pathologies of Power: Health, human rights, and the new war on the poor.* Berkeley, CA: University of California Press, 2003, p. 419.
25. Narayan D. Poverty is powerlessness and voicelessness. Finance and Development, International Monetary Fund, 2000. https://www.imf.org/external/pubs/ft/fandd/2000/12/narayan.htm (Accessed 18 November 2021).

# Learning from low- and middle-income countries  8

Fazle Hasan Abed wanted to give me a simple message.

We were talking on the nineteenth floor of a building in Dhaka from where we could look out over the city. Just below us there was a U-shaped bend in the river, its base near the foot of the building with its arms extending away into the distance on either side. There were three- and four-storey buildings along the outer sides of the U and one could imagine how in another city, or here at some future date, this would be a very attractive place to live with river walks and restaurants, their lights reflecting in the river at night.

At the centre of the U was a slum. It wasn't the largest or the worst slum in Bangladesh, but it was a slum nonetheless. We could see the temporary shacks made of wood and cardboard and plastic and between them the pathways that were no more than muddy channels filled with rubbish. There were more than 2000 urban slums like it in Bangladesh. They were the reasons BRAC existed.

I had come to meet the founder of BRAC in his headquarters and had just asked him how, based on his experience, the world could make faster progress in reducing deaths in childbirth. He replied quietly and without the slightest hesitation: '*Empower the women.*'

> Empower the women.
>
> *Fazle Hasan Abed*

There was a long-running argument in Britain in the late nineteenth century about when might be the right time to give working people the vote. On one side, the reformers argued that they needed to be educated first, so that they would use it wisely. On the other, the radicals simply replied that, if they had the vote, they would educate themselves.

Fazle Abed was with the radicals.

He told me later about how BRAC decided to launch a campaign in 1979 to teach families how to care for children with diarrhoea. They were aware that millions of children in poor countries throughout the world have died simply because nobody knew how to rehydrate

DOI: 10.1201/9781003267706-8

them when they were suffering from diarrhoea. In Bangladesh, with its annual floods, the chances of a child drinking dirty water and succumbing to an easily preventable death were very high.

BRAC used its extensive network of village and women's groups, of schools and classes to teach people about the problem and about how to tackle it. Ten years later 13 million households out of 15 million nationwide had learned to prepare oral rehydration solution. BRAC had empowered the women and the communities.

Deaths of children under 5 in Bangladesh fell from over 86.5 per 1000 to 30.8 per 1000 between 2000 and 2019. It was so much better than the sub-Saharan African figure of 75.8 for 2021, but still massively higher than the British figure of 4.3.[1]

This was a practical lesson in simple solutions and community organisation. It was a story that contrasted very sharply, as I think Mr Abed knew it would, with the technical analysis and complicated planning processes that I had heard about elsewhere. He was deliberately contrasting the simplicity of this self-help approach with the complex processes of international development.

BRAC is a remarkable organisation, involving 90 000 staff and reaching 126 million people with its services. It covers all parts of Bangladesh and has, in recent years, spread its activities and philosophy to other countries.

It runs health clinics and education classes and works with women to help them understand their rights and improve their position in society. It has always focused on the poorest people and those most excluded from the normal life and services of the country, but it also recognises that people need to aspire to the best and has, for example, created a BRAC University to provide wider opportunity for learning and development.

Its approach to empowering people is to help them improve their own lives and to make those improvements self-sustaining. As part of this approach, it uses business methods to achieve its social goals. It helps women learn the skills to run small enterprises, supports them by providing small loans from the BRAC Bank, has created shops to help small enterprises sell their products and founded six farms to provide good-quality chicks to be grown on by small farmers. BRAC is a social enterprise that is a big business in its own right. BRAC Bank alone has 6 million active borrowers, 87% of whom are women, and lent US$4.5 billion in 2020.[2]

BRAC maintains a focus on the ultra-poor, the most disadvantaged in society. It set up the Graduation Initiative in 2002 when it recognised that some of the very poorest people weren't able to make use of their services and didn't, for example, join the village microfinance groups. BRAC plans, by providing additional support to this group in a 'big push', to aim to reach 4.6 million households by 2026, helping them climb out of extreme poverty.[3]

As Abhijit Banerjee, who evaluated the Graduation Initiative for BRAC, said in his 2019 Nobel Lecture: *'What idea is bigger than the idea that the poorest of the poor have enough talent to be self-sufficient? That if you give them a push, they'll stay up?'*

BRAC's version of empowering people is to help them gain economic independence as well as have rights and a voice in their society.

# DIFFERENT IDEAS THAT CAN ENHANCE WESTERN SCIENTIFIC MEDICINE AND HELP IT ADAPT FOR THE FUTURE

BRAC illustrates many of the things that can be learned from lower-income countries. These fall into three groups: firstly, there are different ideas, attitudes and approaches to health and resources; secondly, there are specific innovations in policy or treatment; and thirdly, there is much that can be learned from working together. We start here with the first of these.

In the last chapter we saw how it was the ideas, values and world view of western medicine and society that were imported so effectively into lower-income countries, and which continue to influence them so powerfully in so many different ways today. The most important things that the higher-income countries can learn from lower-income countries, in precisely the same way, are different ideas, behaviours and attitudes. These can help them conceive and conceptualise their world differently and find new solutions to new as well as old problems. They can learn to see the world differently and act differently.

> These can help them conceive and conceptualise their world differently and find new solutions to new as well as old problems.

Lower-income countries simply don't have the critical mass of professionals, the scientists, the commercial activity and the governments' funding of healthcare, which are so essential to our understanding of western scientific medicine. That doesn't mean that progress can't be made, but rather that people have developed another set of ideas for dealing with the problems they face.

These ideas, which have been developed in different countries all over the world, can't replace the science underlying western scientific medicine. Biology is biology and our understanding of it develops through experimentation and scientific study. Treatment of patients and the delivery of services, however, depend on using insights from psychology and anthropology, taking account of cultures and building on insights from traditional sources in ways that are discussed further in Chapter 10. These different ideas complement western scientific medicine and, I will argue, show how it needs to adapt to be even more effective in the years to come.

Figure 8.1 lists seven of these ideas, all of which relate to each other. We have already seen how BRAC has developed an approach that employs the first four of these ideas: using business methods to achieve social goals; working with communities and especially women; empowering people by helping them become economically independent; and dealing with health as part of peoples' lives and not as something completely separate.

We will see later in the chapter how leaders in Africa and Brazil have developed new ways of training and deploying health staff, in the absence of all those health professionals, brought public health and clinical medicine closer together, and made the best use of whatever resources were to hand.

- Developing social enterprises which use business methods to achieve social goals
- Working with communities and especially women
- Empowering people by helping them become economically independent as well as having rights and a voice
- Dealing with health as part of people's lives and not as something completely separate
- Training health workers to meet local needs and not just for the professions
- Bringing public health and clinical medicine together
- Making best use of the resources to hand

**Figure 8.1** A different set of ideas that can enhance western scientific medicine.

Combinations of these seven are already proving vital in many countries. They can have an equally profound impact in even the richest and most powerful countries in the world. It is interesting to note that BRAC and organisations in other countries have had a practical appreciation of the importance of the social, environmental, economic and political determinants of health well before the carefully garnered research evidence brought them to the world's attention. It is also worth noting that they go beyond narrow definitions of frugal or reverse innovation.

These key features combine a pragmatic common sense and respect for tradition with vision and creativity. All the examples given over the next few pages use a combination of two or more of these approaches in the way they work.

Bangladesh might seem an unlikely place from which to learn. It is a fascinating country, but it has very serious problems. Poor, it comes at 133 out of 189 on the Human Development Index Ratings.[4] Overcrowded, with 163 million people in 148 thousand square kilometres, it is the tenth most densely populated country in the world and the only large country anywhere near the top of a list headed by Macau, Monaco, Singapore and the Vatican. Its traffic congestion in my experience, however, probably comfortably tops the world rankings.

A large part of Bangladesh floods each year. This is beneficial in providing the vital water and nutrients it needs for its crops. In a bad year, however, the run-off of melting snow from the Himalayas and the monsoon of summer can turn a routine annual flood into catastrophe. Following the great improvements in oral rehydration and similar successes on immunisation, the biggest single killer of children is now drowning.

Bangladesh will be very badly affected by climate change and rising sea levels. Addressing this will be particularly difficult in a country where politics is highly contested, with periodic violence and political differences that are further entrenched by familial and dynastic ties.

Despite all this, Bangladesh has a very strong spirit of enterprise and community action and has produced some other remarkable social enterprises. Muhammad Yunus's Grameen Bank, the pioneer of microfinance and microcredit, has had enormous influence and impact internationally. There are now many large and small microfinance institutions around the world that are able to lend small sums of money to people, mainly women, to set up or run small enterprises and help them to save money for use later.

These enterprises are capable of having enormous impact. A World Bank study found that 40% of the entire reduction of poverty in rural Bangladesh was directly attributable to microfinance.[5] There is a long tradition of such schemes elsewhere in the world and in 2018 they lent over US$124 billion to 134 million people, 85% of whom were women. These figures do not take account of many smaller and more local schemes.[5]

There are many other smaller organisations in Bangladesh that embody the same spirit and this same social enterprise approach of using business methods to achieve social purposes. They appear to sit comfortably alongside other commercial organisations. I asked people in Bangladesh why there was this spirit of self-help and community entrepreneurship. They suggested it had grown out of their battle for independence from Pakistan when they had to rely only on their internal resources and their community solidarity. Wherever it comes from, it is very powerful and gives a sense of hope to a country facing such a difficult and uncertain future.

> There are many other smaller organisations in Bangladesh that embody
> the same spirit and this same social enterprise approach of using business
> methods to achieve social purposes.

Bangladesh is not the only country where these developments have occurred. Urmul, 1000 miles away in Rajasthan in India, had been established in 1986 to promote the economic and social development of remote communities in the Thar Desert. Established explicitly on Ghandian principles of self-determination, one of its early projects was the development of a cooperative among the weavers of the area.

More than 300 self-employed weavers, each working on a loom at their own home, had built an organisation that allowed them to share the purchasing of raw materials and the marketing, production planning and sales that kept them in business. Together they create many of the wonderful and bright cloths worn by Rajasthan women that are so characteristic of the region.

Arvind Ohja, a man of medium height in his 50s, with the beard common to all men in the area and wearing a long woollen waistcoat, woven locally, as an outer garment, was my guide to the organisation. He is intellectual and both passionate and eloquent about the organisation of which he was one of the original members. I asked him how he had become involved and, in a story with biblical overtones, he told me that he had been working in local government when he met the founder. Within an hour he had decided to join him and, 15 years on, he has never looked back or regretted it.

Urmul expands into the areas where it is needed. Eye health was one. Eyes suffer in the dry, dusty and often windy conditions of the desert. Urmul went into partnership with Sightsavers International to run eye camps, bring treatment to remote areas and find ways to rehabilitate people who had become blind. Arvind Ohja took me to a single-storey house made of concrete blocks miles from the nearest town and introduced me to Manohar Kanwar, who had been blind from childhood and lived with her mother and sister. Thanks to Urmul and Sightsavers, she had learned to cook and look after herself and earned money sewing edging onto material prepared by the weavers.

The same themes that we saw in BRAC are evident here: social enterprise, economic empowerment and the treatment of health alongside other issues. Urmul, and Arvind Ohja himself, have a very powerful vision for what they are aiming to do: to lead the poor towards self-reliance by making available to them '*a package of development services that they themselves decide on, design, implement and eventually finance*'.

> A package of development services that they themselves decide on, design, implement and eventually finance.
>
> *Urmul vision* as reported to me by Arvind Ohja

In Nicaragua, another inspirational group, the Movimiento Comunal Nicaragüense (MCN), was created in 1978 to improve living conditions through social and community development, gender equality and environmental protection. They work in about half the country, mostly in rural areas, and have a presence in 120 municipalities and 2000 local communities. Like BRAC, they are able to mobilise thousands of people, mostly women, such as community leaders, teachers and midwives to improve public health.

The group's efforts have led to advances in literacy, polio eradication and reduction of maternal and child mortality rates. Most recently, MCN has centred its efforts on young people, aiming to improve gender relations, wipe out violence, prevent sexually transmitted infections (STIs) and reduce teen pregnancies.

Urmul and MCN may be half a world apart, but both of these organisations are a world away from the usual professionalised models of development.

## TRAINING PEOPLE FOR THE JOB THAT NEEDS DOING

Training people for the job that needs doing and not just for the professions is one of the biggest and most important and far-reaching ideas – and the one that is most challenging to the health professions around the world. As we saw in the last chapter, there is a critical shortage of health workers in many countries and, as a result, there has been a great deal of effort put into finding ways to fill the gap. We will move to Africa and Brazil over the next few pages as we explore some of the solutions people have found. All of them have in common that they are training people for the job that needs doing with reference, but not deference, to the established health professions.

I wasn't surprised to hear that BRAC had links with some of these developments in Africa. Colin McCord, a young American surgeon, worked at BRAC in the 1970s and subsequently moved to Mozambique, where he became involved in training non-medical staff to undertake obstetric surgery.

Mozambique, war-torn and very poor, had very few doctors and an appalling health record. Thousands of mothers died in childbirth each year and thousands of babies and young children perished. In 1984, carefully selected health workers were recruited from various rural settings for a 2-year course to become *técnico de cirurgia* and be able to undertake obstetric surgery.

These *técnicos de cirurgia* in Mozambique might be called obstetric surgeons or clinical officers or medical officers or medical licentiates elsewhere in Africa. They are equivalent to what Europeans or Americans might call surgically trained assistant medical officers. Development workers and academics tend to use the terminology 'mid-level workers' in order to distinguish them from much lower-skilled community health workers and from the traditionally educated health professionals such as doctors, nurses and midwives.

These *técnicos* have over the years become the mainstay of the country's obstetric service in rural areas. A study published in 2007 showed that 92% of caesarean sections, obstetric hysterectomies and laparotomies for ectopic pregnancies performed in all district hospitals in the country during the course of a year were carried out by *técnicos de cirurgia*.[6]

A second study, also published in 2007, tells a remarkable story about how the training and employment of *técnicos* is having an impact on the perennial problem of retaining skilled health workers in rural areas. It showed that 88% of *técnicos de cirurgia* from the three graduating classes surveyed were still working in rural areas 7 years after graduation. None of the doctors, by contrast, who graduated in the same 3 years, were working in rural areas 7 years after graduation.[7]

Earlier studies had shown that there were no clinically significant differences in postoperative outcomes between surgeries undertaken by *técnicos* and by doctors and that postoperative mortality rates for 10 258 patients operated on by *técnicos* were very low, at 0.4% for emergency surgery and 0.1% for elective.[8,9] In laypeople's terms: the work was done as well as doctors would have done it – if there had been any there to do it.

> In laypeople's terms: the work was done as well as doctors would have done it – if there had been any there to do it.

There are other medical as well as surgical *técnicos* in other countries of the world playing a vital role in health systems. More work needs to be done to understand how they operate, build a research base and strengthen support for mid-level providers to be used more extensively.

This extraordinary success story is mirrored elsewhere in Africa.

I visited the District Hospital in Jinja in Uganda on behalf of Sightsavers and met some of the students being trained there as ophthalmology assistants. At the end of the year they would be able to assess their patients and do a range of operations including ones for trachoma, that awful disease of the eyelids that causes great pain and leads to blindness. After 1 year's further experience they could return to Jinja for further training with the eventual prospect of becoming cataract surgeons.

I talked with 12 bright, young people in their classroom: a concrete block-built single-storey building no different from thousands of other schoolrooms in Africa. Their learning aids were a single overhead projector and, most important of all, access to the nearby eye ward where their teacher, Dr Bantu, operated.

I asked them about themselves and their hopes and fears for the course. They were high school graduates who had all done 1 year of some health-related work before coming on the course. They were proud to be there and looking forward to a future working in their home districts. They laughed and joked with each other as they talked about going home and taking up a job with the responsibility for looking after the eye health needs of a local population. It was obviously both exciting and nerve-racking at the same time. These young people were going to carry a lot of responsibility.

Sightsavers, as is its normal practice, had set up the course in collaboration with the government and, while it paid for the training, the government guaranteed the students subsequent employment, provided they passed their exams. Dr Bantu, a middle-aged man of Asian ancestry approaching retirement, saw his role very explicitly as providing trained health workers to meet the needs of his country and he was therefore very interested in what becomes of his pupils after they leave him.

He showed me a register with the names of all the students who had graduated from his class over its 12-year existence. Going through them one by one, he told me where they were now. He was proud that he had at least one graduate working in each District of the country, even the north, which was still very troubled and, in some parts almost a war zone. Several had gone on to be cataract surgeons and one, to his great pride, had successfully trained to become a fully qualified ophthalmic surgeon.

Sadly, 12 of the 100 or so graduates were already dead, reflecting the AIDS epidemic in his country. One he had lost touch with and one, to his horror, was working in the private sector in the capital Kampala. 'This one,' he said, jabbing at the name on the page with disgust, 'is a deserter!'

While the group I met were on a 1-year course to become ophthalmology assistants, others were trained as cataract surgeons. These surgeons have become the backbone and mainstay of cataract surgery in large parts of East and West Africa. As with the *técnicos*, the cataract surgeons have very low complication rates.

> These surgeons have become the backbone and mainstay of cataract surgery in large parts of East and West Africa.

The moment when a person's sight is restored is a remarkable thing to witness. I met two of Dr Bantu's patients as their bandages were being taken off after a cataract operation. The first, an elderly man, remained impassive for a long instant as if nothing were different, before the beginnings of a smile appeared on his face. '*What do you see?*' he was asked. '*Muzungu,*' he replied: a white man!

The second was a middle-aged woman who reacted immediately when the bandages were removed. Beaming, she stood up from the bed and began a shuffling dance, swaying her large hips and ululating her pleasure. '*What are you going to do now that you can see?*' someone asked. '*Find a new husband!*' she replied. I wondered why all the men had fled laughing as I innocently stood my ground and waited for the translation.

Another man who was very clear about the need to think radically about health workers and, more generally, make the best use of what is available was the Minister of Health for Ethiopia, Dr Tedros Adhanom Ghebreyesus. One of the most successful and long-serving health ministers in Africa, he has gone on to become the Director General of the WHO. I met him several times when he was minister and responsible for health in one of the fastest growing and poorest countries in Africa, where the annual expenditure on health by 2018 had still only reached US$24 per person with by then a population of more than 110 million.[10]

His whole health plan was based on the premise that you train and employ the people you need to deal with the work that needs doing. The foundation of the Ethiopian service is a very large number of health extension workers who work locally and are primarily concerned with health promotion but carry out some treatment programmes. Above them sit the mid-level workers: the emergency surgeons, direct entry anaesthetists, general clinical officers and others who carry out the bulk of the direct patient work. Above them are the doctors and nurses and other clinical professionals and scientists.

> His whole health plan was based on the premise that you train and employ the people you need to deal with the work that needs doing.

Dr Tedros' view in those pre-pandemic days was straightforward: 80% of the burden of disease in Ethiopia was due to communicable diseases, and most cases could be prevented or treated by community and mid-level workers. We must use the assets at hand and provide what we can to our communities. There is no justification for the shortages of community and mid-level workers. All groups of health workers are needed.

Ethiopia, Mozambique, Uganda and other countries need the highest levels of educated scientists and doctors as well as health extension workers. The fundamental questions are about the proportions of the different types of health workers, the relationships between them and, of course, how easy it is to train, develop and employ them.

Brazil can also tell an impressive story. Since the 1980s it has pursued a policy of training family health teams to provide local care for the country's entire far-flung population, many of whom have to travel for days to reach a hospital. Each team consists of a doctor, a nurse and up to six nursing auxiliaries. Almost 40000 teams had been created by 2016 and covered the vast majority of the country's municipalities.[11] One of the central aspects of this development has been the upgrading of the skills of existing auxiliary nurses, taking them into new areas of expertise and skill where they, like the health extension workers, deal with health promotion as well as treatment.

## COMMUNITY HEALTH WORKERS – LINKING PUBLIC HEALTH AND CLINICAL MEDICINE

The earlier discussion has concentrated on the so-called mid-level workers, people who have received the substantial amount of training needed to perform caesarean sections or cataract surgery, and on auxiliary nurses, who are an integral part of a local health team and a local health system. They are all part of a formal health team.

There is also, however, a very strong emphasis on community in the provision of healthcare and the promotion of health in many low-income countries. This goes far beyond the notion of a formal health service. There is no simple picture here and a spectrum of activity from government-initiated schemes to local developments and groups concerned with advocacy and education.

Pakistan's Lady Health Workers Programme is an enormous enterprise that was started in 2005 by the government with the aim of deploying 100000 workers across the country to help improve health at the village level. Each worker is a resident of the community she serves and is attached to a government health facility from which she receives training, a small allowance and medical supplies.

Each worker is a resident of the community she serves and is attached to a government health facility from which she receives training, a small allowance and medical supplies.

India has similar programmes and I met two of India's thousands of Accredited Social Health Activists (ASHAs) in a small brick-built hut in a village 50 miles south of Kolkata in Western Bengal. These ASHAs have been recruited across India to provide advice and information for their neighbours, to promote immunisation and contraception and to track pregnancies, antenatal care and health issues.

The two women showed me proudly the various handwritten charts and tables they kept that recorded the names of the whole population, identified who was pregnant, who was using contraception and whose children had been immunised. In the gloom of early evening, with no electricity and no lamps, they talked with pride about their work and how they kept an eye on the old people in the village as well as on water levels and how they reported it all to the local authorities.

My western eyes noted that there was no attempt to preserve patient confidentiality. I was reminded of the discussions in the UK about who could have access to patient and public records and how this had become more complicated by the existence of electronic records that with a keystroke, intentional or otherwise, could be sent around the world. This was one problem they didn't yet face in western Bengal, although with India's IT industry it might only be a matter of months away.

The theme of health, not illness, pervades the work of community health workers in Africa. Dr Brian Chituwo, formerly Minister of Health in Zambia, himself a clinician – an orthopaedic surgeon trained in London – goes further. He sees them in his country as promoting health, a healthy life and a healthy community; they are a core part of the development and future prosperity of his country.

Minister Tedros in Ethiopia was also very keen to point out that the most local level of his health system is made up of Health Extension Workers whose primary role is promotion of health and prevention of diseases. They do give some treatment, but, as he always stressed, this was secondary. His aim was to create a service founded on health, not disease.

There is a deliberate intention to bring together public health and clinical medicine to the benefit of both. Ghana's 2006 health plan went even further and was based on the idea of involving the whole community and using all its knowledge and energy in laying the foundation for future health. It is one of several that seek to involve the traditional healers, reasoning that they are an extra resource which, engaged in the right way, can help provide information and support the work of the trained health workers. This can be a risky practice, unless healers can be persuaded to forgo many of their traditional practices.

I was told by researchers undertaking a survey on blindness in Nigeria in 2008, for example, that traditional healers treated many people with cataracts by 'couching'. This is an old and painful practice, mentioned by Pliny, where the clouded lens is knocked off the front of the eye with a wooden implement, thereby allowing light but not focused sight to reach the retina at the back. It offers a semblance of improvement with the patient able to distinguish night from day but does so much damage to the eye that only rarely can a new artificial lens be fitted later and sight restored.

Communities can also play a very important role in getting health messages through to individuals and stopping these dangerous practices. I met a group of villagers in Uganda who worked with Sightsavers to take messages about eye health to their own and neighbouring communities. They did it through the African media of play-acting and music.

> Communities can also play a very important role in getting health messages through to individuals and stopping these dangerous practices.

Eight of them played out a scene for me in front of the village's one-roomed clinic. It was a straightforward tale full of drama and humour. A woman with a pain in her eye went to a traditional healer, who gave her a potion to rub in. It made it much worse. She sobbed with pain as she went completely blind. A wise neighbour intervened and took her to the nurse in the clinic. In due course, her eyesight returned and all was well. The play-acting was simply done but very effective.

Traditional birth attendants are frequently involved in care for pregnant women in many countries. They have skills very different from Mozambique's highly technically trained mid-level workers and are unable to provide the level of care recommended by WHO and others. However, they can bring experience, wisdom and care as part of a well-managed and balanced team. In a striking reversal of previous official policy on the continent, the African Union declared a Decade of Traditional Medicine in 2001 and has since adopted a policy for developing its use and integrating it into both policy and practice.

These snapshots from different countries illustrate something of the range and scope of community health work. There continues, however, to be much debate and controversy over whether and to what extent these types of community worker are effective in keeping populations healthy. The evidence is becoming much clearer as researchers bring together the findings from several studies.

Community health workers can improve health outcomes through health promotion and deliver a range of treatments, which include vaccinations, malaria treatment, case management of childhood illness and adherence to treatment regimes. Research has shown that community health workers can contribute to reductions in child mortality[12] and specifically that the Pakistan Lady Health Worker programme has led to more women using antenatal care, having assistance at birth and using family planning services.[13]

The evidence also shows that these community worker programmes are most effective where they are integrated into the wider health system, they can refer on to more trained health workers and they have the opportunity for refresher or further training and supervision. Many community worker programmes have failed for lack of these features.

> These community worker programmes are most effective where they are integrated into the wider health system.

One of the reasons that China's famous 'barefoot doctors' were not in the end as successful as they might have been was that they were largely left to their own devices after their initial training, with no supervision and refresher or follow-up training. In these circumstances, knowledge can decay and bad habits become ingrained. The remnants of the service, established in 1968, did survive into the 1990s, when wholesale privatisation of health services swept them away, with many setting up as individual private practitioners.[14]

## INNOVATIONS IN POLICY AND TREATMENT

These examples have shown something of the way people in lower-income countries have developed different ways of looking at the world, challenging some of the western world's basic assumptions about medicine, professionalism and government responsibilities. There is much to learn from their whole approach. There are also examples of specific policies and practices that the West can learn from.

Matt Harris and his colleagues at Imperial College London have undertaken a wide range of studies on learning from low- and middle-income countries over the last 10 years and established themselves as the UK's leading researchers in this field. They have looked both at the sorts of innovation and intervention that could influence western practice and at the cultural and systemic barriers to their being adopted.

Their work includes, for example, a systematic review of early medical abortion in primary care in low- and middle-income countries, showing that it is safe, acceptable and effective. It is frequently delivered by nurses or even community health workers in these settings. They argue that this approach in the UK would improve timely access to medical abortion services.

Their study on the use of mosquito net mesh for hernia repair, used throughout India and sub-Saharan Africa, found that these are closer in biomechanical form and function to abdominal wall muscle than much more expensive commercial mesh used in the NHS. Their review notes that, although multiple trials demonstrate equivalence in effectiveness and adverse events compared to commercial mesh, it is recommended for use only in low- and middle-income countries and not high-income ones. This, they argue, is a glaring double standard.

Forthcoming publications include a review of Miracradle, a frugal alternative to servo-controlled devices to induce therapeutic hypothermia in pre-term neonates at risk of hypoxic brain injury. They argue there is a strong case for its use in the UK given that it is used in India and is as effective as the more expensive technologies. They have also undertaken a systematic review and realist synthesis of research into Kangaroo Mother Care in the UK, exploring the challenges and barriers to its use.

Kangaroo (or Cangaru) care is a technique originally developed in Columbia in the mid-1970s, where children are strapped to the mother's or another adult's chest, making skin to skin contact, as an alternative to high dependency clinical care. Many studies have shown that it reduces mortality in stable pre-term babies compared to incubator use. It is recommended by the WHO and used in many countries around much of the world. However, it is not routinely practised in the UK, where neonatal intensive care units are ill-equipped to provide families with the necessary space, time and training to practise it.

Other studies of theirs have focused on exploring entrenched biases against innovation or research from low- and middle-income countries. They have, for example, published a systematic review and narrative synthesis of research articles exploring bias based on the geography of author affiliation. They have also published a randomised controlled trial showing how English clinicians rate research from low- and middle-income countries far lower than research from high-income countries, even when the research is identical. Their Implicit Association Test has demonstrated unconscious bias against research from low- and middle-income countries.[15]

Most recently, Matt Harris was one of several co-authors of a commentary at the start of the pandemic arguing that, like many low- and middle-income countries, the UK should have a scaled system of community health workers to support contact tracing and vaccine uptake.[16] The authors argued that *'Experience from Brazil, Pakistan, Ethiopia, and other nations shows how a coordinated community workforce can provide effective health and social care support at scale.'* This has obvious echoes of the Ugandan village COVID groups described in Chapter 3. It also links with the pilot introduction of community health workers in a London borough based on the Brazilian model that is described in the last pages of this chapter.

The speed of vaccine development in response to the pandemic has been very impressive and celebrated globally. With Professor Dhananjaya Sharma at the Centre for Global Surgical Innovation and Low Cost Solutions in Jabalpur, India, and Dr Yasser Bhatti, at QMUL, Matt Harris drew attention to the way COVID-19 has also led to a surge of frugal innovation responses, innovating under resource constraints at pace and scale.[17] We have seen some extraordinary changes, the rapid development of hospitals in China, India and Pakistan refitting train carriages to become hospitals, distilleries manufacturing millions of bottles of hand sanitiser, car manufacturers building ventilators and the UK's NHS leasing private-sector beds and whole hospitals.

As the authors argue, *'These responses bear the hallmarks of so-called "frugal innovation" – that is, doing more, with less, for the many, and being creative, innovative and resourceful in the face of institutional voids and resource constraints.'* High-income countries are learning to respond in ways that low- and middle-income countries have had to do for a long time.

> These responses bear the hallmarks of so-called 'frugal innovation' – that is, doing more, with less, for the many, and being creative, innovative and resourceful in the face of institutional voids and resource constraints.
>
> *Matt Harris and colleagues[17]*

Other examples, not related to the pandemic, come from westerners working in poorer countries, where the resources they would normally use simply aren't available and they have had to be creative. Steve Mannion, who worked part of the year in Newcastle in the UK and part in Malawi, is an orthopaedic surgeon who has changed the way club-foot in newborn children is treated as a result of his experience in Malawi.

The practice in rich countries had been in recent years to carry out a lengthy and difficult operation to realign and straighten the foot. Faced with a vast number of patients in Malawi needing treatment, he cast around for other ways of helping them and came across an old technique invented by an Italian and based on repeated manipulations. In simple terms, the foot is bent as far as possible into the right position each week and bound in place. This is repeated week after week, bending the foot a little further in each case. After several weeks of such treatment, the condition has all but disappeared. This is now the standard treatment in London, Paris and New York as well as Lilongwe and Blantyre.

The way that TB and HIV/AIDS treatments are administered globally is based on experience in Africa where there isn't the infrastructure to manage follow-up clinics and home treatment. This has led to different ways of delivering therapies and, for example, giving as much treatment as possible on each occasion. It was quickly recognised that this would be useful elsewhere and these methods of delivering treatments learned in Africa are now the standard protocols worldwide.

Aravind Eye Care in southern India is now very well-known globally. It has used innovative locally designed approaches, blending them with modern western management techniques, to provide very streamlined and effective treatment. It was set up with the vision of providing services for everyone and has a simple system of cross-subsidy in place whereby the poorest pay nothing and the profits from other patients cover their costs.

Aravind is very impressive in both the range of its activities and the scope of its ambition. Faced with enormous numbers of patients needing cataract surgery and unable to afford the expensive materials and techniques then in use in rich countries, they set out to develop new methodologies and materials. They succeeded. Their intraocular lens is now used in 120 countries around the world; and their operational and other research is world class.

India more generally has a tradition of *jugaad* which means using limited resources – whatever is to hand – in an innovative way. The Oxford dictionary describes it as *'the use of skill and imagination to find an easy solution to a problem or to fix or make something using cheap, basic items'*. It has been used to develop everything from cooking stoves to makeshift vehicles to housing and has been described as a way of life in India. In recent years, management theorists and businesses have adopted it for application to businesses and there is a plethora of books on the subject.

Not all *jugaad* products are good, and some are downright dangerous. The Indian government has banned *jugaad* vehicles from the roads. It is a reminder that we should not romanticise innovations in low- and middle-income countries. Necessity may breed invention, but it can also breed disaster. Nevertheless, the simple message holds that people with limited resources in any country can be enormously creative – and we can all learn from them. This is why universities such as Duke and businesses such as Philips have set up innovation and partnership centres in India. We desperately need inspiration and innovation from wherever it comes.

> Necessity may breed invention, but it can also breed disaster.

COVID-19 is bringing with it a long trail of mental illnesses that will be with us for years to come. Professor Alan Rosen, an Australian psychiatric and public health specialist, has written about comparative studies by WHO, which have demonstrated better long-term outcome for schizophrenia in developing countries.

*'These findings still generate some professional contention and disbelief, as they challenge outdated assumptions that people generally do not recover from schizophrenia and that the outcomes of western treatments and rehabilitation must be superior. However, these results have proven to be remarkably robust, on the basis of international replications and 15–25-year follow-up studies.*

*'Explanations for this phenomenon are still at the hypothesis level, but include: (1) greater inclusion or retained social integration in the community in developing countries, so that the person maintains a role or status in the society; (2) involvement in traditional healing rituals, reaffirming communal inclusion and solidarity; (3) availability of a valued work role that can be adapted to a lower level of functioning; (4) availability of an extended kinship or communal network, so that family tension and burden are diffused, and there is often low negatively "expressed emotion" in the family.'*[18]

I have quoted Professor Rosen at some length because his account deals with the scepticism of his colleagues and suggests some of the reasons why the treatment is so successful. These comments point the way to a new set of approaches to mental health which has been maturing in recent years. A 2021 report from the All-Party Parliamentary Group on Global Health, which I co-chair, argues that the mental health workforce needs to change dramatically both in its composition and in the way mental health specialists work with the wider public and civil society.[19] It quotes Professor Dinesh Bhugra, former President of the World Psychiatric Federation, saying that *'Mental health is too important to be left to the specialist. It is everyone's business.'* All the social factors mentioned by Alan Rosen are central to prevention of disease as well as treatment and care.

> Mental health is too important to be left to the specialist. It is everyone's business.
>
> *Professor Dinesh Bhugra*

There have also been innovations and different ways of thinking about health systems alongside these more specific interventions and service models. Most notably, perhaps, is the way health policy and plans in most low- and middle-income countries are seen as being part of wider anti-poverty or development policy and plans. Education, health and economic growth have gone together in global policy since the era of structural adjustment, when economic development trumped everything else, and education and health were neglected.

Western mindsets have tended to be different, seeing health much more as a stand-alone activity, at least until recent years. This has resulted in many policy conflicts – schools, for example, selling off playing fields or allowing pupils to buy unhealthy food regardless of the health impacts. Efforts in recent years to tackle childhood obesity have proved difficult precisely because of different policies in different departments. When I was the English NHS chief executive, policy relevant to exercise was split four ways between the departments responsible for health, education, culture and sport, and local government and the environment. Cross-cutting targets and plans were largely unsuccessful. There is more focus now on working together but it has taken COVID-19 to make this a real priority.

Some western governments, notably Norway, have been much better at such cross-government working. We have already seen in this and earlier chapters how BRAC has brought so many streams of activity together. Mexico has been another successful pioneer. In the 1990s, the Mexican Ministry of Health had recognised that the poorest people in the population often didn't have the education or motivation to adopt healthy practices, so they started giving people specific payments as an incentive to change their behaviour and, for example, get a medical check-up for their children, attend antenatal clinics or enrol their children in school. This was so successful that Mexico has subsequently tied most of its social welfare programme to these sorts of actions and behaviour changes. In 2002 they set up Oportunidades as, in the current jargon, a conditional cash transfer programme designed to reach all parts of the population.

In 2004, Julio Frenk, the then Health Minister, took this further by establishing a programme of health insurance for the poor called Seguro Popular. His aim was to achieve *'universal access to high-quality services with social protection for all'*. Both the Oportunidades and Seguro Popular have been very influential globally – in richer and poorer countries.[20]

> Universal access to high-quality services with social protection for all.
>
> *Julio Frenk describing the aim of Securo Popular*

Many countries in Latin America, Asia and Africa created similar programmes and they, like Mexico, have developed them further over the years. I spoke with Julio Frenk while writing this book. He is now President of the University of Miami, having previously been Dean of the Harvard School of Public Health, but is still heavily involved in health globally. Together with Lincoln Chen, he has led the work on education health professionals for the twenty-first century which will be described in Chapter 10. Sadly, he told me that the new Mexican President had abolished the whole programme. Instead, he has instigated a system of pensions for poor people that are paid directly to them without any conditions or linkage to other programmes. The pension is presented as though it comes directly from the President and is due to his largesse and concern for the people. It is a perfect example of how populist politicians currently operate, disposing of any system of checks and balances, dispensing public funding as though it were private patronage, bribing citizens with their own money. It is precisely how many autocrats have behaved in the past.

These few accounts illustrate people using the resources they have and finding ways around local obstacles to the delivery of healthcare. This is sometimes described as reverse innovation – a term that I feel is deeply patronising and misleading. Why would we expect innovation to come only from the rich and powerful?

In reality, innovation generally comes from outside the mainstream and from small organisations, individuals, young people and people without formal power. Think of Microsoft and IBM, Turing and computing, high-street shops and the internet. By contrast, those in authority generally have something to lose from innovations that disrupt the status quo.

Frugal innovation at least points to the type of innovation and not to who developed it. Even so, like reverse innovation, it can have connotations of being somehow inferior. I prefer to talk of innovation and to recognise that we can learn from everyone and that we need to source innovation globally and from all parts of our own communities.

## ARE THE RICHER AND MORE POWERFUL COUNTRIES YET READY TO LEARN?

Matt Harris's studies show that western health systems are not yet ready to learn from low- and middle-income countries. There are strong barriers largely because we have such strong professions, regulators and systems and such well-established ways of doing things. It is worth noting that some other sectors and particularly business and commercial and social entrepreneurs are much better at this, largely because they don't have the same levels of these barriers.

There are, however, many individuals and organisations who are keen and ready to learn. I have met many Americans, Britons and other Europeans who, when asked about learning from their experiences in poorer countries, immediately give me examples.

Professor Philippa Easterbrook, for example, sent me a long list based on her experiences in working at the Infectious Diseases Institute in Uganda. It included exploring different models of delivery of care, innovative approaches to the scaling up of counselling and testing through the use of family members and the community, the involvement of people living with HIV as agents of change and a more holistic approach to care. She also remarked on the recognition of the central role of spirituality, as well as music in the delivery of care in Africa, and on the adoption of 'task sharing or shifting' with leading roles for nurses and pharmacists in delivery of ART.

Working abroad as a volunteer, on a placement or in a paid role can be a very positive experience for the people involved, as we already noted with Martin Beed's experience in Ethiopia in Chapter 2. People have told me about becoming more adaptable, being open to new ideas, improving teamwork and returning home refreshed and reinvigorated.

It is, however, very difficult to measure these benefits in objective terms that take account of the experiences of different volunteers and relate directly to the expressed development needs of particular countries. Louise Ackers and colleagues carried out a UK study which focused on the potential direct benefit to the NHS of volunteers working abroad. The study concluded that, while placements abroad were clearly valuable for the individuals involved, there needed to be more alignment between the overseas experience and what the NHS had identified as its staff development priorities. General development and learning were not seen as being valuable enough in itself. They concluded that they couldn't – against this rather narrow criterion – at present justify NHS expenditure on this activity.[21]

This study very helpfully enables us to distinguish between individual-level learning and system learning. Every health system will define its staff development needs in terms of its current perception of its role and aims and some will see this more broadly than others. It is clearly right that public money should be spent on what the system has decided it needs. The difficulty here is that systems also need to be open to ideas from outside their own experience. Unwillingness to learn is a significant barrier to improvement, as Matt Harris and others have shown.

While individual learning is valuable – and some people will learn more than others – what is needed is system-level learning. Fazle Abed's policy of empowering the women and the type of examples I describe as complementing western scientific medicine that were listed in Figure 8.1 are about system-level changes not individual ones. They are about the engagement of social enterprises, involving communities and especially women, helping people become economically independent, linking health into every aspect of lives, training for needs not the professions, bringing clinical medicine and public health together, and making the best use of the assets to hand.

While individual learning is valuable – and some people will learn more than others – what is needed is system-level learning.

I suspect that the NHS, with its new focus on local-level decision making and community and public engagement, may be in 2022 more ready to understand what it can learn from outside its own experience than it has been in the past.

We return to system learning in Chapter 11. By the system I mean the professions, the regulators, the politicians, the managers, and the key partners, everyone who makes it work and the influential outsiders such as the pharmaceutical companies and other businesses, the universities, the government officials, commentators and media. This requires changes in mindset about how we conceptualise health and health systems. Individuals working abroad will undoubtedly help accelerate that change, but they can't do it by themselves.

Most western health systems may not, as yet, have noticed that the world is shifting. Eventually, however, I suspect that it will be costs that will finally force decision makers to understand how policies in high-income countries – particularly about staffing structures – will have to change.

There is no reason, however, to think that the UK or the USA or France or Germany can avoid the issue. Somewhere, sometime, explicitly or by stealth, politicians and health planners will have to alter this over-reliance on the most highly paid professionals and start to introduce many more health workers trained to do the work that needs doing. They will have to alter the balance of their workforce and do what the Africans and South Americans are doing today.

There are already examples: physicians' assistants in the US and elsewhere, for example, and the introduction of nursing associates in the UK following a review in 2015. The NHS describes this new role as follows and notes that it is part of a team and has career prospects: '*Nursing associate is a new role within the nursing team. Nursing associates work with healthcare support workers and registered nurses to deliver care for patients and the public. It is also a stepping stone to becoming a registered nurse.*'[22] As we shall see later, community health workers could also soon be introduced across the NHS.

It is important to note that this can and needs to be done in a way that improves quality and doesn't just reduce costs. The appointment of nursing associates who allow nurses to work to the 'top of their licence' – doing only what they need to do – can improve the quality of nurses' work and enable more people to be cared for. Nursing associates can also provide a quality of service of their own, spending more time with patients, listening and being there for them.

The pyramids in Figure 8.2 compare the workforces in Ethiopia and the UK and illustrate the differences. This figure is not to scale. The UK pyramid would be more than 30 times larger than the Ethiopian one to reflect the greater number of health workers in the country.

This key difference means that, in high-income countries, whatever the structure of their service and its intended operation, the whole dynamic, as we saw in Chapter 5, is to pull more and more activity through to the highest and most specialised level. In countries such as the USA where patients can directly refer themselves to specialists without being referred by a generalist, this is even more pronounced. The result is the expensive and wasteful top-down hospital-based and highly specialised services that are so familiar in high-income countries.

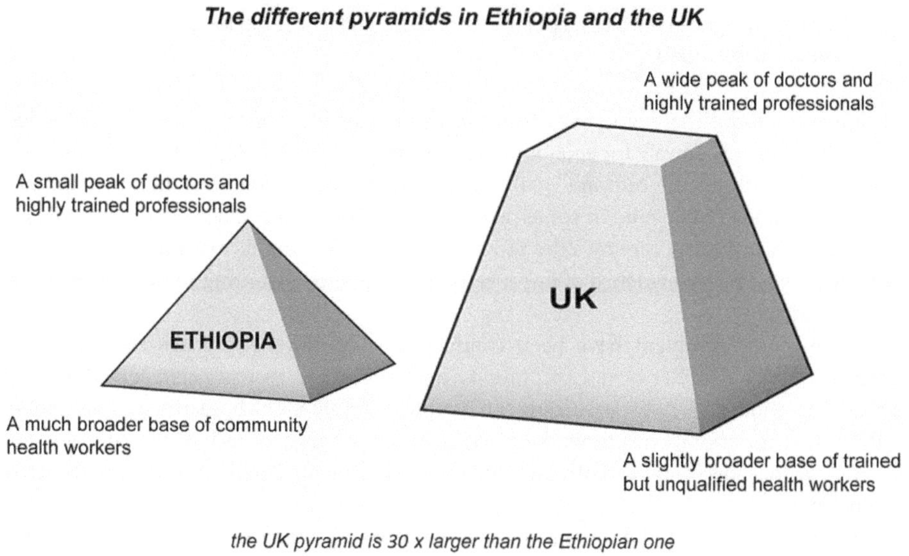

**The different pyramids in Ethiopia and the UK**

A small peak of doctors and highly trained professionals

A wide peak of doctors and highly trained professionals

**ETHIOPIA**

**UK**

A much broader base of community health workers

A slightly broader base of trained but unqualified health workers

*the UK pyramid is 30 x larger than the Ethiopian one*

**Figure 8.2** The different workforce distribution in Ethiopia and the UK.

We will undoubtedly see a similar trend in Ethiopia and other countries as people seek career progression. The world doesn't stand still and the thousands of people who are mid-level workers today will aspire to be nurses and doctors tomorrow. Minister Tedros' successors will have difficulty in keeping the appropriate proportions between the levels of staff in his service. The skill mix will become richer, with greater numbers of qualified people, each of them with a reasonable expectation that their skills will be rewarded with higher levels both of pay and responsibility – and there is no doubt that more health professionals are needed in countries like Ethiopia.

Costs and qualifications go hand in hand from the length of training to the cost of employment. In Mozambique, an economic evaluation of the comparative performance of *técnicos* and doctors in 2007 showed that the costs per major obstetric procedure for *técnicos de cirurgia* average about one-third of physician costs over their careers. The costs of training and deploying *técnicos de cirurgia* is less than one-quarter that of physician specialists.[6] The figures will be different but the pattern similar in other countries.

Making changes in the skill mix of the workforce is difficult, both for good reasons and for bad. The good reasons are concerns about whether patients will actually see the highly trained specialist when they need to or whether they will see a less-trained person who will miss the vital information and fail to make the right diagnosis. This is a real concern and can only be dealt with by making sure that the less-trained person always has access to the higher-trained and knows how to refer and is listened to when they do. This isn't easy to do. It requires sufficient numbers of staff at both levels as well as good training and good systems.

Making changes in the skill mix of the workforce is difficult, both for good
reasons and for bad.

There is no doubt that some ministers and businesses see opportunities to employ less
well-qualified people simply for economic reasons, regardless of quality. They may also seek
to call people without the relevant qualifications nurses or doctors. This is most common
with nurses but also happened in some places with doctors and can be very dangerous. The
other side of this is that sometimes the professions and trade unions resist all change – even
where there is excellent evidence of improvements in quality – wanting to protect their jobs
and their territory.

These types of argument have been conducted in development circles for years, with
controversy about whether or not community health workers, in particular, served a useful
purpose. The evidence is now persuading the doubters. Jeffrey Sachs has strongly championed
the roll-out of community health workers across Africa, arguing for its cost-effectiveness and
efficacy. African leaders have recently adopted the goal of having 2 million such workers across
the continent.[23]

These battles are still to be fought in richer countries. Experience to date shows that they
have not yet really started.

The Brazilian plan, its Family Health Program, has been sustained for 20 years and during
the tenure of successive presidents and governments. This is a remarkable demonstration of
the sustained and consistent political commitment that is the first and most important criterion
for success in any major change in a health system.

It is interesting to note that the successive Brazilian governments have steered a careful path
between taking a radical approach to the training and employment of health workers while
at the same time maintaining the position and status of the traditional health professionals.
The new auxiliary nurses are, in many cases, people who were already undertaking some
kind of health role in an unsupervised and unregulated fashion in the country. Their training
by government brought them within a regulated system. This has created a very welcome
improvement in the quality and continuity of care. It has also meant, however, that the new
auxiliary nurses did not threaten the power and position of the professionals. In some ways
they reinforced the status quo.

The fact that the status quo hasn't changed was well illustrated for me at a meeting I was at
in Africa where the Brazilian Deputy Minister took and made a succession of slightly agitated
phone calls. He told me that the doctors in Brazil were threatening to go on strike because a
minister had suggested that nurses might take on a task reserved for doctors.

Brazil is one of those countries with a very restricted list of roles and tasks that can be done
by professionals other than doctors. Nurses are far more limited in what they can do than in the
UK or North America. This demarcation is enforced by law. The doctors' unions were clearly
not ready for any task shifting. The government was not prepared for a fight on that occasion
and later that day Deputy Minister told me it had backed down.

We need to be careful that we don't see 'task shifting' as a purely temporary expedient, as
discussed in the last chapter, and only necessary until enough staff and money are available.

We need to make sure that we don't think that quality refers only to narrowly defined clinical quality and outcomes or that only highly trained professionals can deliver high-quality care. It depends on what the patient needs and, as we shall discuss in Chapter 10, what *matters to them.*

## PARTNERSHIPS

There is a long tradition of partnerships between hospitals, universities and other organisations in rich and poor countries. At the same time, many individuals have found their own way to work in poorer countries as volunteers or temporary members of staff. Over the last few years, more and more students have gone to spend periods of time working abroad. There is an increasing amount of interchange in person and over the internet and through social media.

At their best, these partnerships between institutions in different countries can be very effective. They can have enormous impact if they are based on the needs of the poorer country and built up through long-term relationships of respect. At their worst, when they are short-term and badly thought through and executed, they can lead to wasted effort by both parties and to people being badly bruised by the experience.

> They can have enormous impact if they are based on the needs of the poorer country and built up through long-term relationships of respect.

I have been shown or told about many examples in Africa and India of equipment sent out from the UK that was not suitable, required parts, maintenance and even power that wasn't available locally and had just been left to rot. I was also told of people flying in to help who did so briefly and then left, having disrupted the hospital for the period of their residence. If people are coming to help, I was told frequently, they need to stay for a longer period or come back regularly to work, train people locally and share their experience and expertise.

There are over 100 UK organisations that have long-term partnerships with others abroad and many more from all over Europe and North America. In the UK they are mainly grouped around the Tropical Health Education Trust (THET), which has developed approaches to good practice.[24] For many years, THET ran a UK Government grant scheme to promote such partnerships but this was completely cut when the Government cut overseas development aid in 2021.

Brazil has built up strong links with the six Portuguese-speaking countries in Africa and shares a development network with them. Each arrangement is individual, but many of these partnerships work on the basis of teams from the richer country going to work for a period in the poorer one, offering training and expertise. This may be followed by people from the poorer country coming back to the richer one for further training and experience, with the whole programme and exchanges being dictated by the needs of the poorer country.

There are other health partnerships in other countries. Memisa is a network of Belgian organisations supporting health programmes in Asia, Africa and Latin America.[25] The ESTHER Alliance for Global Health involves 12 European countries working with partners in other parts of the world and has plans to transition into a more broadly based network over the next few years.[26]

Some of the gains for the poorer country are obvious, such as having skilled people, albeit for a limited but regular period, who can do particular tasks and can train locals. Sometimes these visits have led to new services being developed with continuing support provided by email and phone. The partnerships also provide a more hidden benefit by offering professional support to the, often isolated, clinical and other staff in the poorer country. I have heard people talk of the importance of not being alone and of feeling part of their wider profession and involved in global events.

For the UK and other countries with large numbers of communities from different ethnic groups, this sharing of experience between different countries and traditions can be very important for another very practical reason. Knowledge of their culture, tradition and practices is enormously useful to the clinician in London.

I have described partnerships here as if the only ones involve two parties, one from a higher-income country and one from a lower. There are many combinations, with advantages to be drawn from partnerships involving many parties and ones linking countries with the same needs. There are no boundaries to the arrangements that can be developed.

Partnerships are a recurring theme throughout the book, where partnerships with a particular focus, for example on diabetes or AMR and other more general ones for research, nursing development and climate change will be discussed.

## CONCLUSIONS

This chapter, written about what richer countries can learn from poorer ones, has also demonstrated how much poorer countries can and do learn from each other. Between them, they are creating a new set of ideas that grow out of their own circumstances and experiences.

The biggest theme has been about training people for the work that needs doing and not just for the professions. This is not new. My father-in-law, David Jenkins, who was referred to in the first chapter, reminded me that during the Second World War the British and French had both trained 'field surgeons' in the same way. In Africa, they did the same during the internal conflicts in Ethiopia and Mozambique much more recently.

Meanwhile, I suspect that the full potential of microfinance has not yet been realised. Some existing microfinance organisations already offer wider services and are likely to expand their activities much more extensively into health- and education-related matters, helping people both to improve their health and to cover the effects of what would otherwise be catastrophic illness.

Sheila Leatherman, a Professor from the University of North Carolina who researches and writes on this area, argues strongly that *'microfinance institutions can provide health education, motivation to change health practices, and referrals to good-quality health services, along with credit that stimulates increases in income and assets, while reducing people's vulnerability to financial and health crises'.*[27]

This chapter has also suggested that richer countries can learn from the ideas and approaches being generated in poorer ones. It has explored some of the very biggest themes in health that are of relevance to every country. There is the importance of empowering women, economically as well as politically. There is social enterprise and the bringing together of public health and clinical medicine. There is the understanding of power and the necessity, for good or ill, of political involvement, determination and will. There is, overwhelmingly, a sense of working with and through communities, villages and families and of generating energy to enable people themselves to make change and improve their lives. There is an understanding that health relates to everything else and an absence of rigid boundaries between actions to improve health and those to improve the economy or the environment.

These are all themes that we can find in high-income countries as well as in lower-income ones. However, they are not as prominent or as central. They are not yet fully part of the canon of knowledge and learning and don't yet take their place alongside science, commerce, professionalism and service. In high-income countries we have been failing to notice how the world, even in our own countries, is changing around us. COVID-19 has been a wake-up call.

> They are not yet fully part of the canon of knowledge and learning and don't yet take their place alongside science, commerce, professionalism and service.

This chapter has also started to draw out the creativity inherent in bringing together all the different ways of looking at the world: bringing together different ideas, different experiences and different views. This blend is what I call in future chapters the practical knowledge for the twenty-first century.

The next chapter looks at what can be learned from different communities within our own countries. This chapter ends with a final example of learning from elsewhere – a new venture that transfers knowledge from Brazil to the UK.

## FROM BRAZIL TO WESTMINSTER

Matt Harris, as noted earlier, was one of the authors advocating that the UK adopt a national community health worker strategy as part of the response to COVID-19. Together with Connie Junghens and other colleagues, he has secured funding from Westminster City Council to employ four community health workers in a ward in Pimlico.

These community health workers, closely based on the Brazilian model, are local people, community champions, who know the area well and act as the eyes and ears in the community for the local GPs. The community health workers work in a very different way from other health workers in the UK, by visiting every household in their defined area, around 130 in total, every month.

Every household gets a visit, no matter what their health and social care needs. The workers' responsibilities cover all areas of health promotion and support including updating people on the pandemic, encouraging childhood immunisation, assisting with chronic disease management, breastfeeding, mental health and loneliness, supporting people to navigate the health and care system, offering informal counselling and empathic listening, and keeping digital records of household and community needs. Through regular visits, they aim to build a trusting and continuous relationship with their households, enabling a proactive approach that is unique in the UK.

Their job description, shown in the Appendix, is part of a wider operational manual, developed with Nav Chana, Clinical Director of the National Association of Primary Care. The manual will support other localities to adopt this approach as well. The help and guidance of Brazilian colleagues has been instrumental to this work. The Westminster community health workers have had direct discussions with community health workers in Brazil via video conferencing to share learning and benefit from their years of experience.

This pilot scheme will be reviewed for possible wider extension in Westminster, depending on assessment of the first year's performance, but it has already attracted attention from elsewhere in the country. I suspect that the timing is perfect, coinciding with the introduction of new health and care structures which give a much more local focus to many activities. It could even be the start of something much bigger.

# REFERENCES

1. https://data.worldbank.org/indicator/SH.DYN.MORT (Accessed 19 November 2021).
2. http://www.brac.net/program/wp-content/uploads/2021/06/MF-Factsheet-09-06-2021.pdf (Accessed 19 November 2021).
3. https://bracupgi.org/our-vision#impact/ (Accessed 19 November 2021).
4. http://hdr.undp.org/en/content/latest-human-development-index-ranking (Accessed 19 November 2021).
5. https://www.convergences.org/wp-content/uploads/2019/09/Microfinance-Barometer-2019_web-1.pdf (Accessed 19 November 2021).
6. Kruk ME, Pereira C, Vaz F *et al*. Economic evaluation of surgically trained assistant medical officers in performing major obstetric surgery in Mozambique. *Br J Obstet Gynaecol*, 2007; **114**(10): 1253–60.
7. Pereira C, Cumbi A, Malalane R *et al*. Meeting the need for emergency obstetrical care in Mozambique: work performance and history of medical doctors and assistant medical officers trained for surgery. *Br J Obstet Gynaecol*, 2007; **114**(12): 1530–3.

8. Pereira C, Bugalho A, Bergström S *et al*. A comparative study of caesarean deliveries by assistant medical officers and obstetricians in Mozambique. *Br J Obstet Gynaecol*, 1996; **103**(6): 508–12.

9. Vaz F, Bergström S, Vaz ML *et al*. Training medical assistants for surgery. *Bull World Health Organ*, 1999; **77**: 688–91.

10. https://knoema.com/atlas/Ethiopia/topics/Health/Health-Expenditure/Health-expenditure-per-capita (Accessed 19 November 2021).

11. https://www.google.com/search?client=firefox-b-d&q=how+many+family+health+team+sin+Brazil (Accessed 19 November 2021).

12. Haines A, Sanders D, Lehmman U *et al*. Achieving child survival goals: potential contribution of community health workers. *The Lancet*, June 2007; **369**(9579): 2121–31.

13. Lady Health Worker Programme. *External Evaluation of the National Programme for the Family Planning and Primary Health Care. Quantitative Survey Report.* Islamabad: Oxford Policy Management, 2002.

14. Zhang D, Unschuld PU. China's barefoot doctor: past, present and future. *The Lancet*, November 2008; **372**(9653): 1865–7.

15. Harris M, Marti J, Watt H *et al*. Explicit bias toward high-income-country research: a randomized, blinded, crossover experiment of English clinicians. *Health Aff*, 2017; **36**(11): 1997–2004. https://www.healthaffairs.org/doi/10.1377/hlthaff.2017.0773 (Accessed 19 November 2021).

16. Haines A, de Barros EF, Berlin A *et al*. National UK programme of community health workers for COVID-19 responses. *The Lancet*, April 2020; **395**(10231): 1173–5. https://www.thelancet.com/journals/lancet/article/PIIS0140-6736(20)30735-2/fulltext (Accessed 19 November 2021).

17. Harris M, Bhatti W, Buckley J, Sharma D. Fast and frugal innovations in response to the COVID-19 pandemic. *Nat Med*, 2020; **26**: 814–17. https://doi.org/10.1038/s41591-020-0889-1 (Accessed 19 November 2021).

18. Rosen A. Destigmatizing day-to-day practices: what developed countries can learn from developing countries. *World Psychiatry*, 2006; **5**(1): 21–4. https://pubmed.ncbi.nlm.nih.gov/16757986/ (Accessed 19 November 2021).

19. All-Party Group on Global Health. New directions for the mental health workforce globally. London, 15 July 2021. https://globalhealth.inparliament.uk/ (Accessed 19 November 2021).

20. Frenk J. Bridging the divide: global lessons from evidence-based health policy in Mexico. *The Lancet*, 2006; **368**(9539): 954–61. https://www.thelancet.com/journals/lancet/article/PIIS0140-6736(06)69376-8/references (Accessed 19 November 2021).

21. Ackers HL, Ackers-Johnson J, Chatwin J, Tyler N. International mobility and learning in the UK National Health Service. In *Healthcare, Frugal Innovation, and Professional Voluntarism*. London: Palgrave Macmillan, 2017 pp. 31–66. https://doi.org/10.1007/978-3-319-48366-5_1 (Accessed 19 November 2021).

22. https://www.healthcareers.nhs.uk/explore-roles/nursing/roles-nursing/nursing-associate (Accessed 19 November 2021).

23. https://www.jeffsachs.org/newspaper-articles/y3s3fafpml83natcsaz99k926hxkp9 (Accessed 19 November 2021).
24. https://www.thet.org/wp-content/uploads/2020/10/Guidance-for-New-Health-Partnerships_final-1.pdf (Accessed 19 November 2021).
25. https://memisa.be/en/about-memisa/ (Accessed 19 November 2021).
26. https://esther.eu/ (Accessed 19 November 2021).
27. Leatherman S. Personal communication, 28 September 2006.

# Learning from communities in our own country

**9**

There is so much that can also be learned from communities in our own countries, from people and organisations which are easily ignored or forgotten, the less powerful, less well connected and, often, more disadvantaged. This applies equally to low-income countries, where there is often an elite detached from most of the population, as to the more layered societies of the West, where many different groups have different levels of access to power and influence.

The examples discussed in this chapter are all from the UK but there are many similar projects, programmes, organisations and activities in other countries around the world.

The chapter begins with a brief discussion of government programmes designed to make improvements in the UK's most disadvantaged communities and moves on to describe action that has been taken by people in the communities themselves. Some of them are reminiscent of what Arvind Ohja from Urmul described in the last chapter as '*A package of development services that they themselves decide on, design, implement and eventually finance.*'

The chapter goes on to discuss health creation and look at some of the things that health creators in communities, business and health services are doing to improve health. It finishes by reviewing the behaviours that are characteristic of the many people involved in health creation and which are very much part of what we can all learn from our own communities.

The environments may be very different but there are, sadly, some very striking similarities in the way that some professionals in the UK have treated people in some of the more disadvantaged communities and the way some development partners treat people in lower-income countries. There has been too much top-down problem solving and decision making and too little listening and supporting people to do what they already know needs doing.

There have been many national programmes over the years designed to improve the lives and life chances of people. I was a community worker in Halewood, a large overspill estate outside Liverpool, in the mid-1970s and was employed by a local NGO and funded partly through the Urban Aid Programme, its name reminiscent of overseas aid.

The Halewood estates had been built alongside a small rural village about 8 miles from the city centre and consisted of terraced houses, maisonettes, and a few tower blocks, one of which I lived in, and very limited facilities. It had been created as part of a slum clearance programme which was itself designed to improve lives but involved breaking up inner city communities

DOI: 10.1201/9781003267706-9

with their own strong cultures and moving people to the outskirts where they didn't even know their new neighbours and had to start again from scratch.

Urban Aid and programmes like it had some remarkable successes in some areas and with individual projects – and we would claim some in Halewood for our work with young people – but, despite them, inequality has been growing in the UK for many years and there were no material improvements made in many places.

Much of the reason was structural. Poor facilities, badly constructed housing, some of it now demolished, short-term interventions and high unemployment all contributed. Part of the reason for failure was because change was imposed from outside and not owned by the people directly involved. Community building, like nation building, needs to be bottom-up.

In fact, much of the discussion in Chapter 4 about health and poverty in lower-income countries applies here, too. There are multiple problems which reinforce each other, structural features which maintain disadvantage, and a lack of self-determination and of being able to control your own destiny.

> Much of the discussion in Chapter 4 about health and poverty in lower-income countries applies here, too. There are multiple problems which reinforce each other, structural features which maintain disadvantage, and a lack of self-determination and of being able to control your own destiny.

Britain had a long tradition of strong working-class communities, often with large extended families and people working in the same industry – mining or the cotton mills, for example – and where people generally helped each other. There were savings and welfare schemes and cooperative food stores. The cooperative movement was born in Rochdale with the Rochdale Pioneers of 1844, although the history of cooperation can be traced back to the Hull Anti-Mill Co-op of 1795 and earlier examples. One mutual aid group, the Tredegar Workmen's Medical Aid Society, is often said to be the inspiration behind the formation of the NHS.

In truth, Tredegar was only one such organisation, but its story is instructive. The Tredegar Iron and Coal Company employed a doctor to look after its workers. Money was deducted from their wages to pay for the doctor who, of course, worked for the company. It was the same story elsewhere in the UK and is true today in some industries in other countries.

The result according to recent account was that *'This lack of control was a source of bitterness and workers complained that while they paid the piper, they rarely got to call the tune. So, in the late 1800s and early 1900s, many workers across south Wales took over and workmen's committees set about enhancing the basic features.'*[1]

We must not romanticise the past. There were plenty of places that didn't have this enterprising community spirit and there was awful poverty, ill health and early death everywhere, even in these communities. Sir William Beveridge's 1942 report that provided the blueprint for post-war social policy and the creation of the welfare state spoke of battling against the five giants of idleness, ignorance, disease, squalor and want.[2]

Many communities in London, Liverpool and other big cities were broken up by slum clearance programmes and the rebuilding of bombed areas after the war. The later destruction of the coal, steel, ship building and other major manufacturing industries in the 1970s, 1980s and 1990s broke up many more. Today, with some notable exceptions, the UK is largely a country where people are mobile, live away from their family and may not even know their neighbours. Community often now refers to people linked by common causes, ethnic roots, convictions, lifestyles and has little or no connection with the place where they live.

There are, however, today many people attempting to rebuild communities to suit the current times, just as we were in 1970s Halewood. The importance of place has been rediscovered in recent years and is now promoted by many organisations such as the Town and Country Planning Association and appears in government policy. Regrettably, however, we are still seeing new housing developments and conversions that ignore any pretence about creating communities or 'places' and the proposed deregulation of planning will only add to the problem.

> We are still seeing new housing developments and conversions that ignore any pretence about creating communities or 'places'.

There are also many examples of people trying to recreate something of the pioneering cooperative movements, with food and transport cooperatives, self-help and communal schemes of many different kinds. These sorts of ideals inform several of the schemes discussed in this chapter.

I am reminded of the group of women mentioned at the end of Chapter 1 who, when asked by a researcher how they would describe themselves, replied: *'We are kind, members of the community, we look out for each other, and we want to make the place better.'* That group provided an enormous amount of help in their community during the pandemic, looking after isolated people, checking up on older and disabled people, doing shopping, and being there when they were needed.

They are creating a community in their town and are some of the people we need to listen to.

## LISTENING TO COMMUNITIES

I have written about David Aynsley's story elsewhere, and will only mention the main points here.[3] Sixteen years ago, he was a police sergeant leading a community policing team in Camborne near the furthest tip of Cornwall and was becoming frustrated by constantly chasing young people for minor offences, graffiti and vandalism. It was having no long-term impact. Following a chance encounter with a former health visitor, he met with some of the young people to discuss what they wanted and, as a result, agreed with them to set up a dance club.

David Aynsley listened to them. Sixteen years later the TR14ers, as they called themselves after the town's postcode, are running a thriving dance club which has had more than 3000 members over the years and measurably improved health and well-being among young people in the town. It is now run as a company limited by guarantee and a registered charity by the current generation of young people.

The TR14ers have had to be self-supporting because they have not been able to get sustainable long-term funding and are still having to rent a church hall on an hourly basis.

David Aynsley listened but the NHS and local government didn't. This sort of activity, despite its measurable success, is still regarded as, at best, of marginal interest by the formal health and care system.

In an ironic twist, which has resonances elsewhere, Sergeant Aynsley was criticised by his bosses because his arrest numbers fell – the indicator given the most weighting at the time by the local crime and disorder partnership between the police and the local authority to assess his success as a community police officer.

Hazel Stuteley, the health visitor who worked with him in Camborne, says unequivocally that '*Disadvantaged communities and their people are not the problem – they are the solution.*'

> Disadvantaged communities and their people are not the problem – they are the solution.
>
> *Hazel Stuteley*

This is firmly based on her own experience in Falmouth where she worked as a health visitor from 1990 to 2000. She and her colleague Phil Trenoweth spent most of their time on the Penwerris estate, known locally as Beacon and Old Hill and home to about 6000 people. It was, she says, a deeply troubled and stigmatised area, suffering poor health and violent crime against a backdrop of poverty, unemployment and sub-standard housing. The dockyards had provided much of the employment in the area, but they had lost work to cheaper firms on the continent and closed, leaving many people unemployed.

She told me how, over the first 5 years of their work there, they were fighting against a spiral of decline. There was a patch of green land that separated the two parts of the estate which had literally become a battleground where children as young as 4 threw stones at each other across the divide. A number of families were dealing in drugs – 14 as she later learned from the police and local residents – and intimidated people and used violence against anyone who didn't pay their debts.

It was the killing of a small girl's pet rabbit by one of these families that was the final straw for the two health visitors. They were at breaking point and had received death threats. About 1% of the people on the estate were making life hell for everyone else. They managed to get some extra support from their manager and set out to do something. They didn't have a specific plan in mind but knew they needed to bring the various agencies together to work on the problem and that they had to have local residents owning and supporting the work.

Eventually, after much effort, they found five residents who were willing to work with them and, together with a head teacher, a local councillor and representatives from police and housing, they set up a small group to plan the way forward. Four important things happened which were crucial to their future success.

Firstly, the housing department funded the five residents to go on a training course to become Penwerris Tenants and Residents Association (PTRA), giving them a credible voice and constituted powers, and they came back confident and fired up.

Secondly, the five residents, now PTRA, took on the enormous task of visiting all the homes on the estate, roughly 1500 in total, to tell residents that they had got key service providers together who would listen and now needed to hear from them, the residents, what needed doing.

Thirdly, and as a direct result of this, 120 residents attended an evening 'listening event'. Nothing like this had ever happened on the estate before. At first, it was stormy when the residents vented their frustrations to the police and housing in particular, but cathartic, too. They said they wanted their homes improved, violence to stop and jobs to be created. The local councillor and the housing officer bravely apologised for neglect in the past. The anger dispersed almost immediately, and constructive dialogue began. It was agreed to call the group Beacon Community Regeneration Partnership and that they would collectively seek funding for the improvements needed.

Finally, however, it was PTRA who successfully bid for Capital Challenge Funding, for home insulation and energy conservation. Only tenant groups were eligible to bid. The £1.2 million they received 6 months later was then match-funded by a further £1 million from the local housing department to make a total of £2.2 million. The home improvements transformed people and place and also showed residents that the authorities had truly listened.

Hazel Stuteley told me that the residents gradually took more and more control, insisting on being part of the process for spending the money they had generated and even fundraising themselves. It was at this point, when they began to self-organise and set up family activities for all age groups, even reviving the carnival, that she knew it was going to be successful and sustainable.

Things developed quite quickly from these foundations. The Partnership won a major Health and Social Care award from the Department of Health in 1999 and the local people grew in confidence as positive attention focused on the estate. Table 9.1 shows the truly remarkable outcomes from their work over 6 years in terms of health, environmental, employment and educational outcomes, many of which were totally unexpected.

It is worth spending a moment looking at these figures. They are impressive by any standards: breastfeeding up 50%, postnatal depression down by 77%, boys' school test results in year 2 (Key Stage 1) improved by 100%, and teenage pregnancies down to zero in only 1 year more. Later data not included in Table 9.1 show that unemployment on the estate fell by 32% in the same period. Hazel Stuteley is rightly proud that these are all practical real-life results that everyone could see. As a health visitor, she also pointed out to me the direct link between a mother's postnatal depression and a son's achievement at school.

Hazel Stuteley moved to work in the Department of Health and the Department for Communities and Local Government in order to spread this learning and these methods, and she influenced national thinking. However, and I speak as the Chief Executive of the English NHS at the time, we were too focused on the acute agenda, getting waiting lists down, improving care for priority groups in cancer and heart care, and tackling MRSA to really take up the lessons from her work. Looking back, I am not sure we could have done much more at the time – we were addressing the public's and the politicians' priorities.

Looking back, she says that she felt that people saw her work as *'nice and pink and fluffy'* and, by implication, not a serious priority. Timing is always important in making change and the current changes in the NHS with an emphasis on local partnership could provide a much better environment.

Hazel Stuteley has gone on to found C2 Connecting Communities, which, as its names suggests, is all about strengthening communities and sharing learning.[4] It defines community strengthening as *'enabling communities to increase control over their own lives and local environment'* and it uses five principles developed from their work in Falmouth:

- Place-based partnership working
- Community centred and led
- Strengths- and relationship-based
- Informed by complexity theory
- Health-creating or salutogenic

**Table 9.1** The Beacon Project: health, environmental and educational outcomes between 1995 and 2001. From C2 Connecting Communities

| Health benefits | Environmental outcomes | Educational outcomes |
|---|---|---|
| Increased breastfeeding rates by approximately 50% | £1.2 million generated by tenants and residents + further £1m match funding – £2.2m | On-site training for tenants and residents |
| Postnatal depression rates down 77% | Gas central heating to 318 properties | After-school clubs |
| Child Protection registrations down 60% Childhood accident rate down 50% | Loft insulation in 349 houses: cavity wall in 199; external cladding to 700 | Life skills courses |
| 50% reduction in incidence of asthma and schooldays lost | Fuel saving estimated at £180306 per annum, releasing disposal income to residents | Parent and toddler group |
| 78% reduced fear of crime | £160000 traffic-calming measures | Boys' and girls' Key Stage 1 SATS up 26% |
| Beacon Care Centre providing on-site health advice | Provision of safe play areas and resource centre | IT skills |
| 'Sorted' sexual health service for young people: teenage pregnancy rates ZERO in 2002 | Recycling and dog waste bins | Crèche supervisor training |
| All levels of crime including violent crime reduced 50% | Skateboard park | Boys' SATS Key Stage 1 results up 100% |

C2 Connecting Communities works with many communities around the country and has influenced many people. Three things stand out from this account that are directly relevant to the arguments of this book: the importance of people being in control of their own lives, the centrality of relationships in making progress; and the very practical way the official service providers were brought together with residents to provide a structure in which they could listen and hear what people in the community thought needed doing.

I hope that Hazel Stuteley will one day write her own account of her work. She has influenced many people and there is still more to learn from her experience and insights.

## TAKING CONTROL

Heather Henry is an independent nurse and entrepreneur who has worked in many communities around Manchester in the north-west of England and has based some of her approach on what she learned from Hazel Stuteley.

She had been employed to help improve health in part of Salford when she realised that the large number of fathers, most of whom were long-term unemployed and who would normally be seen as problem, were, in fact, a great asset and strength for the community. She began working with them and helped them form a group called Salford Dadz – Little Hulton and start doing things in their own communities, providing facilities for the children and organising community activities. This all helped bring men together who were often quite socially isolated, and they began talking with each other about personal and emotional things, giving each other support.

Both the fathers' and the children's well-being improved quite quickly. Gradually, over time, she told me, the fathers became more confident and began running the activities themselves, taking the initiative and taking control. She began at the front of the room, as she put it, and moved to the back.

She was working with these men in the same way that Fazle Abed had worked with women in Bangladesh – empowering them, giving them the skills and the confidence to act. What was noticeable here was that there were clear community benefits and the men themselves benefited and several got jobs as a result of the experience.

> She was working with these men in the same way that Fazle Abed had worked with women in Bangladesh – empowering them, giving them the skills and the confidence to act.

Elsewhere in the north of England, Heather Nelson runs the Black Health Initiative which, among other things, has a community café in Leeds. She combines running community activities for the black community locally with advocacy locally and nationally about health and care. Because she is very much part of the black community herself, she is able to listen and understand how people are thinking about disease, vaccination and treatments.

Her organisation provides briefing for NHS planners about how specific diseases are manifesting themselves in the community and how best to ensure that insights about treatments and behaviour are incorporated into NHS policy and services. This vital work takes place in a context where standard diagnoses and treatments are based on research on the white population and where, for example, black skin often isn't included in dermatology textbooks or African pelvic shapes in obstetrics and gynaecology textbooks.

Moreover, the design of standard medical equipment may also disadvantage black people. The standard pulse oximeter, for example, which is used for measuring the oxygen saturation level of the blood – and which has become such a vital tool during the pandemic – is designed for white skin and works less effectively on people with dark or black skin. This may have contributed to poorer treatment and outcomes for these groups.

There are also significant differences in life expectancy and in trust in the NHS between black communities and the majority populations, with the black communities always faring worse. The organisation undertook a survey about vaccine hesitancy within the black community and found that reluctance to be vaccinated was more to do with lack of trust in the NHS and government than about specific concerns with the vaccine. The survey report noted that *'the more participants reported that they were suspicious of doctors, healthcare workers, and medicine, the greater their hesitancy towards the COVID-19 vaccine.'*[5] This cannot be solved easily.

Heather Nelson and the Black Health Initiative play a vital role in channelling views and information to the planners and decision makers and helping match policy and need more closely.

People within public bodies sometimes talk about the difficulty in engaging people. The issue is perhaps even more important the other way round – how do local people get the NHS and other authorities to engage with them? People in local communities very often know what needs to be done but no one listens. The whole approach needs to be turned upside down.

## HEALTH IS MADE AT HOME, HOSPITALS ARE FOR REPAIRS

As I said in Chapter 1, one of the things I have learned from Professor Francis Omaswa is the expression *'Health is made at home, hospitals are for repairs.'* He coined it when he was running the health system in Uganda. It contains the insight that what happens to us at home – and at school, work and in the community – profoundly affects our health and well-being and that everyone in every part of society has an important role to play in health. It also suggests that health can be *created*.

There is now a developing health creation movement in the UK and elsewhere which embraces many organisations in all sectors.[6] There are thousands of groups in the UK which I call 'health creators'. Many of these, like those already mentioned, work in communities and bring people together around different activities and help them engage with their neighbours and in different ways take more control of their lives.

There are very large numbers of groups involved in community gardens, conservation and the environment which encourage physical activity, ease mental stresses and engage people with each other – simultaneously addressing the physical, mental and social well-being elements of the WHO's definition of health. The experience of COVID-19 has encouraged many more people to participate in these activities.

Energy Garden, described in Chapter 3, supports community gardens at railway stations across London. Incredible Edible is a network of about 150 groups in the UK and beyond which grow food in public places, sharing the produce and involving people in swapping recipes and running cookery lessons. People on thousands of allotments around the country do similar things on different scales, informally or in a more organised fashion, with many community allotments now in use.

Pam Warhurst, co-founder of Incredible Edible, talks about propaganda gardens because they spread ideas and bring people together and can lead on to all kinds of other activities that improve health and help tackle climate change. She has written her own account of the organisation that describes her aims and ambitions for the network and tells the stories of many of the local groups.[7] The Royal Horticultural Society, which runs some of the UK's great public gardens and the great gardening shows, is increasingly linking its activities with health and well-being and GPs can now officially prescribe gardening for health reasons as an alternative to medicines and other more clinical interventions.

> Pam Warhurst . . . talks about propaganda gardens because they spread ideas and bring people together and can lead on to all kinds of other activities that improve health and help tackle climate change.

Social and private businesses can also be heavily involved. The Sewing Rooms is a social enterprise that creates jobs and brings socially isolated women together in Skelmersdale. The Big Issue which runs the well-known weekly magazine sold by homeless people – giving them a hand up not a handout – also funds other social enterprises and lobbies for improvement.

Meanwhile, in the City of London, some of the world's biggest financially related companies, including Lloyds Bank, KPMG, the *Financial Times* and the Bank of England, are part of the City Mental Health Alliance, which provides services for employees with mental illnesses as well as aiming to create workplaces where people can flourish.

The Healthy Schools Programme was cut in the years of austerity and Sure Start, which runs centres for parents and pre-school children, had its funding reduced drastically during the UK's years of austerity. However, many schools are running their own schemes, with 13 000 schools now organising for their children and teachers to run their Daily Mile, which involves the whole school running together during one of the breaks in the school day. More than 3.1 million children were doing so at the latest count and the idea, which started at a school in Scotland, is now copied in 85 countries.[8] As the founder of the Daily Mile, Elaine Wyllie, says, in words which apply to so many of these activities, *'Keeping it simple works best.'*

> As the founder of the Daily Mile, Elaine Wyllie, says, in words which apply to so many of these activities, 'Keeping it simple works best.'

Elsewhere, there are Forest Schools where children are taught outdoors, and outdoor education centres, and farms which take school visits. One very experienced organiser of school visits told me that it was often the most difficult children who thrived in these visits and she described how teachers and their peers changed their evaluation of these pupils as they showed their capabilities in the woods and fields.

This impressive list does not include housing associations, religious, conservation and arts groups, and many others. These few examples show that health creation is something that can be led by local community groups, employers, community businesses, or professionals of all backgrounds. Ideally, all these and other parts of a community will be involved and work together to create a thriving community.

There are now several organisations promoting health creation in the UK including Hazel Stuteley's C2 Connecting Communities, the Health Creation Alliance, Wellnorth Enterprises, and the Health Creation Academic Network, which was set up by Heather Henry to bring health creation into the education curricula for health professionals.

All these organisations describe in different ways the importance of people taking control, relationships, confidence and learning by doing. These are among the things that we can all learn from the health creators, and which are discussed at the end of this chapter.

Health professionals can also play a significant role in creating health, with GPs in particular being very well placed to do so. In East Surrey, Dr Gillian Orrow has taken the leading role in setting up a network of community members and local providers called the Growing Health Together group, which has established health-creating partnerships across Redhill, Merstham, Caterham, Oxted, Horley and surrounding areas.

These partnerships aim *'to provide the conditions for local people to improve their own health and well-being'*. Leadership from the professionals has been very important and several GPs and others take a prominent role. As with Hazel Stuteley's experience in Falmouth, it has been important to bring the various professionals together to develop their skills and understanding. There is an important point here about the professionals learning to work together to facilitate and support activities run by local people. In the group's words: *'These partnerships have been nurtured through the formation of a new cross-disciplinary community of practice . . . learning from one another, and from experiences around the country, on how to support the creation of health within our communities.'*[9]

> These partnerships have been nurtured through the formation of a new cross-disciplinary community of practice, . . . learning from one another, and from experiences around the country, on how to support the creation of health within our communities.
>
> *Dr Gillian Orrow*

Figure 9.1 describes some of the many activities being undertaken in different parts of the East Surrey network. These cover a wide range from the arts to active travel (walking and cycling) to gardening and sustainable energy.

---

- Community-led outdoor well-being space for carers, young people with learning disabilities and bereaved survivors of suicide offering gardening, fishing and more
- Inter-generational community garden outside Horley Infant School
- Contributing to new active travel infrastructure plans for Smallfield, with Surrey Highways
- Improving sustainability in Horley, from community tree-planting events through to exploring opportunities for solar energy, retro-fitting and ground source heat pumps on NHS, school and other local buildings
- Establishment of new health-creating partnership in Oxted, involving Patient Participation Group, PCN, Tandridge Voluntary Action, head teachers and local council, who are together exploring future ideas to improve health and well-being within the area
- Collaboration with Surrey Arts around a new sculpture trail with opportunities for walking for health

---

**Figure 9.1** Growing Health Together in East Surrey – examples of activities.

There is a lot of other related activity underway in Surrey, with both the politicians and the officers from Surrey County Council taking an active lead and focusing firmly on tackling inequalities. Jude Middleton, the Project Manager for Transforming Outcomes for People at the Council, talks about the importance of system convening. She writes in an introduction to a new book on system convening that *'In order to achieve our goals of reducing health inequality and greater system integration, we need to be able to make sense of what is often a very complex web of connections.'*

She describes a new role of system convenors, people who can both stimulate change and accelerate its pace. They are the facilitators, sense makers, and what the French call *'animateurs'*. As Simon White, Executive Director of Adult Social Care for Surrey County Council says, *'We are not looking for . . . heroic individuals who can do what we cannot do ourselves. The vision for the future and the ability to deliver it rests with us, working as a system.'*[10]

## JOINING THE DOTS

Lord Andrew Mawson is a serial social entrepreneur who came to east London from Bradford more than 30 years ago to take up post as the minister of a Nonconformist church. He rapidly became involved in the local community, bringing together voluntary organisations, businesses, schools and other local institutions to enhance the local area. Joining the dots, he calls it.

Andrew Mawson is well known within the NHS for developing the Bromley by Bow Centre, which includes a primary care surgery where Dr Julia Davis, Sir Sam Everington and other GPs began a social prescribing programme almost 20 years ago and long before it was official policy. There are now four linked health centres across East London, but Bromley by Bow is much more than a health centre. It is a community hub from where people can access social and sporting activities, cultural events, education, skills training, and the development of social enterprises as well as health and social support.

The Centre's chief executive Rob Trimble told me that they were engaged in building a community and emphasised their four active values: be compassionate, be a friend, have fun, and assume it's possible – a combination that is very different from the average public sector body. The Centre used all these values in rising to the challenge of COVID-19 by supporting isolated people, organising food supplies and support, and constantly building up a sense of belonging and community while doing so through the plan they created and called *'Thriving not Surviving'*.[11]

> Building a community . . . their four active values: be compassionate, be a friend, have fun, and assume it's possible.

How, one might reasonably ask, are some of the things happening in low-income countries described in earlier chapters different from these sorts of development?

The biggest difference is whether these developments are absolutely central or not to the health system. BRAC in Bangladesh, Urmul in India and the Village COVID groups in

Uganda – all of which bring different groups together around shared issues – are absolutely central to the national or regional health and planning system.

In countries like Bangladesh, with little public or state provision, these organisations become the mainstream. In countries like the UK, however, they are generally still seen as peripheral. They are typically fitted in around the main business, which remains firmly the preserve of the professions.

In writing up his own story about the achievements and frustrations of the last 30 years in developing these programmes, Andrew Mawson describes how he has almost always found it difficult to be taken seriously by the authorities, despite the growing scale and obvious success of most of his ventures. It is about the mindset, the way of thinking and doing things in officialdom. It has been a constant struggle to make progress through the official processes and to find allies who 'get it' and can help move things on. This struggle continues today.[12] Despite these problems, he has used the learning from Bromley by Bow in other developments in London and played an active part in securing the legacy from the 2012 London Olympics, which was based nearby. In 2015 he set up Wellnorth Enterprises to release potential in other parts of the country by using the learning from Bromley by Bow and elsewhere.

Andrew Mawson has also succeeded in securing both public and private-sector investment into communities to improve services and facilities and create employment and new businesses. As noted earlier, much of the reason why so many government interventions have failed in the past is that they did nothing to deal with poor facilities, badly constructed housing, and high unemployment, poor schools and other structural failures. The other part, of course, was that the initiatives were imposed from outside without listening to the community.

Andrew Mawson is still innovating. In an inspired and rather counter-intuitive initiative, Professor Brian Cox and he co-founded the Science Summer School in 2012 at a secondary school in east London which had experienced extremely challenging circumstances for years. It was a revelation, with young people thriving as they discovered the excitement of science directly from leading scientists. Several have subsequently done well in exams and gone on to study related subjects at leading universities. He says: *'Connecting education, careers, science and health was the impetus for rebuilding an entire community and inspiring young people to have confidence in what they can achieve in life.'*

> Connecting education, careers, science and health was the impetus for rebuilding an entire community and inspiring young people to have confidence in what they can achieve in life.
>
> *Lord Andrew Mawson*

The first Skelmersdale Science Summer School was held in July 2021 in partnership with West Lancashire College and the West Lancashire Partnership. It was designed to encourage young people to pursue careers in science, technology, engineering, arts and maths (STEAM) subjects. Four hundred pupils attended and speakers included astronaut Major Tim Peake, civil engineer Ayo Sokale, medical doctor and scientist Professor Lord Robert Winston, cosmetic science expert and entrepreneur Flow Adepoju, mechanical engineer for Airbus and Mars

Rover Abigail Hutty, and Dr Kate Black, a chemist and tech entrepreneur, as well as Brian Cox.[13,14] Other summer schools will undoubtedly follow.

Andrew Mawson brings people and organisations which can influence the situation together. In many cases, if you can, for example, get local businesses, the council, the education, health and police authorities pointing in the same direction and acting together, you can make enormous progress. This is not about setting up committees with representatives from all the organisations in an area but finding the people who understand the bigger picture – not just the view from their own agency – and are willing to act. The movers and shakers. They may not be the obvious people. It's not about job descriptions but about personality and commitment.

It's a very important lesson. All the stories in this chapter demonstrate the importance of starting with people and relationships and not with setting up organisations and systems.

## LEARNING FROM COMMUNITIES IN OUR OWN COUNTRIES

I have met and talked with more than 60 health creators over the last 3 years and, as a result, identify ten things we can learn from them – all of these are about their behaviour and approach. These are listed in Figure 9.2. Some have already been mentioned in this and earlier chapters. Brought together in this way, they represent a very different approach from the formal authorities, but they need not be any less professional or rigorous in their application.[15] These are all common sense ideas and can be described very simply in a few words.

1. Taking off your NHS spectacles means not seeing health through the lens of the NHS. Don't assume health is the sole province of professionals or that it's about hospitals and services. We know in our normal life that it isn't, but it is easy to slip into lazy assumptions.
2. Almost all the health creators address mental and physical health, even though our health systems keep them separate. The everyday question of 'How are you feeling?' of course embraces both.
3. Start with building relationships. Relationships trump systems. They can help you get things done in the system and sometimes despite it. They create strength and help us develop new ideas.
4. Build on strengths not weaknesses, positives not negatives, abilities not disabilities. This is about achieving potential and not just coping, important as that can be.
5. Communities are important for our health and well-being. They shape our daily experiences, encompass many of our relationships, and can provide support and give meaning to our lives.
6. In health-creating activities, people are doing something that motivates them, and their actions have meaning and purpose. They are not just following a plan or obeying orders.

There are dull and repetitive tasks in every activity but even they can be meaningful if people believe in the end goals.

7. Connect and communicate mean just that and are central to all relationships. Join the dots and keep them joined.
8. The built and natural environments are very important for everyone's health. Damp and cold homes can be killers, while the natural surroundings can be actively life- and health-enhancing.
9. Learning by doing, being entrepreneurial, applying the scientific method of trial and error are all vital when you are breaking new ground or finding new ways of dealing with a problem or creating new opportunities.
10. Being in control is in itself good for your health, helping people to be in control, self-organise, take the initiative and own a change are essential for success.

A quick glance at this list shows that it is unsurprising that people from the official bodies and large businesses find it hard to work with the health creators. Their approaches are so different.

Moreover, these examples are not about the NHS or local authorities being in charge and engaging with communities and civil society on their terms. They are not about social prescribing, for example – valuable as that is – where local activities are co-opted by the NHS. This is not business as usual. The people running them, the health creators, are not responding to other people's plans but doing things for their own reasons.

> The people running them, the health creators, are not responding to other people's plans but doing things for their own reasons.

Nevertheless, the examples earlier in the chapter show how the official bodies can learn to work with local people and health creators without compromising their necessary emphasis on business planning, proper systems, audit and accountability. The five agencies that worked with Hazel Stuteley in Falmouth, for example, and the GPs from East Surrey with their cross-disciplinary community of practice are doing that.

1. Taking off our health system spectacles
2. Addressing physical and mental health together
3. Starting by building relationships not systems
4. Building on strengths not focusing on weaknesses
5. Recognising the importance of communities
6. Imbuing actions with meaning and purpose
7. Connecting and communicating
8. Recognising the importance of the natural environment
9. Learning by doing
10. Taking control and helping others to take control

**Figure 9.2** Ten lessons from health creators.

The experience of COVID-19 brought many people together who didn't normally even meet each other and enabled new relationships, plans and approaches to be developed. The new NHS structures provide the opportunity to build on these successes.

## HEALTH CREATION

This approach means we need to think about health in new and broader ways, and address three separate but linked areas of activity planning for health. These are: health services led by health professionals and health systems; disease prevention and health protection led by government; and health creation led by wider society. Health workers have a role in all areas and need to be equipped with the different skills required.

I define health creation as being about providing the conditions to be healthy and helping or enabling people to be so. It is what parents do, good teachers, good schools and good employers as well as good communities. And it is what good architecture, design and planning can help do, too. It is about enabling people to develop as resilient, social, competent, confident and healthy individuals. It is about all these qualities and more because health is not an add-on to normal life. I think of it as being about human flourishing.

And health creation is vital in the fight against inequality. A study of the Sure Start programme showed that some of its effects lasted well into the teenage years, with improved health as a result of early interventions. It also showed *'that impacts of the programme are strongest among children living in the 30% poorest areas of the country.'*[16]

The science behind this approach is becoming clearer; Sir Michael Marmot and others have demonstrated how the social and political determinants of health affect life expectancy and life chances across whole populations. Often, this work is thought of as identifying the barriers to health – and, indeed, it does – but we can also turn it the other way up and see how it can identify the causes of health and use the insights it offers to promote and create health.

There are also many studies which show how environmental factors – being in a green environment, for example – and social factors, such as relationships and stress, affect individuals and alter their chances of illness and recovery.

The three essential sets of health and care activities are shown in Figure 9.3.

National government, local authorities and planners need to think about communities and health in this wider way, recognising the value of health creation and supporting it alongside service provision, disease prevention and health protection.

This simple framework can guide them in supporting local action as well as undertaking action themselves both nationally and locally.

---

**Healthcare services** – with the professionals and health and care systems in the lead
**Health protection and disease prevention** – with governments in the lead
**Health creation** – where everyone and every part of society has a responsibility and a role to play

---

**Figure 9.3** The three essential sets of health activities.

## ACTION BY GOVERNMENT

Health creators need to be supported by health and care workers but there also need to be changes in policy and, in many cases, investment in order to reduce inequality and build a health-creating society.

Poor housing, poor infrastructure, poor schools and poor transport systems need to be replaced or upgraded as part of a sustained improvement in life in the UK. The two disasters of the pandemic and climate change should be taken as an opportunity and a reason for doing so.

There also needs to be proper financial and other support for the health-creating groups described in this chapter. It is absurd that long-standing and clearly effective groups such as the Bromley by Bow Centre and TR14ers are still left existing hand to mouth.

Support for local action and health creation should include:

- Providing direct support for local initiatives through grants and help in kind as appropriate – listening to what local people and communities believe needs to be done. Some authorities already provide grants for local initiatives, but these are mostly short-term. If successful, these should be carried through into formal commissioning alongside other activities – as is now happening, for example, in Salford.
- Finding better ways for local groups to engage directly in local authority and NHS decision making and activity. This covers everything from membership of committees and consultation processes to direct service provision.
- Supporting local communities' own assessment of what their needs are and planning for improvement.
- Bringing cross-sectoral groups together, including businesses, public bodies and voluntary and community groups, to identify and act on local priorities.

One of the first steps in building healthy communities is to recognise the importance of health creation and to build a health-creating society where all groups and organisations can play their part. Without it, all new initiatives are likely to be unsustainable. I have watched too many fail over the years since I worked in Merseyside in the 1970s. More than 50 years later, we should be able to do better.

The UK Government published its response to Danny Kruger MPs report 'Levelling Up Our Communities: proposals for a new social covenant' in February 2022 just as this book was going to press. It represents another opportunity to make progress with supporting local communities to make improvements – provided, of course, lessons are learned from history.[17,18]

## REFERENCES

1. https://theconversation.com/nhs-was-not-solely-modelled-on-a-welsh-workmens-medical-society-98024 (Accessed 20 November 2021).
2. https://www.parliament.uk/about/living-heritage/transformingsociety/livinglearning/coll-9-health1/coll-9-health/ (Accessed 20 November 2021).

3. Crisp N. *Health is Made at Home, Hospitals are for Repairs: Building a healthy and health-creating society.* Billericay: SALUS, 2020, pp. 53–8.
4. https://arc-swp.nihr.ac.uk/research/projects/c2-connecting-communities/ (Accessed 17 February 2022)
5. https://irp.cdn-website.com/18199a76/files/uploaded/27977%20YSJ%20COVID-19%20 Vaccine%20Hesitancy%20Report%20%28Final%29.pdf (Accessed 20 November 2021).
6. Crisp N. *Health is Made at Home, Hospitals are for Repairs: Building a healthy and health-creating society.* Billericay: SALUS, 2020.
7. Warhurst P, Sikking A. *Incredible Edible – Seeds to Solutions: The power of small actions.* Todmorden: Incredible Edible CIC, November 2021.
8. https://thedailymile.co.uk/ (Accessed 20 November 2021).
9. Growing Health Together update for July 2021. https://twitter.com/GH_together (Accessed 20 November 2021).
10. Oppenheimer J, Warren S. *Systems Convening: A crucial form of leadership for the 21st century.* London: Lankelly Chase Foundation, September 2021.
11. Crisp N. *Health is Made at Home, Hospitals are for Repairs: Building a healthy and health-creating society.* Billericay: SALUS, 2020, pp. 222–3.
12. Mawson A. *The Social Entrepreneur – Making communities work.* London: Atlantic Books, 2008.
13. https://wellnorthenterprises.co.uk/?s=Summer+school (Accessed 20 November 2021).
14. YouTube video. Science Summer School 2021. https://m.youtube.com/watch?v=J73ri1 HDh6I&pp=sAQA (Accessed 20 November 2021).
15. Crisp N: *Health is Made at Home, Hospitals are for Repairs: Building a healthy and health-creating society.* Billericay: SALUS, 2020, Chapter 13, The big ideas, pp. 173–83.
16. Cattan S. Conti G, Farquharson C *et al.* The health effects of universal early childhood interventions: Evidence from Sure Start. IFS, 13 August 2021, p. 3. https://ifs.org.uk/ uploads/WP202125-The-health-effects-of-universal-early-childhood-interventions-1.pdf (Accessed 20 November 2021).
17. https://www.dannykruger.org.uk/files/2020-09/Kruger%202.0%20Levelling%20Up%20 Our%20Communities.pdf (Accessed 7 February 2022)
18. https://www.gov.uk/government/publications/government-response-to-danny-kruger-mps-report-levelling-up-our-communities-proposals-for-a-new-social-covenant (Accessed 7 February 2022)

These next two chapters bring together some of the learning from countries and communities all over the world: high-, low- and middle income, the wealthy elite and the poorest and most disadvantaged. We need insights and contributions from everyone if we are to confront the great challenges facing us all.

I have called the two chapters 'Practical knowledge' because they are about things that people are actually doing and can do and not just the theory, the hopes and the wishes. Theory matters and so do campaigning and calling out injustices. They are all vital in moving on our thinking and influencing policy and practice. In the end, however, it is what people do, how they behave and act, that will make a practical difference to our health. It is the day-to-day actions of millions of people that count. There are no magic solutions.

This chapter concentrates on people, communities and health workers; the next addresses technology, equity and health and care systems. This one starts with the relationships between patients, communities and professionals. It goes on to review some of the new approaches being taken to strengthen that relationship and concludes by discussing the changing roles and educational needs of health and care workers.

## WHO REALLY MAKES THE DECISIONS?

The indigenous people of Alaska have some important things to teach us. I became exposed to their thinking through Doug Eby, the Southcentral Foundation (SCF) senior physician executive, who works for them. He and others from SCF speak about their transformed system of care that now provides very good outcomes for significantly less cost. They believe that clinicians and people running health services don't pay anything like enough attention to what patients think and, even more importantly, what they do. Their system is, in their words, *'customer-owned, customer-designed, and customer-driven'* at both the individual and system level.

SCF is an Alaska Native-owned, non-profit healthcare organisation serving approximately 65 000 Alaska Native and American Indian people living in and around Anchorage. Its vision links health with related services, spirituality, culture, and empowering people to take

DOI: 10.1201/9781003267706-10

control of their lives: *'Southcentral Foundation's Vision is a Native Community that enjoys physical, mental, emotional and spiritual wellness; its Mission is to work together with the Native Community to achieve wellness through health and related services. The organization has developed and implemented comprehensive health-related services to meet the changing needs of the Native Community, enhance culture and empower individuals and families to take charge of their lives.'*[1]

The Foundation is a truly remarkable organisation which has been widely recognised as a leading example of successful healthcare redesign and is a recipient of the Malcolm Baldrige Quality Award. It now offers consultancy, support and training in its Nuka System of Care and whole system transformation to other organisations nationally and globally.

Doug Eby is a doctor who moved to Alaska in 1995 to work in support of the Alaska Native-run health system and has been there ever since, settling into a community made up of Alaska Native people, non-Native individuals, adventurers and oilmen. Based on long conversations with the patient community, he maintains that whatever their doctor says, in most cases the patient is going to decide what will happen next. All his experience, in Alaska and other parts of the United States, tells him this.

> Whatever their doctor says, in most cases the patient is going to decide what will happen next.

He and the Foundation point out that it is only in relatively extreme, high-acuity cases that the professional is fully in charge of the situation and can get the patient to do everything he or she wants. This is true, Doug explains, when the patient is in a coma, anesthetised or collapsed; but the lesser the symptoms, the greater the chance that the patient will do what he or she wants to do and will take the professional's advice selectively at best. He gave me the SCF graph reproduced in Figure 10.1, which shows there is a crossover point from patient to clinician control. *'Health professionals simply won't be able to do our jobs properly'*, Doug says very firmly, *'if we succumb to the myth that people normally obey doctor's orders.'* They don't. As patients, we don't.

Many healthcare planners and clinicians talk about the importance of empowering patients. They generally mean by this giving people the knowledge and the skills to look after themselves, have choices and make decisions. They mean that clinicians shouldn't just do things to and for patients. These are all very important points, but the SCF graph shows that we are starting in the wrong place. We need to see the world the other way up and start by recognising that, in general, patients have the control.

Looking at this the other way up, we can see that, too often, the behaviours of clinicians and the way systems work tend to disempower patients. This happens in all sorts of both subtle and obvious ways.

The language used by clinicians and the environment of hospitals and clinics may be alien and intimidating. As patients, we may feel disempowered because we are dealing with people who know so much more than we do and with institutions that seem to embody all the knowledge of science. The chances are that we are probably already anxious about our health when we go to see a professional. With our confidence dented by our surroundings, we may not have the courage to mention those other symptoms, which may be minor – or they may not be – or to ask the questions that are really worrying us. There may not even be the time to do so.

Control: Who really makes the decisions?

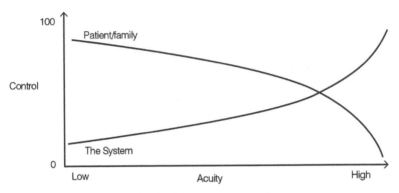

1. Control who makes the final decision influencing outcomes?
2. Influences family, friends, co-workers, religion, values, money
3. Real opportunity to influence health costs/outcomes influence on the choices made behaviorial change
4. Current model tests, diagnosis, treatment (medication or procedures)

Southcentral
Foundation

**Figure 10.1** Who really makes the decisions? Source: https://www.southcentralfoundation.com/

Most clinicians understand these points very well and professional education has incorporated them for 30 years and longer. We may very well find ourselves being looked after by a clinician who listens to our story and reflects on our insights into the problem. We may easily not. Even if we do, however, we may both find it difficult to communicate with each other and we may find that the system makes it harder for the clinician to respond.

There are really three practical questions here for clinicians and for health planners. How do we empower patients? How should we not disempower them? And the deeper question of how do we secure their trust sufficiently for them to empower the professionals?

Patients very often refuse, in practice, to take on the role that the health system ascribes to them of being the passive as well as patient recipients of services. People make their own trade-offs and decide what they are going to do based on what is important to them. This is not just about lack of trust but about a whole range of attitudes, perceptions and beliefs. These may mean that patients don't even look for help in the first place or accept it when it is offered.

> People make their own trade-offs and decide what they are going to do based on what is important to them.

This doesn't just happen in western countries, where greater affluence and better education are producing generations of people accustomed to questioning authority. A research project in Ethiopia looked at why patients didn't seek care when they needed it. The researchers worked in and around Jimma, an agricultural and university centre with a population of around 160 000 in the south-west of the country. The warmer, wetter climate of this area means that the land is more fertile and the population are generally better off than people in the highlands of the north.

There is a university hospital in the town and, while Ethiopia then had only about US$5 per head per annum to fund its services, there was a range of services available. In these circumstances, the researchers wondered why so many people, particularly from the countryside, failed to seek help for conditions that could be dealt with by the local health system.[2]

The researchers asked about the patients' perception of illness, whether they thought the treatment was worthwhile and would work, and about costs, including the indirect cost of travel and loss of income.

Unsurprisingly, the researchers concluded that patients were much more likely to seek care when they understood the severity of the illness, appreciated the quality of the service and believed that the benefits of treatment outweighed the costs. Whether or not they sought help depended on their perceptions, beliefs and knowledge.

These patients appear to be no different from patients anywhere. Many studies have shown patients not seeking care when they need it, put off by cost or long queues, or by not realising how serious their problem was. One result is that a consultation or treatment is offered, and resources are later wasted with patients not attending clinic appointments or not taking the medications they have been given.

The Medical Director of one Blue Cross organisation, a health insurance business in the USA, told me that their research showed that as many as 30% of people didn't even fill the prescriptions they had been given. They simply didn't take the prescription to the pharmacy and purchase the drugs. Part of this in the US context is because of the cost, but another big part, he thought, was that the patients simply hadn't been convinced that the drugs were worthwhile or worth the trade-offs between their cost and effort and the likely benefit. They made their own decision on the facts as they saw them. Researchers in the UK make a similar analysis, although costs do not play such a significant role.[3]

Trust plays a significant role here. The research undertaken by the Black Health Initiative into vaccine hesitancy described in Chapter 9 concluded that *'the more participants reported that they were suspicious of doctors, health care workers, and medicine, the greater their hesitancy towards the COVID-19 vaccine.'*

The way that people behave is by no means straightforward or necessarily consistent. Some people may ignore the doctor's advice to change their lifestyle. Others may not take their prescriptions for any one of a number of reasons from thinking they don't need them to reasoning that they probably don't work to not understanding what they are meant to do to, forgetting about them or simply being too disorganised, forgetful or just lazy.

Others, of course, may go out of their way to seek and follow advice, self-prescribe, buy health foods and supplements and adhere to the strictest of healthy regimes. Commerce and the media help them to do this by constantly reminding them of their anxieties and marketing to them the newest products and ideas. The formal health system of doctors, hospitals and prescription drugs is a multibillion dollar industry but so, too, is the informal health economy of healthy living, diets, supplements, exercise and meditation.

The point here is very simple: every patient is different, and everyone is an individual whose behaviour and beliefs affect the way health professionals can care for them. Patients, consciously or unconsciously, make the big decisions.

## THE PRIMARY DIAGNOSIS IS SOCIAL

Patients, people, all of us are influenced by our family and friends and our wider community. The Alaska Native SCF experience and thinking can once again offer us insight. They listen and learn from the community they serve; in fact, they talk a lot about being customer-driven and customer-designed. They also draw on generations of wisdom held by the tribal elders about what makes people do what they do and how to influence them to do it differently.

Doug Eby is a compelling speaker. I have heard him talk about learning from native leaders and his own experience that, for many patients, *'The primary diagnosis is social.'*

His and SCF's point is crushingly simple. The old man may have Parkinson's disease but his biggest and most immediate problem is that he is isolated, lonely, not eating and washing properly and starting to wander physically and mentally. You should deal, SCF believes, with the personal and family social issues as the primary diagnosis and, then only as part of the whole package, treat the Parkinson's. Most patients, the worried well and the genuinely sick alike, they assert are like this.

I have been in audiences of clinicians and health managers who have loved every word Doug and his colleagues have spoken and enjoyed his style and presentation, but I have wondered if anything changed or if they went home and just continued running their systems in their old ways.

It must seem very difficult to work out how you are going to employ this insight back home in the well-structured environment of a healthcare system geared to treating the illness and only the illness. Everyone working in healthcare is familiar with the problem of how best to meet the needs of people with significant social problems: the homeless, the addicts, and the elderly people who have deteriorated to the point where they can't go home and have no carers to look after them.

SCF has applied their thinking in their own area and has produced its own, much more sophisticated, version of the simple 'life belt' model I described in Chapter 5, where the patient at the centre can draw on services from different areas as they are needed. It can be done, and SCF is doing it. The Alaska Native SCF model believes that we should start thinking about all our patients, not just this group, as if the first concern, the primary diagnosis, was their social situation. If we do so, we will change the way we design their services.

There are many reasons why people don't apply the SCF approach in practice. After all, they may even want to rationalise, they are working in a very different location. Other people don't behave like the Alaska Native people. That is true, but it doesn't mean that social issues are unimportant.

Few, if any, healthcare systems in rich countries are geared to taking social factors fully into account. Their first concern is for the acutely ill not the chronically ill. Health systems are resourced to look after people when they are in the acute phases of illness. They are not generally able or willing to deal with the longer-term problems of rehabilitation or, for example, to help an elderly lady weakened by her illness live safely at home. *'We are not social workers,'* I have heard some hospital doctors complain when faced with a patient of this sort. *'This isn't our business.'*

It is, however, fast becoming our business.

As we saw earlier in Chapter 5 about 'Health and wealth', the so-called 'lifestyle diseases', associated with our behaviour and our appetites, are increasing and clinicians treating us will need to understand more about our social situation. The increase in chronic diseases and the ageing of the population in rich countries is making us need to focus on how to provide continuing support for middle-aged and elderly people as they have periods of acute illness and come in and out of hospital over the years.

SCF is right. We need to pay much more attention to the social diagnosis. This has become our business.

## COMMUNITIES AND CULTURE

The story of the research in Jimma was also about culture. It was about how people thought about their illness. Did they see it simply as a physical phenomenon or did they perhaps think that someone or something caused it? Was it retribution or punishment? What about the treatment that was on offer? Did people believe in the medicines available?

Culture, beliefs, traditions and ways of looking at the world all affect what we believe we know and how we act. These questions aren't new. Benjamin David Paul, for many the founding father of medical anthropology in the USA, wrote in 1955: *'If you wish to help a community improve its health, you must learn to think like the people of the community. Before asking a group of people to assume new health habits, it is wise to ascertain the existing habits, how these habits are linked to one another, what functions they perform, and what they mean to those who practice them.'*[4]

> If you wish to help a community improve its health, you must learn to think like the people of the community.
>
> *Benjamin David Paul*

All the aspects of habits that Paul draws attention to are important. Our beliefs and habits don't exist in isolation from everything else about us. Improving health is not as simple as just changing one belief or one habit.

Susan Scrimshaw, former President of the Sage Colleges in the USA, illustrates this in writing about efforts to treat HIV/AIDS in sub-Saharan Africa. She draws attention to gender roles and different cultural traditions, describing how it is the different combinations of cultural, social and economic factors that can make it so difficult to treat AIDS patients and restrict its spread.[5]

She describes the secrecy regarding HIV/AIDS that is common within the region. It is a source of shame and something to be denied, as it is in most cultures of the world. She also draws attention to specific examples of how people think about AIDS. In some areas, for example, there is a superstition that having sex with a virgin will cure an HIV-infected man. In other areas, it is seen as a curse from the gods, resulting from the people having adopted western ways.

These perceptions can manifest themselves in many different ways. In parts of southern Africa, for example, women don't register for antenatal care because they know that they will be tested for HIV/AIDS and that, if they prove positive, they will be ostracised and perhaps abandoned by their husband, family and friends. The stigma is so powerful that they risk their lives and health not only from increased risk in childbirth but also, if they are HIV-positive, by forgoing the treatment.

The difficulty in tackling AIDS in South Africa was made worse for many years because the health minister and president denied the existence of AIDS as a separate condition and argued it could be dealt with by diet and other non-medical approaches. The truth is that cultural and behavioural approaches are needed alongside medical treatment and drugs. The South African government set back AIDS treatment in their country by many years.

Culture is not always a barrier. It can also accelerate health improvement.

There is now a growing literature about the health of indigenous people around the world which is both leading to and reflecting new ways of delivering services. These use and respond to indigenous knowledge and beliefs alongside western scientific medicine.

The Toronto Birth Centre is a wonderful example of the sort of services now being developed. It was founded by and is led by Indigenous community members. Its vision, very similar to that of SCF, is for *'people, families, and communities to access culturally rich and culturally safer birthing care, rooted in the resurgence and celebration of the knowledges and cultures of First Nations, Métis and Inuit peoples'.*[6]

Roberta Pike, the Centre's Executive Director, told me that it was founded to provide a safe space for Indigenous people away from the racism and discrimination that they routinely faced in using maternity services or other health mainstream facilities. This negative impetus was matched by the positive desire to create a place where people could feel that their care was being centered, they belonged, and that allowed for the full expression of ceremony based on their culture and beliefs.

The Centre is accredited by those who have been educated in western scientific medicine without any barriers and is led by midwives and Indigenous community workers who work with both western and Indigenous knowledge. However, as Roberta Pike explained to me, the way the Centre and the staff work is based on *'a different way of seeing, being, doing and relating'* which influences how they are governed and led, and how they conduct themselves and make decisions. They have four core values – the right to self-determination, dignity, justice and equity – and their decisions are shaped by the importance of always thinking about the impact of what they are doing today on the future seven generations.

The Centre is impressive and inspiring and provides high-quality care for its users. As Roberta Pike says, there is a great deal that others can learn not only from the Centre itself but from their whole approach to life – and living the values of self-determination, dignity, equity and justice.

There are four broad points that are exemplified by these examples and come out of the literature on indigenous health which are very relevant to this chapter. Firstly, health needs to be seen as part of the wider picture and wider goals. It doesn't stand alone. It needs to be seen as contributing to indigenous success or, in the words of Professor Mason Durie from New Zealand, helping create indigenous resilience and moving from disease and disadvantage to the realisation of potential.[7] Improving health is about improving life more generally.

Secondly, this could only happen if everything done to improve health was fully aligned with all other aspects of society, such as family relationships and cultural and religious beliefs. Working to tackle a particular disease, for example, wouldn't work well and might even be counterproductive unless all the actions fitted in with other things that were happening. Communities could reject the efforts, as we saw in the earlier example from Ethiopia, for any one of many different reasons of trust, beliefs or perceptions.

Thirdly, health professionals need to consider all the different sorts of evidence they are presented with, the social as well as the scientific, and to find ways to evaluate how they can be used to improve health.

The final point is about how health systems handle data and are organised and run. It is important to understand people's experience of health and healthcare as part of the planning process. This is not a simple or token process of consultation but a much deeper activity if their experience is to be fully understood and captured in the data. Dr Janet Smylie and colleagues argue that *'current systems of population health data collection, management, analysis and use are too often disconnected from the communities being described and whose data are being collected'*, continuing that *'communities need to be fully and centrally involved in data decision making'.*[8]

This approach should mean working with people locally both to gather the data they believe is necessary and to find the best way forward. This will empower communities as well as improve health. Failure to do this and therefore using planning data which ignores differences can be unintentionally racist and discriminates against groups within a wider population.

> Using planning data which ignores differences can be unintentionally racist and discriminate against groups within a wider population.

Different ethnic groups may experience different conditions very differently. It is vital to disaggregate data to understand populations properly. There is also now evidence that shows that minority ethnic groups in a population experience 'weathering' – a continuously raised level of stress – which damages health in the longer term and reduces life expectancy.

These four points may all seem to be very much common sense and as if they should apply to every health system in every country. In reality, they are not how most health systems operate. Individual clinicians may well try to take account of all of these factors; however, the health systems within which they work in western countries will typically focus on the disease or condition, use aggregated data that applies to the whole population – falling into the averages and aggregates trap mentioned in Chapter 2 – and pay little or no attention to the rest of a patient's life or to the barriers to good health which they face.

These all explain why pioneering programmes such as the Toronto Birth Centre are so important not only for the people they serve but also in showing what alternatives might look like. They are very deliberately constructed within the culture of their people and are about reasserting identity and taking control for themselves. They are not an exact model for anywhere else, but they offer insights to all of us.

## WHAT MATTERS TO YOU?

Given this discussion, it may seem obvious that clinicians need to find out what matters to people before they treat them. The *What Matters to You?* movement has spread rapidly around the world since the question first appeared in an article in 2012.

The idea of asking patients *'What matters to you?'* as well as the more traditional *'What's the matter with you?'* came from two researchers seeking to increase clinicians' awareness of important issues in their patients' lives that could drive customised care plans.[9]

It is a very simple idea with profound implications, and one which has obvious links with the ideas already discussed in this chapter. The IHI has publicised it extensively as a means for *'creating deeply personal engagements with patients and their family members, a deeper understanding of what really matters to them, and is the foundation of developing genuine partnerships for co-creating health'*.[10]

The question unlocks the primary 'social diagnosis' and brings culture and beliefs into every contact. It opens new possibilities for solving problems and has since spread to 49 countries all round the world. There is now a global movement and a *'What Matters to You?'* Day on 9 June.[11] It is in many ways a similar approach to that adopted by indigenous health leaders in the very different context of the individually focused health and care systems and societies of the West.

This approach is an important part of the efforts that organisations need to make to change the relationship between clinicians and patients and, in the wider context, to educate, engage and empower people – and remove barriers to health. It is very much in the dominant western tradition of focusing on the individual and empowering them and doesn't in itself address the wider issues of empowering communities – although it may, in practice, lead on to people recognising common and shared issues.

## INDIVIDUALS AND COMMUNITIES

Governments, public health authorities and private health insurers alike have a shared interest in understanding how to influence people on health and promote healthy behaviour. The Nuffield Council on Bioethics drew up the very useful 'intervention ladder' summarised in Figure 10.2.[12] It sets out very well the escalating choices available to them – from doing nothing at the bottom, through education, incentives and finally legislation at the top. Their report discusses each in terms of a set of ethical principles designed to help steer people through the difficult choices and trade-offs involved.

These efforts are all top-down and will not be fully successful unless they are able to transfer ownership and power to the public and patients – to go with the ultimate decision-making power that they already have. Even the successful implementation of legislation, the top rung of the ladder, depends on whether people accept it or not – in everything from speed limits to the illegal use of drugs. It is worth remembering that most of us take our opinions and our beliefs from our peers, from those people we see as 'just like us'.

> Most of us take our opinions and our beliefs from our peers, from those people we see as 'just like us'.

| |
|---|
| **Eliminate choice.** Introduce laws that entirely eliminate choice, for example through compulsory isolation of people with infectious diseases. |
| **Restrict choice.** Introduce laws that restrict the options available to people, for example removing unhealthy ingredients from foods, or unhealthy foods from shops or restaurants. |
| **Guide choice through disincentives.** Introduce financial or other disincentives to influence people's behaviour, for example increasing taxes on cigarettes, or bringing in charging schemes to discourage car use in inner cities. |
| **Guide choices through incentives.** Introduce financial or other incentives to influence people's behaviours, for example offering tax-breaks on buying bicycles for travelling to work. |
| **Guide choice through changing the default policy.** For example, changing the standard side dish in a restaurant from chips to a healthier alternative, with chips remaining as an available option. |
| **Enable choice.** Help individuals to change their behaviours, for example by providing free 'stop smoking' programmes, building cycle lanes or providing free fruit in schools. |
| **Provide information.** Inform and educate the public, for example through campaigns to encourage people to walk more or eat five portions of fruit and vegetables a day. |
| **Do nothing or simply monitor the current situation.** |

**Figure 10.2** The intervention ladder. Source: Nuffield Council on Bioethics.[12]

We have seen during the pandemic just how much rumour and misinformation – intentional or otherwise – influence behaviour and attitudes. Social media can spread all kinds of anti-vaccination messages as well as conspiracy theories and be manipulated by people or governments to their own ends. As we have seen throughout this book, restoring trust, healing the splits in our society and improving access to knowledge are all vital for the future – and all depend on listening to people and learning to think like the people of the community we are working with.

Internationally, non-smoking campaigns have used all the steps in the intervention ladder from campaigning with the public to change their behaviour and the incentives of 'sin taxes' to legislation to restrict advertising and smoking in public places. This has, after more than 50 years, brought about significant changes of behaviour among some populations in richer countries, but not all. These approaches risk alienating the public, with accusations of 'nannying' and patronising people or interfering with people's rights to behave as they wish within the law.

There has been an increase in social marketing in recent years whereby marketing messages are aligned with social habits and ways of thinking. Groups in the population are targeted with specific messages designed just for them. It is much easier to get people to accept a message if it fits in with their preconceptions, habits and beliefs. This approach relies to some extent on the idea that we tend to do and think what our friends do and think and are more inclined to believe, as noted earlier, what we are told by 'people like us'.

Nudge theory takes this a step further. This uses positive reinforcement and indirect suggestions as ways to influence behaviour. Often-quoted examples in health include putting the fruit bowl at the front of the school canteen to encourage children to buy more fruit, adding a citrus smell to soap containers to encourage hand washing, and changing the default option so that people have to opt out of organ donation, rather than opt in. Governments have become increasingly interested in this area, with the UK Government, for example, setting up a Behavioural Insights Team in 2010 to guide government policymaking.

Other approaches are to work with people who have themselves become expert over the years on their own diseases, and with mothers – the people who are most likely to be able to affect the health of others and, of course, who are experts on their own children.

Fazle Abed's dictum 'Empower the women', described in Chapter 8, holds good throughout the world. A mother's education is absolutely key. In Malawi, for example, each additional year of maternal education means that her children have a 10% lower probability of dying. In Uganda, the odds of dying for children of women with one additional year of education are 16.6% lower.[13] A child born to a mother who can read is 50% more likely to survive past the age of 5 than a child born to an illiterate woman.[14]

The crucial fact is that the mother has some education – any education, not specifically about health. Even just 5 years' primary education gives the mother a greater ability to think for herself and understand more about the world. It makes the world a safer place for her baby. This education, of course, should also enable a woman to take more control of her own life and her own fertility. 'Empower the women' is about empowering women in all areas of their lives.

There are schemes, projects and policies in every part of the world which work to educate parents, improve their health literacy and empower them. The Sure Start programme in the UK is designed to help parents give their children the best start in life. Other programmes make use of the patient's own expertise. In the UK, for example, the Expert Patient programme worked with patients with chronic diseases, such as arthritis or chronic obstructive pulmonary disease (COPD), and who understand their own condition very well to help others to learn about how to control their condition and to train professional staff.

Mothers to Mothers, (M2M), in southern Africa, has a very extensive programme of mentor mothers working with inexperienced mothers and has played a pivotal role in reducing mother to child transmission of HIV. They bring to their work an understanding that is different from but complementary to the professionals.

These sorts of approach are even more important where there are minority groups within a dominant majority culture. Health workers who are culturally attuned to the group they are working with can reach more of the population and understand how best to link the needs of this group into the wider health system, which will, no doubt, reflect the culture and practices of the majority. Asian women, for example, are more likely to be able to influence other Asian women about diet and exercise.

These top-down initiatives need to be complemented by others that are bottom-up. There is often discussion of professionals trying to engage the population, but the population also needs to be able to engage with the professionals.

> There is often discussion of professionals trying to engage the population, but the population also needs to be able to engage with the professionals.

People, however expert, aren't always able to get their messages across or to influence policy and help shape services. I was privileged to meet Polly Arango who lived in New Mexico, where she and her husband looked after their son, Nick, who had a progressive neurological condition without a name. Over the years, Polly became a true expert on her son's condition and on the sort of services people like him need. She faced difficulties at every turn but ultimately was able to put together a package of the support Nick needed.

As a result of her own experiences, Polly became the Co-founder and, for a long period, Executive Director of Family Voices, a US-wide network of families and friends whose aim is to improve health and related systems for children and youths with special health needs.[15] It now has family-led Family-to-Family Health Information Centers in every US state and in several territories and tribal communities.[16] It also provides advice for policymakers and health leaders.

There are many other people around the world who could tell other stories of fighting to be heard. Some have had Polly's success. Some haven't. The messages from all these schemes for policymakers are similar and straightforward. They should empower. They should enable people to get an education and think for themselves. They should also stop disempowering people by treating them as passive recipients of their wisdom and treat them as fellow citizens and experts in their own right.

In 2001, Derek Wanless, a prominent British banker, was asked by the UK Government to examine future health trends and identify the factors determining the long-term financial and resource needs of the NHS to 2002. He developed three scenarios:

- 'slow uptake', where new technologies and drugs were only brought into use slowly
- 'solid progress', where technology and costs grew together
- 'fully engaged' scenario, where patients themselves contributed much more to improving their health and healthcare.

Derek Wanless concluded that the 'fully engaged' scenario would not only produce the best health outcomes but be the least expensive. Patients who adopted healthy lifestyles would be healthier and incur fewer healthcare costs, whilst the evidence showed that patients who were directly involved in their care often had better outcomes and used less medication. The report was adopted by the Government and became part of the justification for a substantial increase in funding for the NHS.[17]

This and other reports contributed to a spate of innovations in the NHS that included the use of patients' panels to help determine policy in contentious areas, the involvement of patients' representatives on policy bodies, changes in practice towards greater shared care between patient and doctor, the offering of more choice to patients over their treatment and the development of more 'expert patient'-type schemes around the country. Some of these approaches were very successful but there were practical difficulties, which, although they were particular to the NHS, have wider relevance.

My observation as the NHS Chief Executive of the time was that there were three practical difficulties, and that all of them were related to the difficulties described in Chapter 5 of introducing change into an existing system with its own history, culture and processes as well as a very busy agenda.

Firstly, this wasn't our only major policy, and we were deeply involved in implementing others at the time. Secondly, health systems like ours were very heavily invested in traditional practices, which generally excluded patient involvement. Thirdly, the way that money was allocated and spent simply didn't encourage or even allow for greater patient involvement.

These practical problems meant that making significant change would be a massive cultural, financial and logistical exercise. We were not as radical here as we were in other areas. We needed to turn the world upside down.

## TURNING THE WORLD UPSIDE DOWN

The UK has, however, in recent years developed several new approaches which include giving people some control over the money spent directly on their health and by supporting social prescribing. Both have echoes of what is happening in lower-income countries.

Long-term disabled and seriously ill people in England can now receive personal budgets which allow them to buy the services they consider they need to help them. They choose between, for example, spending the money on aids for independent living or on extra care. They can select and employ their own carer directly, rather than simply having the one picked for them by the authorities.[18]

Not everyone eligible wants a personal budget or is able to manage one. However, 55 000 people had received personal budgets by May 2019, with many more eligible. As a result, they have greater autonomy and independence.

This approach has similarities with developments around the world, where people have been using money to incentivise changes in behaviour and increase patient control. The basic concept of giving people money to deal with their immediate needs is not new in any of the countries that have some form of welfare state. Parents receive child benefits in the UK and the equivalent in other countries to help with costs of child rearing. There are unemployment benefits and disability allowances. All these schemes give the recipient some power to spend the money as they see fit, unlike the types of programme more familiar in the USA, where vouchers or items of food, clothing and furniture may be provided but recipients have limited discretion over spending.

The difference is that, for really the first time, these ideas are being introduced in health where the professions and the institutions have for so long controlled the purse strings and held the power. They directly challenge the status quo and respond to the need for control described in Chapter 9.

> These ideas are being introduced in health where the professions and the institutions have for so long controlled the purse strings and held the power.

The English NHS has also developed social prescribing over the last decade and more, whereby GPs and others refer patients to activities in the community to address their health needs. These can include swimming, dancing or singing clubs, gardening or conservation or other activities. They may become involved in volunteering, befriending, cookery, group learning or anything else which will help address their health needs and promote healthier activity. These activities are particularly useful for people with long-term conditions, are lonely or isolated, have complex social needs affecting their well-being or need support with their mental health.[19]

The Bromley by Bow Centre, described in Chapter 9, was one of the pioneers of social prescribing and uses it in conjunction with its many other community-based activities. As noted there, social prescribing is a top-down activity. The clinician prescribes. I talked with Dr Sir Sam Everington, one of the pioneers of the whole movement, who explained that they had used the term 'prescribing' because it was something that doctors were familiar with, and it would therefore be easier to persuade them to be involved. Doctors as well as patients have to be tempted to engage. The term is also probably useful for some patients because it adds authority to an activity and encourages them to participate.

Social prescribing is now fully integrated into NHS policy and practice, social prescribing link workers have been funded to work with GPs across England and an Academy for Social Prescribing formed. The Academy's aims are very broad: *'We work to create partnerships, across the arts, health, sports, leisure, and the natural environment, alongside other aspects of our lives, to promote health and wellbeing at a national and local level.'*[20] The English NHS is being reshaped in ways which bring some decision making more locally, involve more partners, and encourage prevention – if not yet health creation – and many areas are creating health and well-being centres of different kinds. There are many parallel activities taking place in other countries. Amid all the uncertainty and difficulty of the current time, there are some very positive developments.

## AGENTS OF CHANGE

I had worked closely with nurses for many years, but it was only when the All-Party Parliamentary Group that I co-chair carried out a review of nursing globally that I understood quite how undervalued nurses were within health systems and what potential they had for the future. Nurses, of course, understand this very well.

The *Triple Impact* review of nursing showed that developing nursing will have the triple impact of improving health, promoting gender equity and supporting economic growth.[21] The report argued that the combination of nurses' education – which addresses biological, psychological and social factors – their patient-centred values and their role in providing continuity of care made them particularly well suited to take more of a leading role in dealing with the major health problems of today. It came to three conclusions:

- Universal health coverage will not be achieved globally without strengthening nursing.
- Nurses are too often undervalued and unable to achieve their potential.
- Developing nursing will promote gender equity and economic development.

The report recommended that the WHO, the Commonwealth, another international body, or even the UK Government should set up a global initiative to raise the profile and status of nursing and, as a result, realise an enormous health dividend. None of them was interested, some because they had other priorities and some because they didn't want to support an initiative involving only one profession.

We argued that nurses were half the health workforce globally and at the heart of almost all healthcare teams. Healthcare is a team activity and developing nurses and enabling them to work to the 'top of their licence' would enhance the team and also allow everyone else to work to their own full potential. We also pointed out that, while nursing is not a gendered profession, around 80% are women and developing nursing would promote gender equity. It would also give women in low-income countries more opportunities, status and money and thereby boost the local economy.

> Healthcare is a team activity and developing nurses and enabling them to work to the 'top of their licence' would enhance the team and also allow everyone else to work to their own full potential.

We also appealed to economic reasons. We argued that it was an enormous waste of resources for nursing, the biggest part of the workforce and one of the largest single investments in health, not to be able to contribute to its full capacity and capability.

It was all to no avail.

However, Baroness Mary Watkins, herself a nurse, and I decided we would launch our own initiative. As well as contacting nurses for their advice, I wrote to four very experienced doctors around the world to ask if they would support it: Lincoln Chen in the US, Enrique Ruelas in Mexico, Srinath Reddy in India and Francis Omaswa in Uganda. They were unanimous in their support, telling me that it was not only important to do but also very timely. In general throughout the campaign, senior doctors were very supportive, knowing from their own experience how much benefit this could bring.

The new WHO Director General Dr Tedros became an enthusiastic and committed supporter and we launched the three year campaign in February 2018 in association with the WHO and the ICN. This gave the campaign accountability to the two relevant global democratic structures that involved the countries of the world on the one hand and most of the national nursing associations on the other.

We kept the organisation and administration as simple as possible by attaching ourselves to an existing organisation. The Burdett Trust for Nursing very generously allowed the campaign to operate as a committee of the Trust – giving us an instant governance structure – and the Trust's chair Alan Gibbs and chief executive Shirley Baines were both extremely supportive throughout the campaign. The Trust provided about half the funding for the campaign and enabled the appointment of a small group of staff.

The campaign had a number of global successes including securing 2020 as the Year of the Nurse and Midwife (using Florence Nightingale's bicentenary as a very useful hook), helping have a Chief Nursing Office appointed at WHO, and a new Nursing and Midwifery strategy which was agreed at the end of the campaign in May 2021.[22]

We also published a number of reports globally, the most important of which advocated for more nurse specialist and nurse practitioners, for nurses and midwives to play a leading role in primary care, strengthening nurses' and midwives' roles in promoting health and well-being and for *'making nurse-based and nurse-led services the norm for the management of most non-communicable diseases.'*[23]

> Making nurse-based and nurse-led services the norm for the management of most non-communicable diseases.
>
> *Crisp N, Brownie S, Refsum C.*[23]

The campaign's main focus was at national and local level. This is where change needed to happen – in the policies and practice of nursing and face to face with patients. It took off much quicker than we had expected and, by the time we drew the campaign to a close in May 2021, a few months later than planned because of the pandemic, there were 750 self-funding Nursing Now groups in 126 countries. Each of them supported our vision and had agreed their own local priorities and plan of action. East African countries were the first to establish local and national groups, with the final three national groups – China, Russia and Saudi Arabia – all joining in the last few months of the campaign.

The campaign's final report showed something of the extent of activity around the world – without, of course, being able to capture more than a tiny amount of what was happening in 126 countries driven by passionate leaders.[24] It shows that 24 countries invested more in nursing as a result of the campaign, new curricula were developed in several countries, workforces grew, more innovative services were established, and more nurses took on leadership roles at national and local level.

The campaign left a legacy of strengthened nursing nationally and globally. It also led to the Nursing Now Challenge, a development programme for young nurses and midwives which had been established as the Nightingale Challenge by the campaign and involved more than 30 000 young nurses and midwives. It is continuing for at least 2 more years and aims to involve 100 000 young people.[25]

These very practical results were achieved by the hard work of individuals in their own countries and not by the campaign as such. It was passion, determination and graft that brought about change rather than slogans and publicity, while social media helped mobilise people very effectively.

There are a number of lessons here for other campaigns. Some of them relate to the behaviours I observed in the UK health creators which I described in Figure 9.2 in Chapter 9. These included starting by building relationships not systems, learning by doing, being vision-led not plan-led, and reinforcing local control and autonomy. Having relatively little money was, perhaps surprisingly, an advantage as it meant people locally had truly to own their local activity rather than just doing what we asked because we funded them. We couldn't fund anything.

Three extra points are worth drawing out. Firstly, timing was important. Secondly, we were successful partly because change was already happening in some places, and we very deliberately set out to publicise it and accelerate it. Finally, the leadership had a broad base and was broadly representative. We had a board of 21 with members from 16 countries. Two-thirds were nurses, one-third non-nurses. Two-thirds were women, one-third men. Young nurses were included on the board and in the main decision making, not in a separate group by themselves. And Sheila Tlou, a nurse and former health minister for Botswana, co-chaired the campaign with me.

One of the most important points was that we adopted the approach I had learned from IHI of *'waste no will'*. This meant that we were ready to welcome everyone who wanted to help as long as they bought into our vision of raising the profile and status of nursing. We weren't exclusive, we didn't require people to have particular views on specific issues, and we weren't trying to impose a UK or American or any other model of nursing. Diversity was strength and the energy and momentum grew with everyone who joined in.

> **Diversity was strength and the energy and momentum grew with everyone who joined in.**

The inclusivity of *'waste no will'* seems to me to be a vital part of the future for improving health globally. We must not seek to impose solutions on others. We need to find the commonalities not the divisions and celebrate diversity of views and approaches as well as diversity of backgrounds.

At the end of the campaign, I was even more convinced of the importance of the growing role of nursing, and of enabling every other profession as well, to work to its true potential. We will all benefit. This approach needs to be built into all plans for strengthening health systems and improving health.

We called Nursing Now's final report *Agents of Change* as a direct reference to the *Lancet* Commission on the Education of Health Professionals for the 21st Century chaired by Julio Frenk and Lincoln Chen and of which I was privileged to be a member. Its report was published in 2010, a century after the Flexner Report which had led to radical changes in medical schools through integrating modern science into their curricula.

The central theme of the Commission report was that professional education should be *'systems based to improve the performance of health systems by adapting core professional competencies to specific contexts, while drawing on global knowledge.'*[26] The report made many important recommendations about, for example, basing professional education on competences, using ICT more effectively with new ways of delivering education including Massive Open Online Courses (MOOCs), and promoting inter-professional education and trans-professional teams involving non-professionals such as community health workers.

The most relevant point to this discussion is that professionals need to be concerned with the health system as well as with the patient in front of them. The report described three levels of education:

- *Informative learning* is about acquiring knowledge and skills.
- *Formative education* is about socialising students around values and the production of experts.
- *Transformative education* is about acquiring leadership attributes in order to produce enlightened change agents.

> **The most relevant point to this discussion is that professionals need to be concerned with the health system as well as with the patient in front of them.**

This idea that health professionals should be agents of change is very powerful. It applies to the single psychiatrist in a region of an African country who needs to mobilise what support they can from governments, civil society and communities to provide care, prevent disease and create health, as well as providing direct care to their patients. It applies as much to the UK GP who reaches out to help create health and wellness activities or health-creating networks in their area as well as being clinicians. And it applies to nurses building and running a new service for COPD patients or homeless people. At its most extreme, it applies to the Myanmar clinicians desperately trying to create services for their population as described in Chapter 3 – and being fired on by the army as a result.

At the time of writing, Julio Frenk and Lincoln Chen are undertaking a review of progress over the decade since the publication of the report and will publish an update in the coming months. I believe that this will be even more relevant today when, as they say, the pandemic has accelerated advances in technology, changed health systems and revealed inequalities.

They report that globally, medical and nursing graduates have increased markedly over the past decade, nearly doubling for doctors and tripling for nurses/midwives. Expenditure on educating the two professions now amounts to about US$110 billion. They also describe how technology has the potential to widen access to professional education and to health more generally.

Their conclusion fits very well with the themes emerging from this book. Health and care professionals play the major part in shaping how we think about health, and we will return to the idea of them as agents of change in the final chapter of the book. They conclude that *'How education responds to social inequalities and nurtures the heart and soul of the healing professions in the years ahead will determine our ability as a global community to progress towards a more just and safe world.'*

> How education responds to social inequalities and nurtures the heart and soul of the healing professions in the years ahead will determine our ability as a global community to progress towards a more just and safe world.
>
> Correspondence from *Julio Frenk and Lincoln Chen* in 2021

The Commission's approach and ideas resonate very strongly with the work of Professor Ged Byrne who has used his role as Director of Global Engagement for Health Education England to pioneer some very important approaches to learning between different countries and cultures. He was responsible, among other things, for the creation of the Uganda UK Heath Alliance and was a major influence behind the development of the Kenya UK Health Alliance described in Chapter 11.

He explained to me that education is partly about the subject matter, partly about the teacher, and partly about the context in which the learning is implemented. The health professional visiting a different country learns a great deal from understanding the environment and different problems but most importantly from what people actually do in the different context. They can learn new ways of thinking as well as new ways of acting and influencing – as agents of change.

This applies as much to the clinician from an African country working in a western country as it does to western professionals in a low-income African country and is the basis of a very wide suite of programmes of exchange and mutual learning run by Health Education England.

Figure 10.3 which shows an outer ring of education, a middle ring describing the activities health professionals need to perform, and an inner ring of the competences they need to do so is based on the Commission on the Education of Health Professionals for the 21st Century and is used by Ged Byrne in his work.

A recent study reveals just how important context is. Oliver Johnson and colleagues interviewed 27 Sierra Leone doctors in a qualitative study of leadership in Sierra Leone which described the very difficult challenges of working as a leader in the country. The authors argue that international leadership models were relevant but that contextual issues were even more important and required very distinctive leadership qualities. They wrote: '*Context-specific factors included health system breakdown, politicization in the health sector and lack of accountability, placing importance on skills such as persistence, role modelling and taking initiative.*'[27]

I talked with Oliver Johnson about the study and he told me that doctors in leadership positions were often placed in almost impossible situations which challenged their own values

**Figure 10.3** Education, activities and competences. Drawing by Professor Ged Byrne, in private communication

and ethics. Some felt that the choice was to leave the country or get broken by the system. Those who stayed had to become very skilled at navigating all the complexities – '*bending without breaking*'.

The study concludes by arguing that governments and development partners need to work to create a supportive and enabling environment.

This is a salutary reminder of how difficult it can be to work in many countries and how easily people can become disillusioned – or of course choose to emigrate. It reinforces the *Lancet* Commission's whole emphasis on the importance of health systems in the way that professionals practise and are educated. The development of health systems and professional education need to go hand in hand. Agents of change need some help from their environment.

It is also a reminder that achieving universal health coverage is about more than money – important as that is – and that culture, behaviour, values and leadership have important parts to play. And it also reminds us that planners must not ignore the, sometimes ugly, reality of the real situation in a country when they draw up the plans – something that is easy to do in a distant government department and even easier to do from faraway Washington, London or Tokyo.

We return to discussing health and care systems in the next chapter.

## REFERENCES

1. https://scfnuka.com/about-us/ (Accessed 23 November 2021).
2. Petricca K, Mamo Y, Haileamlak A *et al*. Barriers to effective follow-up treatment of rheumatic heart disease in rural Ethiopia. A grounded theory analysis of the patient experience. [Unpublished paper.]
3. Crome P, Kelly S, Steel J. Have you taken your tablets this week? *Clin Med (Lond)*, 2009; **9**(1): 12–13. doi: 10.7861/clinmedicine.9-1-12.
4. Paul BD. *Health, Culture, and Community.* New York: Russell Sage Foundation, 1955.
5. Scrimshaw SC. Culture, behavior & health. In Merson MH, Black RE, Mills AJ (eds). *International Public Health: Diseases, programs, systems and policies*, 2nd edn. Sudbury, MA: Jones & Bartlett Publishers, 2006.
6. https://torontobirthcentre.ca/ (Accessed 23 November 2021).
7. Durie M. Pacific Region Indigenous Doctors Congress, 2006.
8. Smylie J, Lofters A, Firestone M, O'Campo P. Population-based data and community empowerment. In O'Campo P, Dunn JR (eds). *Rethinking Social Epidemiology: Towards a science of change.* New York: Springer, 2012. https://link.springer.com/book/10.1007/978-94-007-2138-8 (Accessed 23 November 2021).
9. Barry MJ, Edgman-Levitan S. Shared decision making – the pinnacle of patient-centered care. *N Engl J Med*, 2012; **366**: 780–1. https://www.nejm.org/doi/full/10.1056/NEJMp1109283 (Accessed 23 November 2021).
10. http://www.ihi.org/Topics/WhatMatters/Pages/default.aspx (Accessed 23 November 2021).
11. https://wmty.world/ (Accessed 23 November 2021).
12. Nuffield Council on Bioethics. *Public Health: Ethical issues.* London, 2007, para 3.37, p. 42. Available via https://www.nuffieldbioethics.org/publications/public-health (Accessed 23 November 2021).

13. https://link.springer.com/article/10.1007/s13524-019-00812-3 (Accessed 23 November 2021).
14. https://www.prb.org/resources/the-effect-of-girls-education-on-health-outcomes-fact-sheet/ (Accessed 23 November 2021).
15. https://familyvoices.org/about (Accessed 23 November 2021).
16. https://familyvoices.org/ (Accessed 23 November 2021).
17. https://www.yearofcare.co.uk/sites/default/files/images/Wanless.pdf (Accessed 23 November 2021).
18. https://www.england.nhs.uk/personal-health-budgets/what-are-personal-health-budgets-phbs/ (Accessed 23 November 2021).
19. Buck D, Ewbank L. What is social prescribing? London: Kings Fund, 2020. https://www.kingsfund.org.uk/publications/social-prescribing (Accessed 23 November 2021).
20. https://socialprescribingacademy.org.uk/about-us/what-is-social-prescribing/ (Accessed 23 November 2021).
21. *Triple Impact – How investing in nursing will improve health, improve gender equality and support economic growth.* All-Party Parliamentary Group on Global Health, London, October 2016. https://globalhealth.inparliament.uk/news/triple-impact-how-investing-nursing-will-improve-health-improve-gender-equality-and-support (Accessed 23 November 2021).
22. WHO. The WHO global strategic directions for nursing and midwifery (2021–2025). https://www.who.int/publications/m/item/global-strategic-directions-for-nursing-and-midwifery-2021-2025 (Accessed 23 November 2021).
23. Crisp N, Brownie S, Refsum C. Nursing and Midwifery: the key to the rapid and cost-effective expansion of high quality universal health coverage. https://ecommons.aku.edu/eastafrica_fhs_sonam/232/ (Accessed 7 Februray 2022)
24. Nursing Now. *Agents of change: The story of the Nursing Now campaign.* London: Burdett Trust for Nursing, May 2021. https://www.nursingnow.org/wp-content/uploads/2021/05/Nursing-Now-Final-Report-Executive-Summary.pdf (Accessed 23 November 2021).
25. https://www.nursingnow.org/ (Accessed 23 November 2021).
26. Frenk J, Chen L, Bhutta ZA *et al.* Health professionals for a new century: transforming education to strengthen health systems in an interdependent world. *The Lancet*, December 2010; **376**(9756): 1923–58. doi: 10.1016/S0140–6736(10)61854–5.
27. Johnson O, Sahr F, Begg K *et al.* To bend without breaking: a qualitative study on leadership by doctors in Sierra Leone. *Health Policy and Planning*, 2021; **36**(10): 1644–58. doi: https://doi.org/10.1093/heapol/czab076 (Accessed 23 November 2021).

# Practical knowledge (2) – science, equity and systems

**11**

This chapter, like the last, is about some of the practical things we can learn from each other by pooling our knowledge and experience from around the world. It provides a brief overview of some of the recent advances in technology and science. The main focus of the chapter, however, is on health equity and on how health and care systems need to adapt for the future. It finishes with a discussion on quality and safety.

The chapter begins with data and technology being put to good use in an architecture practice in Bradford, England. Yeme Architects has developed a new platform which brings together data from publicly available sources to create a multi-layered map of a neighbourhood, town or city. Amir Hussain, the chief executive, demonstrated to me how you can move a cursor across a map on a screen to reveal the location of facilities and services.

He showed me how he could identify, for example, all the community assets and activities within two miles of where he was that, as he put it, *'could lead to opportunities for human interaction'* – things such as shops, schools, restaurants, pubs, green spaces, allotments or community gardens, evening classes, places of worship, choirs, food banks, social clubs and community groups of all kinds. These are all the sorts of things that help make a community function.

The map could be adjusted to cover a smaller or larger area and then be overlaid with data on employment, educational attainment, income, health status and much more so that it could begin to reveal a whole, almost living and breathing, picture of real communities – of what's there and, just as importantly, what is not.

The platform shows us what we already know – that, for example, areas of lower income have fewer facilities, poorer health status, fewer activities and less green space. But it also shows us things we may not know – levels of very local social activity, community activities, groups doing similar things only a few streets apart, underused facilities, and small areas with particular problems – all of them things that were hidden from our normal view of the world.

Above all, perhaps, it reveals opportunities for residents and health planners alike. It could show planners how and where to target their interventions – areas with low COVID-19 vaccination rates, for example. They could see where people meet and identify potential allies who could help promote health literacy and support programmes to tackle isolation, poverty and inequalities more generally. They can see where new facilities could be best sited and how

DOI: 10.1201/9781003267706-11

to join up green spaces to create green pathways through the city. And local people, of course, could use the platform to find out what's going on in their area and join in or create other activities.

The platform brings live data from multiple sources together to provide a rounded picture which we can explore in all its richness. Other technologies bring other sorts of data together, from different imaging modalities, for example – CT, MRI, PET scans and more – so surgeons can visualise precisely what is happening within our bodies and even practise the surgery they are planning to carry out. AI can even help us predict what will happen next inside our bodies or in the community.

> The platform brings live data from multiple sources together to provide a rounded picture which we can explore in all its richness.

The application of technology to the diagnosis and treatment of individuals is developing fast. We are beginning to see the introduction of personalised or precision medicine with treatments designed for individuals, for their precise variant or personal manifestation of the disease, as well as gene therapy that may save them from years of pain or early death.

There is increasing use of sophisticated wearable monitors that track physiological data, provide feedback to patients and their clinicians and carers and can help head off disease or acute episodes. All of these promote independence and give people more control over their lives, as does the introduction of controllable prostheses and other supports for people with disabilities.

The development of vaccines in the last 2 years has been spectacular and is itself based on earlier work in genomics and information technology. It has been accompanied by the development of new equipment, drugs and practices. Elsewhere, AI has enabled new insights into protein misfolding, which will have major implications for the study of many diseases including Alzheimer's.

The use of data and 'big data' gathered from multiple sources is also of increasing importance in public and population health. It can provide a deeper understanding of the needs of different groups in society and is beginning to be used to stratify risk and target interventions. Elsewhere, there are developments in construction technologies and materials, and in ways of improving insulation, heating and cooling, and reducing pollution. All these contribute to healthy homes and healthy communities, towns and cities.

Health systems and health services are changing and will continue to do so in even more dramatic fashion. We are all accustomed to remote consultations now. This has been taken much further in China where there are now more than 20 internet hospitals where consultations and prescriptions can be provided online, and only initial diagnosis and hands-on physical treatments need to be done in person.[1] These open up many different possibilities including linking together different facilities of all sorts – hospitals, pharmacies, care homes – and allowing doctors who are physically based elsewhere to consult within the facility.

We can expect that this is only the beginning of further technological developments which will revolutionise the way people access healthcare in the future. They will be accompanied by greater use of robotics in surgery, logistics, bioengineering and, even, caring.

All of this means that the life sciences, biotech, bioengineering and all the associated sciences and technologies from materials science to behavioural science have become very high profile, very political and very big business. This has brought with it ethical, social and economic dilemmas most of which go way beyond the scope of this book. They have become even more important at a time when so many people are questioning science and scientists and when science itself has become so visibly a part of political and geopolitical manoeuvring.

COVID-19 has brought one of these dilemmas – health equity and the impact of social inequalities – into dramatic focus. As I write, infections are rising in at least 20 African countries and there are very few vaccine doses available for their populations. Meanwhile, some of the richest countries in the world are offering their citizens a fourth 'booster' injection.

Before discussing health equity, it is important to recognise that there are some major drawbacks to relying on science and technology to save us from either disease or climate change. This dizzying array of scientific and technological advances may encourage us to paint a very positive picture of the future, but there are important caveats.

> This dizzying array of scientific and technological advances may encourage us to paint a very positive picture of the future, but there are important caveats.

Firstly, not everyone will be able to access these new types of service. This will include many older people, people who are mentally ill or have dementia, and, of course, the very sick – leaving aside people who can't for reasons of cost and availability of these services. These developments may simultaneously open up access to many and exclude others. It is not all about technology, of course. People will still be needed – clinicians, carers, families and friends – to guide, explain, assist in decision making as well as diagnose, treat and provide care.

Secondly, progress is very often over-hyped, over-sold and over-promised. Introducing a practical application may take years following an original discovery and, even then, may not fulfil its initial promise. Not all interesting-looking developments will end up having any useful purpose. I have attended two very large meetings on digital innovation in India in recent years. It was not at all clear which innovations on display might be effective and which not – and which might be actively harmful. Discovery, development – and especially marketing – were racing far ahead of evidence and evaluation.

Alternatively, we may have the knowledge and technology we need, and the evidence about its effectiveness, but do we actually know how to apply it in practice? And is there the political will to make it happen? This is not as easy as it may seem. A significant number of the 5.2 million children who die each year do so from simple causes such as dehydration caused by diarrhoea. Many of their deaths could be prevented. More than 90% of blind people live in low- and middle-income countries; 75% of blindness is avoidable or treatable. We know what needs to be done but we are still not doing it at scale.

The application of knowledge is not just a problem for low- and middle-income countries nor is it just about resources. There is, for example, an enormous divide between hospitals providing high-cost low-quality care and those providing low-cost, high-quality care in the United States.[2] Knowledge simply isn't being applied and spread.

These new advances may also create new problems, the unexpected and unintended consequences of progress. Will we see new diseases and conditions created? Will we see lab escapes? And will scientists, in relieving humans of one disease, make them more vulnerable to others?

Perhaps the biggest question of all from a global perspective is of who benefits from the science and the technology. Is it kept with a closed circle of wealthy countries and individuals? Is it the closely guarded intellectual property of private companies that is only available at exorbitant costs? Will it be used for political purposes – for state control as well as vaccine diplomacy?

## HEALTH EQUITY AND THE RIGHT TO HEALTH

Inequality in access to health and healthcare has become a very high-profile and highly charged issue and runs throughout this book. Health equity is about removing the differences in health outcomes and access to health services that are unfair and unjust. The WHO describes health inequities as *'the unfair and avoidable differences in health status seen within and between countries. In countries at all levels of income, health and illness follow a social gradient: the lower the socioeconomic position, the worse the health.'* It goes on to point to a 19-year life expectancy difference between people born in countries with a high human development index and those born in countries with a low human development index.[3]

> It goes on to point to a 19-year life expectancy difference between people born in countries with a high human development index and those born in countries with a low human development index.

Typically, these differences are linked to ethnicity, gender, disability, income, employment status, sexuality, access to food, education, and living in a conflict zone or a rural area. This list by itself shows clearly that this is a much wider issue of social justice – as we have noted elsewhere – and cannot be dealt with simply through health interventions.[4] The health system is, in effect, both contributing to and responding to wider social issues.

A starting point for tackling health inequalities, as described in Chapter 10, is to make sure that health data is disaggregated so the differences can be seen and interrogated, and we can begin to understand the nature of the differences and the reasons for them. It is very easy for differences in access and outcome to be overlooked if this is not done.

In the end, however, it all depends on there being the political and public will nationally and globally to make change happen – and to do so in ways that address all aspects of the problem through cross-sectoral action. The UK provides an interesting example of action being taken in the health and care system but being undermined by other aspects of government policy.

The English NHS had handled health equity partly through explicitly allocating funding on the basis of a calculation of need and, more recently, through increasing levels of local engagement in decision making and priorities, thus enabling more focus on local issues often linked to equity. It also, in 2020, created the NHS Race and Health Observatory which *'works to identify and tackle ethnic inequalities in health and care by facilitating research, making health policy recommendations and enabling long-term transformational change'*.

However, policies in other areas such as education, housing, social care and welfare benefits – particularly during the years of austerity – have undercut those efforts. The current Government has announced a policy of 'levelling up' with ambitious targets to address these wider issues but there is little or no detail yet as to how this might be achieved in reality.[5]

Globally, health equity has been an expressed goal of health initiatives for 40 years and there have been many projects and programmes to address it in that time. Some have had considerable success. The fact that there is no incentive for private companies to create products for the poorest countries and populations – who cannot themselves pay for them – led to the creation of the International Financing Facility for Immunization and the Advanced Market Commitment in 2005 following a proposal from the UK Government.

These arrangements fund the development of vaccines and drugs for the major communicable diseases that mainly only affect low-income countries. They create a viable business model for pharmaceutical, biotech and other companies to invest in the long and expensive period of research and development. The latest round of funding in early 2021 issued US$750 million for GAVI and the global vaccine initiative COVAX.[6]

There have been ten other innovative financing schemes which mobilised US$8.9 billion between 2002 and 2015. The funds raised were channelled mostly through GAVI and the Global Fund, and used for programmes for new and underused vaccines, HIV/AIDS, malaria, TB, and maternal and child health.[7]

At the same time, prolonged campaigning has led to some commercial organisations changing their own business models so as to provide the same drug or product at cheaper prices in low- and middle-income countries. Some therapies are now much more widely available than they were. AstraZeneca, to its credit, has agreed to provide its COVID-19 vaccine on a non-profit basis in perpetuity to low- and middle-income countries.

> AstraZeneca, to its credit, has agreed to provide its COVID-19 vaccine on a non-profit basis in perpetuity to low- and middle-income countries.

This discussion underscores the importance of the relationship between commercial interests in emerging markets and government action in developing countries in creating and using knowledge and together helping lift the poor out of poverty. Some governments and philanthropic institutions such as the Wellcome Trust and the Gates Foundation fund research into diseases that are prevalent in low- and middle-income countries, from HIV/AIDS to TB and the, so called, neglected tropical diseases.

There are also organisations such as PATH in the US and researchers in many countries focusing on developing technologies and treatments specifically for these populations. In the UK, Dr Helen Lee of Cambridge University, for example, has an extensive programme of developing simple and inexpensive technologies suitable for use in making diagnoses in the environment and conditions of poor countries.

Science and technology can help in very many ways. Mobile phones have provided an extraordinary boost in lower-income countries. Within health, mobile phones, the internet and the power of microprocessors have opened up the opportunities to diagnose, advise and treat patients at a distance. Digital health and telemedicine in all its forms can make a huge difference in poor countries.

Most of these positive developments came out of a period when world leaders and governments were outward-facing and positive about global cooperation. Now, many have turned inwards and recent events, such as the pandemic, the retreat from Afghanistan and heightened tensions, are making politicians insular and defensive. Inequalities are growing.

The drive towards health equity is underpinned by the continuing development of human rights policy and legislation. The right to health potentially has profound implications, but it is still a long way from being put into practice in anything like a universal or consistent fashion.

The 1948 General Assembly of the United Nations set out that *'Everyone has the right to a standard of living adequate for the health and well-being of himself and of his family [sic], including food, clothing, housing and medical care and necessary social services, and the right to security in the event of unemployment, sickness, disability, widowhood, old age or other lack of livelihood in circumstances beyond his control.'*

Other declarations have gradually deepened and clarified the detail. The EU asserted in 2000 that *'Everyone has the right of access to preventive health care and the right to benefit from medical treatment under the conditions established by national laws and practices.'* Meanwhile, the African Union's Africa Health Strategy 2007 to 2015 takes health being a human right as one of its central principles.

Over the last 70 years or so the notion that health is a human right has gradually become accepted in much of the world. While there is much more to do to win the argument everywhere, attention has shifted to asking what this really means in practice in an area where there is massive scope for misunderstanding and confusion.

Paul Hunt, as the UN Special Rapporteur on the right to health, took the definition of health as a human right further by pointing out that this is not, for example, about the right of an individual woman to have the gynaecologist of her choice but the right of a population to have access to healthcare.

Mary Robinson, the first woman to be President of Ireland and a former United Nations High Commissioner for Human Rights, set up Realizing Rights to try to address these practical issues and in order *'to put human rights standards at the heart of global governance and policy-making and to ensure that the needs of the poorest and most vulnerable are addressed on the global stage'.*[8]

> to put human rights standards at the heart of global governance and policy-making and to ensure that the needs of the poorest and most vulnerable are addressed on the global stage.
>
> *Realising Rights*

Realizing Rights existed between 2002 and 2010. Its approach took the assertion of rights a step further by setting out the values that should inform the actions of governments and world leaders. These values provide a framework for action that:

- acknowledges shared responsibilities for addressing global challenges and affirms that our common humanity doesn't stop at national borders
- recognises that all individuals are equal in dignity and have the right to certain entitlements, rather than viewing them as objects of benevolence or charity
- embraces the importance of gender and the need for attention to the often-different impacts of economic and social policies on women and men
- affirms that a world connected by technology and trade must also be connected by shared values, norms of behaviour and systems of accountability.[8]

These refinements begin to make the grand proclamation of the 1948 UN General Assembly practical and achievable by moving the debate away from impossibly impractical-sounding notions of individual rights and individualism to the rights we share and our right to partake in shared resource, shared entitlement and shared progress. It bridges our independence and our interdependence.

The right to health finds expression in Britain's NHS and other European and European-style health systems that have at their heart the idea that the health of all citizens is important to us all – that in economists' terms, health is a public good – and that health services should be available to all. The UK has been explicit both in the original 1946 Act establishing the NHS that healthcare should be available to all equally and, more recently, in the NHS Constitution, asserting that the NHS belongs to the people.

The right to health and the associated idea that basic health services should be available to everyone without user charges have gathered momentum in recent years and resulted in the great movement towards universal health coverage. This perspective sees the provision of healthcare to the poor as no longer being about aid and service but being about rights and entitlement. As the Commission for Africa says, *'It is a journey from charity to justice.'*[9]

> It is a journey from charity to justice.
>
> *Commission for Africa*

Linked to rights, but separate from them, is the demand for greater openness and accountability at every level of authority from the individual clinician to the pharmaceutical company, the government or intergovernmental organisation and the media.

The universal demand is for transparency and accountability with civil society groups that focus on this growing rapidly around the world. While the roots of this activity go back decades and perhaps centuries, there is a pronounced shift now taking place towards a different sort of politics, which takes place outside formal institutions, and the creation of a more networked and engaged democracy.

The British civil service is non-political and has traditionally seen part of its role as speaking truth unto power. Turning this upside down, we can see the civil society movements are beginning to create mechanisms for making sure that power speaks truth unto us.

## HEALTH SYSTEMS STRENGTHENING

One of the effects of the COVID-19 pandemic has been to put a renewed emphasis on the importance of strengthening health systems. Rob Yates of Chatham House, a leading advocate for universal health coverage, told me that, although serious damage had been done to many health systems by the pandemic, there are reasons to be hopeful in the longer term because more countries were recognising that they needed strong and resilient systems. He pointed to new developments in Cyprus and South Africa and also noted that major advances in health systems had very often come out of crisis. National systems were created in much of western Europe and in Japan after the Second World War. New Zealand's pioneering developments followed the depression in the 1930s and Sri Lanka's after major malaria outbreaks 50 years ago.

He emphasised the importance of developing universal systems that were based on primary care and public health and which were able to reach all parts of a population. There was a danger, he told me, of simply introducing US-style personal health insurance which would reimburse people for hospital treatment but not for any of the care, prevention and health maintenance activities undertaken outside hospitals. This is precisely what is happening, for example, in India where the national government's policy of providing insurance for hospital coverage for its poorest citizens is driving people and income towards the large private hospital systems – and away from primary and community care.

Delhi State, on the other hand, and in opposition to the national government, has created community clinics throughout the city, developing them in areas of greatest needs. These Mohalla (or community) clinics were established in 2015 *'to provide primary healthcare at the doorsteps of the common people'*.[10] There is interest from other states in copying the model, against the political opposition of the national government. Here, as elsewhere, raw politics is influencing health policy.

> Mohalla (or community) clinics were established . . . 'to provide primary healthcare at the doorsteps of the common people.'

These examples illustrate the need for planners to concentrate on what the health system can deliver and how it functions and not just on building capacity or increasing funding. At its worst, a poorly functioning small health system would be replaced by an equally poorly functioning large one. Political pressures may well drive short-term visible gains such as new buildings, equipment or staffing rather than the careful building up of a fully functioning system.

We had precisely this problem in the NHS in 2000. We had short-term targets for increases in staff and longer-term targets for outcomes, such as reduction in deaths from coronary heart diseases. We were very conscious of the risk and set up the Modernisation Agency as an internal change agent to help improve our practices and use the new money and the new staff to best effect. We were generally successful but, with hindsight, I would have slowed recruitment and matched it more closely to service change and the development of new roles.

There is another danger for countries introducing universal coverage. They may well be very tempted to introduce practices and ready-made solutions from other countries that simply don't suit their circumstances. Moreover, as they will be receiving lots of advice (and possibly funding) from higher-income countries, it will be very easy unconsciously to adopt the ideas and ideologies that accompany the money and the scientific knowledge.

As importantly, there needs to be a focus on quality and patient safety. Standards can be poor in some low-income countries due to lack of resources and trained staff. A successful implementation methodology needs to have quality improvement and patient safety at its heart. The same, of course, is true in high-income countries where standards can also be very variable.

The next four sections discuss the way the central features of western scientific medicine need to be adapted to be fit for the future before we return to these difficult questions of implementation and quality. Western scientific medicine was described in Chapter 2 as depending on the four features of greater professionalism, biomedical science, commercial innovation and increased funding. They are discussed in turn below.

## PROFESSIONALISM

The health professions developed enormously during the last century. As a result, highly capable doctors, nurses, midwives and other professionals have conquered many conditions and contributed to our health and longevity. This has reinforced the power of these groups. Specialism and skills have given them knowledge and power over the layperson and gifted them an unrivalled position in negotiating with governments and authorities. Monopoly power has been accredited alongside the knowledge. Sometimes, of course, it has been abused.

While most professionals, through their own humanity and training, relate to their patients with the utmost sensitivity, the systems they work in, as we have noted many times in this book, reinforce their status and power and tend to disempower the patient at every turn. Despite this, as discussed in Chapter 10, patients very often don't do what they are advised or even told what to do.

In practice, it is the other way up. Patients are expert in subverting professional power and are very often, in reality, the people who empower and enable the professionals to act effectively, rather than the other way round. There is a total shift in perspective here from the idea that professionals always know best to the idea that the professionals' competence is enhanced and enabled by the patients and communities they serve.

Attitudes are changing rapidly. In the hierarchical British NHS even 20 years ago it was not uncommon to hear doctors complaining about patients' demands or about how they wanted to question or dispute the doctor's conclusions. Nowadays, it is very different, driven partly by training, partly by generational change and partly by external factors such as politics, stronger management and the fact that, in some countries at least, patients can sue.

It was also quite common 20 and more years ago to hear doctors complaining about protocols, guidelines and checklists encroaching on their clinical freedom. Attitudes have moved on and today the opposite danger applies, and the bigger risk is that clinicians blindly follow the protocol without pausing to think. At its best, however, this is liberating medicine. It allows a clinician to see what normal practice is, what their peers believe works best, and what the best available evidence shows. They can then take a measured decision to follow the protocol or not – and, if not, to be able to justify their reason for taking another course of action.

The boundary between professions has also been shifting in recent years. The idea that nurses should work to the 'top of their licence', as discussed in Chapter 10, applies to every profession including doctors. They don't need to do things that others can do as well, or sometimes, better. I remember some of the arguments surrounding the introduction of prescribing by nurses and other non-medical professionals while I was chief executive of the

English NHS. Eventually we got the change through and today, more than 15 years later, it is just an uncontroversial part of ordinary life.

> The emphasis is now much more on each professional doing what they do best within a team.

Some doctors have recognised this for years. Sir Keith Willett is Professor of Trauma Surgery at the University of Oxford and Medical Director for Acute Services in NHS England where he has been leading the NHS response to the pandemic. I recall him telling me in the 1990s that, when you were in theatre or the emergency room, everybody had to leave their professional background outside the door. Inside, everyone used the skills they had. Who did what depended on who was most skilled at doing it, and not on their professional background.

It was this same attitude that led him and colleagues to decide that only nurses could discharge patients from the trauma wards. The nurses spent more time with the patients and were better able to judge when they could go home. The surgeons' unique contributions were made in the clinic and the operating theatre. It was an approach that turned traditional practice on its head and, for a time at least, greatly upset some of Keith Willett's more traditional colleagues.

Doctors, nurses, midwives, pharmacists, scientists, therapists, social workers and other professionals each have their own specific areas of expertise in things which only they can do – and so, too, do the non-professionals, the community health workers, carers, experts by experience and many others. The challenge for the future is about ensuring good teamwork, good communication and enabling everyone to work to the top of their licence.

Professionalism has served us well. Today, however, we need to think about the patient/professional relationship differently and conclude that greater professional competence is achieved through patients and communities empowering and being empowered by the professionals together with a greater emphasis on teamwork.

This, like the other changes advocated in the next three sections, has very practical consequences for how health and care systems are developed.

## SCIENCE IN SOCIETY

The biomedical sciences have delivered enormous health benefits for individuals and whole populations and there is undoubtedly much more to come in the future, from both the biomedical and the social sciences.

Knowledge of culture, society, psychology, politics and economics are central to successful application and the disciplines of operational research and implementation science rely on behavioural understanding and on experimentation in the real and untidy world. Biology is biology wherever you are in the world but how to apply knowledge depends on culture and environment.

The ideas and approaches of western science are themselves conditioned by their social context. They represent one way of looking at the world and, in doing so, can discount or ignore insights that may be available from other perspectives and other traditions of medicine. Practitioners working in traditional societies argue that clinicians should look at and evaluate all the evidence, from traditional sources as well as from western science. This is a sophisticated approach that lays the stress on evaluation and evidence. A clinician who evaluates the evidence will throw out the nonsense and keep the sense from both traditions.

More generally, clinicians need continually to evaluate the evidence, even if they work exclusively within the western scientific tradition. In many cases, there may not be very good evidence and clinicians may rely on a mixture of taking a logical and pragmatic approach and using their own experience. Even the gold standard research methodology – the double-blind clinical trial – is limited in scope because they are based on patients who do not have multiple conditions and complicating factors. The diagnosis and treatment of an elderly patient with three or four conditions, for which they are taking a mix of medications, is no simple matter you can just look up on the internet.

> The diagnosis and treatment of an elderly patient with three or four conditions, for which they are taking a mix of medications, is no simple matter you can just look up on the internet.

There are also choices to be made about what research to promote and fund and about how to use the knowledge generated by science. Science has always been political from the time of Copernicus and Galileo to the development of nuclear weapons and the race for space. It has however, become even more highly political in recent years. Many countries including India, Singapore and the Korean republic, and more recently the UK, have made science a core part of their future national strategies. India started its investment in technical education 70 years ago and Singapore is preparing for the future now by introducing computer programming into primary schools. The vaccine diplomacy during the pandemic is surely only one example of many instances to come when countries use science to compete for influence and positional power.

Scepticism about clinicians and biomedical science has developed over recent years and, as we noted in Chapter 3, has been accelerated by the pandemic. Creationism, anti-vaccination movements, controversy over genetically modified crops and fears of technology for many different reasons have become more significant in recent years. Part of this is linked to levels of trust in government. A healthy level of mistrust, of course, is justified both by history and current experience, with abuses ranging from experiments on unwilling people to using technology to imprison and re-educate whole populations.

There is a pressing need to explain and promote science better, to engage and educate people more and, very importantly, to create ways in which it can account publicly for its activity and applications.

The biomedical sciences have served us all very well. Today, however, we need to think about things differently and recognise that scientific discovery is made relevant by our understanding of society and cultures and of how to apply it. It also requires public support and needs to be accountable publicly for its activity and applications.

## COMMERCIAL ACTIVITY AND PUBLIC BENEFIT

Scientific discovery and commercial interests have very often gone hand in hand in medicine. Commercial businesses have contributed enormously to research and the development of drugs, devices, services and facilities that have greatly benefited the public. Competition and the commercial drive for innovation have worked well in the past, although monopolies, price gouging and unscrupulous marketing have all also played their part. Many enterprises have reaped rich rewards, with health and healthcare now a significant segment of all stock markets and at least 16% of the world's largest economy dedicated to it.

Commerce works by identifying needs and gaps and creating products by exploiting the results of scientific and technological research. It has focused very largely on personal healthcare, selling products to be used by clinicians in looking after individuals rather than concentrating on population and public health. It has in health, as elsewhere, followed the money. That is, after all, the point of commerce.

The capacity to innovate can come at a price to society. Businesses that ally themselves with science and, particularly, with clinicians are in a very powerful position when it comes to marketing and sales. Patients and purchasers are often ill-equipped to challenge them. Doctors advocating the purchase of particular drugs or treatments on television must be among the most powerful advertisers for any business in the world.

Regulators and purchasers need to develop good systems to sort out the good from the bad and to make sure that they and the patients are not purchasing snake oil. The two systems of the USA and the UK have gone down different routes, with other countries adopting positions in between the two.

> Regulators and purchasers need to develop good systems to sort out the good from the bad and to make sure that they and the patients are not purchasing snake oil.

The US has relied on a licensing system run by the Food and Drug Administration (FDA) to ensure products are safe and then developed an extraordinarily bureaucratic insurance system that dictates what insurance companies will or won't pay for. This insurance system has itself added an overhead of 15% to the total costs of the system and involved countless patients in long hours of negotiation. In addition, individuals may choose to go outside the system and pay directly for any therapy licensed by the FDA.

The UK has a similar licensing authority, the Medicines and Healthcare Products Regulatory Agency (MHRA), but has also introduced another check in the National Institute for Health and Care Excellence (NICE), which compares therapies and, using both patient and scientific input, makes judgements about what therapies offer sufficient value to be worth using and paying for in the NHS. Patients may insure themselves separately as in the USA and go outside the NHS altogether and pay for any product licensed in the UK that their clinician is willing to prescribe.

The establishment of NICE was really a 'no-brainer'. The NHS needed to know it was getting value for the £10 billion it spent each year on pharmaceuticals. In practice, however, the operation of NICE has been very contentious, with pharmaceutical companies and some patient groups arguing that it has denied patients drugs that could benefit them. Others, however, have argued that it stopped money being spent on drugs, which may be safe but which had marginal if any benefits and then only in a few of the patients treated.

An alternative way of seeing it is that access to medicines in the US is rationed by cost and the private commercial decisions of insurers, access in the UK is rationed through public discussion and open decision making.

NICE is a true world leader which has generated interest in every country that is trying to control expenditure and counter commercial marketing. Over time, its operation and relationship with businesses have changed and new agreements are being reached where pharmaceutical companies agree to demonstrate specified levels of benefit to NHS patients from new drugs before NICE approves them for use in the NHS. It has also expanded its role over the years to include publishing guidelines and providing evidence. The assessment of therapies is only one of its many important roles. While regulation is well established in high-income countries, and overburdensome in some cases, it is very underdeveloped and even absent in many lower-income ones. The fact that it is the poorest people who are most likely to be cheated, given counterfeit drugs or dangerous treatments has led even the staunchly business-orientated World Economic Forum to argue that the most important role for government in lower-income countries is to regulate healthcare so as to drive up quality and drive the quacks and cheats out of business.[11]

At the global level, regulation is much more complex because it involves so many different countries and authorities and because it involves value-based arguments about what value is placed on public goods as opposed to private ones. This is well illustrated by the continuing debates about the ownership and patenting of genetic material, where commercial interests patent genes and scientists from the rich world have gone 'bio-prospecting' for genetic material among the diverse populations of the poor countries. Reports from the WHO and others have argued that the monopolies awarded to commercial organisations by allowing them to patent genes are not in the public interest.[12]

> Reports from the WHO and others have argued that the monopolies awarded to commercial organisations by allowing them to patent genes are not in the public interest.

In 2007, the Government of Indonesia objected strongly to having to purchase expensive vaccines for bird flu from overseas companies when they had been created from biological samples from its own population. As a result, it stopped providing virus samples to the WHO and instead entered into a commercial agreement with a US company for the local development of and manufacture of vaccine.[13] It was criticised by the WHO for upsetting the worldwide virus-sharing network arrangement.

The Convention on Biological Diversity has provided some clarity in parts of this field. It developed the Cartagena Protocol on Biosafety and the Nagoya Protocol on Access to Genetic Resources and the Fair and Equitable Sharing of Benefits Arising from their Utilization to provide *'critical guidance to Parties, IPLCs and other stakeholders on actions to promote the conservation and sustainable use of biodiversity, while equitably sharing the benefits from the use of genetic resources'.*[14]

The COVID-19 pandemic has brought questions about intellectual property and public good into focus. The rejection by major western nations of the India and South Africa proposal for the temporary suspension of intellectual property in the manufacturing of vaccines during the pandemic, as noted in Chapter 3, will undoubtedly have long-term consequences.

The pharmaceutical industry lives with a paradox: it is responsible for creating medicines that provide enormous benefit to the public, offering hope of relief from pain and suffering, yet the pharmaceutical industry itself is among the least trusted and the most criticised, even reviled, industries in the world. The public want to believe in their drugs, yet there has been a history of half-truths, of concealed research findings and of hard selling. These practices may apply to only some parts of the industry, but they have contaminated the image of the rest.

> The pharmaceutical industry lives with a paradox: it is responsible for creating medicines that provide enormous benefit . . . yet the pharmaceutical industry itself is among the least trusted . . . industries in the world.

A significant part of the problem lies in their business model. Pharmaceutical companies have to invest for many years in the development of a product, which may fail at any stage. They then have a limited period in which to sell the product before it comes out of patent. There are huge sunk costs and enormous risks before any drug comes to the market. This model is always likely to induce certain behaviours. There is little wonder that some companies spend 40% of their turnover on sales and marketing and target individual doctors with gifts as well as product information.

It is also likely to lead to a culture of secrecy, where the details of the development of a drug are kept out of the sight of competitors and the information given to the market is very carefully managed. At best, this secrecy is sensible commercial behaviour and, at worst, it can lead to the concealing of important information, the failure to ask questions that might affect the future of the drug and ultimately to the harming of patients. It can certainly lead to mistrust.

This is not, however, just to do with the business model. The UK's Competition and Markets Authority reported in 2021 that Auden Mckenzie and Actavis UK had increased the price of a 10 mg packet of hydrocortisone tablets by more than 10 000%. The rise increased the cost of a pack of 10 mg hydrocortisone tablets from 70p in April 2008 to £88 by March 2016, a 12 471% increase. The price of a pack of 20 mg tablets rose from £1.07 to £102.74 per pack, a 9501% rise.[15] Here is just one example of extreme price gouging by companies that had not been involved in the development of the drug but were simply exploiting a monopoly position.

The relationship between private business and government goes beyond simply regulation if for no other reason than that government is so often its biggest, if generally indirect, customer. Much of healthcare is subsidised by governments around the world. Even in the USA, where healthcare provision is largely private, the US Government pays approaching half the cost. Government can reasonably expect to have considerable influence over what commercial companies do.

There is also a new vein of innovation coming from philanthro-capitalism, where foundations and individuals use their wealth to promote new enterprises, and from organisations like the World Business Council for Sustainable Development, which believes that governments, businesses and international not-for-profit organisations cannot achieve sustainability on their own.

Private businesses, governments, NGOs and social enterprises all play significant roles in health and healthcare. They often work in partnership with each other and, increasingly, within large-scale and complex groupings and alliances. The relationships and boundaries between them all are shifting as people search for ever more effective ways of delivering services and working with patients and the public. There are parallel developments in other sectors, not least in tackling climate change.

There are many positive developments but, sadly, as many negative ones. Governments and public institutions need to be able to pick and choose which commercial organisations they want to work with and to set the terms via regulation or commercial contracts as appropriate. Almost every country will have a mix of public and private, not-for-profit, cooperative and social enterprises. All can have a role to play. The mix will vary from country to country but, in every case, it offers enormous scope to expand and improve healthcare.

Government has a far wider responsibility in this than the purely commercial contract they may have with a healthcare provider. Citizens reasonably expect government to be looking out for them, to ensure their health and, if regulation fails, to step in. This is about a social contract, rather than a commercial one, and about government's responsibility to act for health as a public good and secure our right to health.

> Citizens reasonably expect government to be looking out for them, to ensure their health and, if regulation fails, to step in.

Commercial endeavour is a very powerful part of the western scientific medicine paradigm. Linked with science and professionalism it has driven both innovation and costs. It needs, however, to be part of a far wider effort to improve health. Commercial innovation is at its most effective when it is undertaken in partnership with health systems, properly regulated, and linked with wider societal goals which promote health alongside human rights and the rule of law.

## FUNDING AND VALUE

The other main feature of western scientific medicine has been the relentless demand for more expenditure throughout the last 100 years – with the apparent supposition that more is always better, despite much evidence to the contrary. This feature is as ingrained into the psyche of health workers as much as any of the others and is as difficult to influence.

Francis Omaswa from Uganda gives the lie to this when he says, '*Rich countries may be able to tolerate waste in their health systems, poor countries can't.*' When money is short, every penny counts. It is only in affluent countries that we can afford to be profligate, throwing money at problems and failing to search out value.

> Rich countries may be able to tolerate waste in their health systems, poor countries can't.
>
> *Francis Omaswa*

The rapid growth of costs in health is not a new issue. Many attempts have been made over the years to try to define productivity in healthcare and use this to control costs, although with little success. Many of the formulas used were borrowed from industrial production models and are misleading and simplistic. At their worst, they can make policymakers focus on units of activity and not outcomes as being the end goal of healthcare.

A simple example from the UK illustrates the problem. A hospital may be paid each time a patient, let us say an elderly woman, is admitted to hospital during a cold winter, but it receives little or nothing if a smart clinician works out how to keep her fit and healthy at home. If we think in terms of simple productivity, then the more admissions the better. If we think in terms of health outcomes, home is almost certainly best. The incentives are wrong.

There is an important place for traditional measurements of productivity in, for example, making sure that facilities are well utilised, and these sorts of production model are useful in considering utilisation rates and downtime in operating theatres. However, it has become increasingly clear that we need to think in wider terms of value and with costs as only a part of the issue.

Sir Muir Gray, who led the development of evidence-based medicine in the UK, has now built on that foundation to be a leading advocate for value-based healthcare. He argues that all health services worldwide face cost pressures due to demography, innovation, patient expectations and much more. They also share five common problems: patient harm; unwarranted variation in quality, safety and outcome, activity and costs; inequalities and inequity; failure to prevent preventable disease; and waste. Tackling these issues will create value and use resources to best effect.

He argues that the real focus now needs to be on value and not costs and defines value-based healthcare as the *'equitable, sustainable and transparent use of the available resources to achieve better outcomes and experiences for every person'*. The centre he founded is supporting the NHS with vital evidence and guides on the practical application of these ideas.[16] Public Health England and others have helped provide the data, for example, in measuring variations in diagnostic usage across the UK.[17]

I have no doubt that Muir Gray is right that adopting a rigorous approach to value-based healthcare is essential for the future of health systems everywhere. Discussion about the future of the NHS in England almost always dissolves into arguments about the funding model. The real issue is the value achieved. This has to be a priority for every country committed to universal healthcare. The EU has defined value as having four dimensions, all of which are important:

- *'appropriate care to achieve patients' personal goals (personal value)*
- *achievement of best possible outcomes with available resources (technical value)*
- *equitable resource distribution across all patient groups (allocative value)*
- *contribution of healthcare to social participation and connectedness (societal value).'*[18]

This approach is complementary to the development by the IHI of the Triple Aim, which brings together the three goals of improving individual experience, improving population health and controlling per capita cost. No one or two of the aims are good enough by themselves; all three are necessary. As citizens, we want all three. However, as Tom Nolan, one of the founders of the programme pointed out in speaking of his own country, *'The root of the problem in health care is that the business models of almost all US health care organisations depend on keeping these three aims separate. Society on the other hand needs these three aims optimised (given appropriate weightings on the components) simultaneously.'*

These two developments should help us to think about healthcare systems differently and they apply in every country around the world. The many developments described elsewhere in this book – such as primary care, disease prevention, the engagement of populations and other sectors, and technological innovation – will all help control cost, but they also need to demonstrate value.

More funding will be needed in most countries, but it needs to be accompanied by greater value and less waste. As part of this, measures of input spending and activity need to be replaced by measures of the social and economic value achieved and the impact on population as well as individual health.

Taken together, these conclusions represent a very different picture from the simple model of western scientific medicine that we started with – with its belief in the power of biomedical science, its all-powerful doctors, its use of the market to create improvement, and its reliance on ever-increasing sums of both public and private money.

All these core features need to be turned upside down, as shown in Figure 11.1. This new approach to how western scientific medicine and its related health systems need to change is an important part of rethinking health and understanding how we need to work with it in our changing world.

---

- Greater professional competence is achieved through patients and communities empowering and being empowered by the professionals together with a greater emphasis on teamwork.
- Scientific discovery is made relevant by our understanding of society and cultures and of how to apply it. It also requires public support and needs to be accountable publicly for its activity and applications.
- Commercial innovation is at its most effective when it is undertaken in partnership with health systems, properly regulated, and linked with wider societal goals which promote health alongside human rights and the rule of law.
- Measures of input spending and activity need to be replaced by measures of the social and economic value achieved and the impact on population as well as individual health.

---

**Figure 11.1** The core features of western scientific medicine need to be turned upside down to improve health and health systems.

## IMPLEMENTATION AND QUALITY IMPROVEMENT

Effective implementation starts with a good understanding of how systems function in health and elsewhere. Don Berwick, formerly President of the IHI, puts it very simply: *'Our approach to quality improvement views healthcare as a large, complex system of interdependent actors (patients, care providers, payers, policymakers) and organisations (hospitals, primary care, public health entities, communities). This approach views performance as an inherent property of the system, linked inevitably to its design. Just as the top speed of a car is a property of that car, the waiting times in a healthcare organisation or the maternal death rates in a community are properties of that organisation and that community as they are currently designed.'*[19] The key is to adjust the system so that it produces better results.

IHI has over the last 20 years established an international reputation for quality improvement in health and for spreading good practice. It does so by applying the quality improvement methods developed over years in other industries through the work of people such as Deming, Juran, Feigenbaum and others to healthcare.

Where health planners typically start with the big picture of what needs doing and work downwards, IHI starts at the local level with the actual clinical practice and works up. Where health planners may try to solve the whole problem in one go by thinking through all the aspects and producing a master plan for success, IHI will more likely start by looking at the detail, understanding how the local system works and what influences it, changing a part, seeing what happens and changing something else. They deal in the practical reality of clinical practice. They turn the world upside down.

> They deal in the practical reality of clinical practice. They turn the world upside down.

Over the years, IHI has developed and refined its approaches so that it is now able to teach people how to improve quality with the aid of well-tested approaches and techniques. In response to demand from medical students, it established the IHI Open School, which provides access to its ideas and approaches to thousands of students and others.

The IHI's ideas and methodologies are now being spread and used around the world. We learned a great deal from them in the UK and these methods are being used more extensively in low- and middle-income countries. Value, safety and quality are absolutely foundational elements of any health system and need to be fully incorporated into all plans for universal health coverage.

New technology and the availability of data is making it possible to understand in real time what is happening within a complex health system and allows for what has become called system learning or the creation of learning health systems. This is about generating evidence that can transform and improve services. '*A "learning health system" (LHS) continuously analyses data which is collected as part of routine care to monitor outcomes, identify improvements in care, and implement changes on the basis of evidence.*'[20]

I suspect we will hear much more about LHSs in the future. The use of data will transform care and treatment.

There is another new development, too, which is a new interest in kindness and compassion. Unsurprisingly, this has gained momentum due to the pandemic. The science, the data, the business methods, the economic language – and even the systematic approach to safety and improvement – all depersonalise the language of health and care. But in the last analysis it is about human contact, clinician to patient, health worker to health worker. Clinicians learn how to manage their emotions, putting their professional face forward, but the experience of COVID-19 in particular has broken through some of those barriers and everywhere people have needed space and time to decompress and recover.

Bob Klaber, consultant paediatrician and Director of Research at Imperial College Healthcare NHS Trust has argued that '*Cultivation of kindness is a valuable part of the business of healthcare*'[21] and that '*Sometimes, whatever our role, we can forget that simple acts of kindness can mean more to people than anything else.*'[22] Elsewhere, Shams Syed of WHO, who has long experience of organising international partnerships for learning and development, described to me the role of compassion as a science and the need for the equation of awareness + empathy + action applying to policymaking and practice at every level.

These are important reminders in a world of health that sometimes appears to be all about technology and economics.

## CONCLUSIONS

These last two chapters have looked at how some of the learning from different parts of the world can be brought together to create practical knowledge that can be applied to improve health and health systems in the real world.

The next chapter considers some of the underlying frameworks and ways of thinking that can inform us for the future. It will also return to equity and global concerns. Many governments are turning away from global commitments, as noted earlier, but many citizens are becoming more engaged in the need for global action on climate change and much more. There is a great deal to play for.

## REFERENCES

1. https://www.lek.com/insights/internet-hospital-china-current-trends-and-future-directions (Accessed 25 November 2021).
2. https://www.dartmouthatlas.org/ (Accessed 25 November 2021).
3. https://www.who.int/health-topics/social-determinants-of-health#tab=tab_1 (Accessed 25 November 2021).
4. Jensen N, Kelly AH, Avendano M. Health equity and health system strengthening – time for a WHO re-think. *Glob Public Health,* 10 January 2021. https://doi.org/10.1080/1744169 2.2020.1867881 (Accessed 25 November 2021).
5. https://www.gov.uk/government/publications/levelling-up-the-united-kingdom (Accessed 7 February 2022)
6. https://iffim.org/ (Accessed 25 November 2021).
7. Rifat A, Silva S, Knaul FM. Innovative financing instruments for global health 2002–15: a systematic analysis. *The Lancet Global Health,* July 2017. https://doi.org/10.1016/S2214-109X(17)30198-5 (Accessed 25 November 2021).
8. Realising Rights: the ethical globalisation initiative. Mission quoted at https://www.sourcewatch.org/index.php/Realizing_Rights:_The_Ethical_Globalization_Initiative (Accessed 25 November 2021).
9. Commission for Africa. Our common interest; 2005. https://web.archive.org/web/20090 207181601/http://commissionforafrica.org/english/report/introduction.html (Accessed 25 November 2021).
10. Khanna A, Srivastava S. Role of Mohalla (Community) clinics in providing primary healthcare: a study in Delhi. *J Sci Res, Varanasi,* 2021; **65**(4). https://www.bhu.ac.in/research_pub/jsr/Volumes/JSR_65_04_2021/5.pdf (Accessed 25 November 2021).

11. World Economic Forum. Strengthening healthcare systems in sub-Saharan Africa. June 2006. https://www.weforum.org/agenda/2006/05/strengthening_h/ (Accessed 25 November 2021).

12. WHO. *Genomics and World Health*. Geneva: WHO, 2002.

13. Shimbo I, Ito Y & Sumikura K. Patent protection and access to genetic resources. *Nat Biotechnol*, 2008; **26**, 645–7. https://doi.org/10.1038/nbt0608-645 (Accessed 25 November 2021).

14. https://www.cbd.int/process/ (Accessed 25 November 2021).

15. Beioley K. Pharma companies fined after 10000% price rise for life-saving drug. *Financial Times*, 15 July 2021. https://www.ft.com/content/5079783f-e74a-44e3-a225-4b107d79c793 (Accessed 25 November 2021).

16. Hurst L, Mahtani K, Pluddemann A *et al*. *Defining Value-based Healthcare in the NHS*. CEBM report, University of Oxford, April 2019. https://www.cebm.ox.ac.uk/resources/reports/defining-value-based-healthcare-in-the-nhs (Accessed 25 November 2021).

17. http://www.exactproject.net/site/index.php/partners/oxford-centre-for-triple-value-health-care-ltd (Accessed 7 february 2022).

18. https://ec.europa.eu/health/sites/default/files/expert_panel/docs/024_defining-value-vbhc_en.pdf p28 (Accessed 25 November 2021).

19. This came from an unpublished paper by Don Berwick which was given to me by Joe McCannon, but I have heard him make these points many times.

20. https://www.nuffieldtrust.org.uk/files/2019-05/learning-health-systems-v3.pdf (Accessed 25 November 2021).

21. Klaber RE, Bailey S. Kindness: an underrated currency. *BMJ*, 2019; 367. doi: https://doi.org/10.1136/bmj.l6099 (Accessed 25 November 2021).

22. https://www.imperial.nhs.uk/about-us/blog/make-kindness-your-new-years-resolution (Accessed 25 November 2021).

# Some conclusions

12

*Turning the World Upside Down Again* asks us to challenge our own ideas and perspectives, to rethink health and well-being, to discard some of our old ideas – even some that have served us very well in the past – and to gather new hope, new ideas, new energy and new momentum to tackle the extraordinary challenges that face us in a time of pandemics, climate change and political turmoil.

This chapter brings together many of the themes in the book. There is a great deal we can learn from lower-income countries and from different communities in our own countries. The chapter considers what this means for how we think about health in all its aspects from individual health and well-being to the health of communities, societies and the planet. It goes on to discuss the implications for the design of health and care services and concludes with a discussion about the role of health and care professionals as agents of change.

One thing we can learn is to listen better and to a wider range of people, going beyond our own safe spaces. We need to duck down below the spin of politics with its new initiatives, the clever marketing that sells us ideas and products, and the noise of all the fashionable causes and people and listen to what people are telling us – and what some people have been saying for years.

COVID-19 and climate change are showing us the cracks in our system, the fault lines in our societies where reality doesn't live up to the politics and the promises. The problems were there all along. It is no surprise that the pandemic hit some groups harder than others – people from ethnic minorities, older and disabled people, people who are chronically sick, unemployed people and those on zero hours contracts, people living in poor housing, and women, children and young people from the least affluent households.

There have been excess deaths in some of these groups and high levels of morbidity. Most have lost income and globally an estimated 150 million people have been driven back into extreme poverty. Many have suffered from isolation during lockdowns. Domestic violence has increased. Children and young people have lost education and opportunities. Mental illness is on the rise.

The pandemic may be the immediate cause of these problems, but their roots go far deeper into social and economic structures, history and culture. We have heard different voices in the book talking about the impact of poverty, corruption, poor standards of healthcare,

DOI: 10.1201/9781003267706-12

governments *'floating above us like a helium balloon tethered by the flimsiest of strings'*, and telling us that *'Poverty is humiliation, the sense of being dependent on them, and of being forced to accept rudeness, insults, and indifference when we seek help.'*

The idea of global solidarity in health, nurtured during the previous two decades through bold actions on HIV, childhood vaccinations and the MDGs and the SDGs has proved weaker than we may have thought and hoped. High-income countries may too often have failed to deliver on the promises they made at summits and high-level meetings, but so too have other governments – including the African heads of state who agreed the Abuja Declaration in 2005 and committed themselves to spending 15% of their budgets on health. Only two have done so.

We should not, however, as I said in the Introduction, succumb to cynicism and narrow individual concerns – or, worse, to populist politics – but try to create a new vision and narrative for health globally that can energise and unify as we work to tackle the great health problems of today in our own countries and the world.

Global solidarity, I wrote, may be difficult to imagine now at the national level but it's not hard to find at the individual level – person to person, health worker to health worker, scientist to scientist – as so many of the stories in this book show. It is there, I believe, that we should begin to construct a new vision, with individuals and communities, and our interdependence globally at its heart.

Governments may be to some extent retreating into themselves, but I don't believe that people are.

## PERSPECTIVES MATTER

Tom Stoppard's play *Jumpers* is about twentieth-century philosophers and their intellectual gymnastics. At one point in it, the great Austrian philosopher Wittgenstein asks why people thought that the Sun went round the Earth. He was told that it was because it looked like it did – you could see the Sun moving across the sky. Yes, he replied, but what would it look like if the Earth went round the Sun?

> What would it look like if the Earth went round the Sun?
>
> Tom Stoppard, *Jumpers*

The same thing can be perceived, and described, in completely different ways. This is not just about where we are standing to look at it but about our mindset, preconceptions and beliefs.

It matters how we see the world because it determines how we act. People thought and acted differently when they believed that the Sun went round the Earth, and that humans were at the centre of the universe. When they began to get new evidence that contradicted that perception – and began to believe that the Earth went round the Sun – it caused havoc with the established beliefs of the day. The Catholic Church and other authorities reacted with outrage and violence.

I don't want to overstretch the parallel, because there is more to it than this, but the change from seeing doctors and other professionals at the centre of health – with the whole world of health revolving around them – to recognising that it is actually the patient and citizen who are there, and who have been there all along (whatever it looked like to us at the time), will change the things we believe and the way we act.

We no longer believe, to parody only a little, that the doctor is always right, science will give us all the answers, we can leave everything to the state or the market, and that more expenditure means better health. We can begin to see all these things differently now. The twentieth-century ideas about health and health services are coming up against the discoveries, inventions and, above all, real-life experiences of the twenty-first-century world.

Many people understand this intuitively. They don't need to be told that the world is changing. Young people, for whom this is the whole world they know, migrants and others with experience of different systems, and technology pioneers all understand the scale of the change while policymakers grapple with its consequences.

The new way of looking at the world is no more neutral or value-free than any other. There are other perspectives that may be based on very different values, drawn from religion, culture or tradition. Different perspectives will lead people to believe very different things and take very different actions.

## HUMAN FLOURISHING

It is very clear from all the discussions in this book that we need to think about health in very broad terms which recognise our connections with each other and the way in which all the social, environmental and wider determinants of health shape our health and well-being. It must also reflect our need to be in control and shape our own destiny.

The WHO definition which saw health as *'a state of complete physical, mental and social well-being and not merely the absence of disease or infirmity'* provides a good starting point.[1] However, as Machted Huber and colleagues point out, it ignores our own agency and the growth of non-communicable diseases which mean many people can never attain a state of *'complete wellbeing'*. They argue, as quoted in Chapter 3, that *'Just as environmental scientists describe the health of the earth as the capacity of a complex system to maintain a stable environment within a relatively narrow range, we propose the formulation of health as the ability to adapt and to self-manage'*.[2] Healthy humans are able to adapt and self-manage in the face of social, physical and emotional challenges.

> Healthy humans are able to adapt and self-manage in the face of social, physical and emotional challenges.

This approach is a very helpful way for us to think about the health of communities and wider society as well as the health of individuals.

At the individual level, as noted in Chapter 3, this relates to the concept of homeostasis. A healthy body has, for example, the ability to regulate its temperature and blood sugar, reacting to outside events and adjusting as necessary. While this is done unconsciously, we can also consciously manage our own activities and responses to external pressures – maintaining for ourselves a healthy lifestyle that suits our own needs and capabilities.

We can, by analogy, think about the health of communities and society in similar terms as a search for a balanced stability and an ability to adapt and self-manage in response to outside events. It captures the extraordinary creativity and adaptability of communities which I have described in so many places in this book – people finding a way to deal with problems and achieve a fulfilling and secure way of life, often against the odds. It also describes the more formalised processes in more affluent societies and the search for global security and governance.

Underpinning all this are the importance of relationships and the integration of our health as individuals with the health of the wider social, cultural and physical environment.

Gill Orrow, whose work in East Surrey was described in Chapter 9, sees health explicitly in ecological terms and talks about improving *'local access to conditions for health and wellbeing. Just as every part of an ecosystem contributes to the health of the whole, we look to ensure all those living or working in our area who wish to, may both benefit from and contribute to the creation of healthier places.'*[3]

Bringing all these ideas together, I now see health as being about three things – our physical, mental and social well-being, our relationships with our communities, wider society and the planet, and our ability to self-manage and exercise control over our lives.

Health and care professionals specifically and other professionals more generally have an important role to play in enabling us to help ourselves, helping communities and societies to heal themselves and helping the wider natural environment to heal itself. Sometimes, of course, they have to intervene directly to deal with disease and injury in all of these areas from the individual to the planet.

More generally, I think it is useful to see health as contributing to human flourishing. The Greek philosopher Aristotle wrote more than 2300 years ago about living well and about *eudaimonia* – normally translated as 'human flourishing' – which he saw as the ultimate purpose of a good life.[4]

The next four sections discuss the health of individuals, communities, wider society and the planet in turn.

## INDIVIDUALS – WE ALL HAVE SPECIAL NEEDS

There is a great deal that disabled people can teach us about the right to health, rights and social justice from their experience and perspective.

Policymakers, too, often treat disability as a simple one-dimensional problem in which people need to overcome their particular disability. It is, of course much more complicated than that. Blindness or mental illness can have devastating consequences for individuals and throw whole families into poverty.

Amartya Sen, the Nobel laureate, argues that policymakers fail to understand the complications and implications of disability because of the way they look at the world, starting, as most of us probably do, with the idea that policy should be constructed around the needs of 'normal' people with exceptions made for those with disabilities of any kind. The result is that their every policy reinforces the disadvantage experienced by disabled people.[5]

> The result is that their every policy reinforces the disadvantage experienced by disabled people.

Baroness Jane Campbell of Surbiton is a friend who has influenced my thinking and had a powerful impact on several aspects of UK social policy. She has, among other things, helped shape the policy of personal budgets described in Chapter 10.

When I was chief executive of the English NHS, I arranged to film an interview with her about her experience of healthcare and hospitals. I played it to a conference of the chairs and chief executives of all England's NHS hospitals and health authorities as a reminder of how far we were from really being people-centred.

Baroness Campbell has been severely disabled from birth. She is small, with limited movement, regularly needs help with breathing and is all too often admitted to hospital for long periods. She is also very bright with a powerful mind, iron determination and a sense of humour, qualities that make her such a successful social commentator and campaigner and so effective a member of the UK's House of Lords.

She told the camera that, on her last stay in hospital, she had been in intensive care for a long period. One day, as she lay there, she heard a doctor say to a nurse that if she 'crashed', there was really no need to resuscitate her as she had such a poor quality of life. Jane was appalled. She would be the judge of her own quality of life.

She acted. She made herself stay awake for the next 48 hours so that she could keep an eye on the staff and sent her husband home to get a picture of her receiving her PhD to place at the end of the bed. The person in the picture was the person the doctor was talking about, she said; he shouldn't be misled by the appearance of the poor person struggling with her illness in the bed before him.

Nine hundred powerful men and women stayed very still and silent when the film had finished. I didn't need to say anything. Baroness Campbell had exposed some of our most basic assumptions and revealed the way power operated in our hospitals.

A long-term campaigner for the rights of disabled people, she has argued consistently for the transformative public services that will overcome the social inequality that disabled people experience. She does not want to be viewed as a vulnerable person in need of care but rather as an active, valued citizen in charge of her own life. Disabled people have the same rights as everybody else.

In a lecture at Cambridge University in April 2008 she set out a distinctive new approach: *'The challenges we now face demand that our slogan, "Nothing about us without us", must speak less of our separateness and difference and more of our interdependence and connection with others. Critically, it must be about seeking to share control and responsibility, not simply taking control. Redressing injustice still requires a politics of recognition, but this should no longer be reduced to a question of group identity or allegiance. It requires a politics aimed at overcoming barriers that prevent all individuals, families and communities participating as full members of society.'*[6]

Her argument is very powerful: *'The ideas of the disability movement – barrier removal, reforming public services to give people greater control over their own lives, and equality legislation based on accommodating difference rather than ignoring it – are the blueprint for the next stages of promoting equality and human rights overall.'*

> The ideas of the disability movement – barrier removal, reforming public services to give people greater control over their own lives, and equality legislation based on accommodating difference rather than ignoring it – are the blueprint for the next stages of promoting equality and human rights overall.
>
> *Baroness Jane Campbell, lecturer at Cambridge University 2008*

Jane Campbell is surely right. We all want greater control over our own life, and we all have our own special needs.

I remember Dr Jeremy Cobb, the very independent-minded former Public Health Director for East Berkshire in the UK, telling me that the crucial end point that health professionals should be working towards is to help people function as independently as possible, physically, psychologically and socially. In other words, to be in control, to self-manage and adapt as they see fit and, within the constraints of their disability or illness, to flourish.

In the absence of such a unifying end goal, people go their separate ways. I recall him trying in the 1990s to get all the professions to assess their patients in terms of their independence. They mostly didn't like it. The nurses wanted their own assessment and had goals to do with care and comfort. The doctors thought in terms of clinical outcomes; social work, as they saw it, still wasn't their business. Only the occupational therapists really reflected on how their patients would eventually manage to resume their old lives.

I have heard Jeremy Cobb rail against the separate professions, the doctors, nurses and therapists who all insisted on assessing patients their own way and, in those days, holding separate notes. It led him into plenty of conflict with his more traditionally minded colleagues. That didn't faze Jeremy. He liked the fight. Years later he believed there has been some progress, but that clinicians and health systems still generally think and talk just in terms of clinical outcomes and the outcomes of care and not in terms of how well the patient can function.

Independence and control are, in practice, what most of us want for our families and ourselves. We want to be able to live as normally as possible with our diseases and disabilities. We don't want to be 'in care' or dependent on others and we don't want to be forced to be 'carers' earlier than we need be. Jane Campbell's experience reminds us that, however disabled we may seem to be to others, we may still want to live and make our own judgements and decisions. We can value life at every stage of it and we can ask our physicians and carers to help us to be as able and as independent as possible at every stage.

We can measure independence and understand it and, crucially, we can apply our own values to it. We alone can judge how much we want to be dependent on relatives and friends and institutions. What may be too much dependence for one person may be independence for another. In this context, what human flourishing means depends on the individual human.

> In this context, what human flourishing means depends on the individual human.

In some ways, Jeremy Cobb's insistence on the end goal being independence is another version of Doug Eby's assertion that the primary diagnosis is almost always social. Both men are looking at the individual in the round. Both men are asking the same questions: what does that individual really want? Or to use the words that are now being used more and more, as we saw in Chapter 10, what matters to you?

It also resonates with Amartya Sen's view that the goal of international development is for people to have the freedom to live a life that they have reason to value. He does not attempt to judge for them what that life might be or how to judge its value. The important unifying goal is freedom.[5]

Human flourishing is, of course, the freedom to live a life we have reason to value.

## COMMUNITIES – HEALTH IS MADE AT HOME

These reflections already bring out some of the connections between individuals and their communities. The life we have reason to value is about our culture, our relationships and our experiences as well as our personal feelings of physical or mental well-being.

There were many examples in Chapters 8 and 9 of people improving their communities or working with groups within them to improve health and well-being. The examples of the Penwerris estate in Cornwall and Salford Dadz both showed how working to improve the community led to improvements in confidence and health among the people involved. People need healthy and stable communities if they are to thrive and grow.

Francis Omaswa's saying that health is made at home, hospitals are for repairs encapsulates ideas about how health is created by the people around us – our families, neighbours, teachers, employers and others – and our relationships and experiences. The concept of *ubuntu*, which means in broad terms that the identity of each person is bound up with their community – I am who I am because of you – is widely used in Southern Africa.

Stable and positive communities contribute to human flourishing but, equally, dysfunctional and damaged communities damage individuals and their life chances. Sir Harry Burns, former chief medical office for Scotland, puts it very clearly: *'a chaotic early life leads to a reduced ability to manage stress and behave appropriately . . . the biology is very clear chaotic difficult circumstances lead to increased risk of physical ill health'.*[7]

He went on to quote Jimmy Reid, a leader of the Upper Clydeside shipbuilders in the early 1970s, talking about alienation: *'It is the cry of men who were the victims of blind economic forces beyond their control. It is the feeling of despair and hopelessness that pervades people who feel with justification they have no say in shaping or determining their own destinies.'*

> It [alienation] is the cry of men who were the victims of blind economic forces beyond their control. It is the feeling of despair and hopelessness that pervades people who feel with justification they have no say in shaping or determining their own destinies.
>
> *Jimmy Reid*

Healthy communities and a healthy society have an enormous role to play in human flourishing.

## A HEALTH-CREATING SOCIETY

There has been much more research done on unhealthy communities and on the damage done by social forces and societal structures than on healthy communities and healthy and health-creating societies. Sir Michael Marmot and others have anatomised the way in which social, economic and political structures damage health.[8]

Modern societies with their dependence on cars, fast food and sedentary pursuits and their stressful jobs and environments are perfectly designed to promote ill health – and do so very successfully in terms of rising levels of obesity and of diabetes and other non-communicable diseases directly linked to lifestyles. Sir Michael's work also demonstrates the way that inequalities in all aspects of life from education to income affect health with a clear social gradient between the long-lived healthy and affluent population and the poorest groups with greater morbidity and earlier deaths.

Part of the answer, of course, is to change the structures that create these inequalities and control these factors that are the causes or drivers of ill health. Another part, however, is to promote healthy environments and activities and all the drivers and causes of health. National and local governments have a central role in this in improving housing and creating healthy towns and cities, strengthening education and supporting parents with under 5-year-old children, and improving working conditions and promoting prosperity in all parts of society.

The civil society health creators described in Chapter 9 and elsewhere can play a part but, ultimately, governments set the framework and provide the context in which health can be created – or destroyed.

Health and a sustainable economy are also intimately linked – and sustainable prosperity must be an important part of human flourishing. Emily Blanchard, Associate Professor at Tuck School of Business, Dartmouth College in the US, describes human capital as *'among the most important drivers of long-run economic growth yet it is frequently overlooked . . . This is a mistake. Economic growth is fuelled by people. An economy's capacity to produce is driven by the vitality, skills and innovation of its population.'*[9] Dame Sally Davies makes the related point, as quoted in Chapter 2, that health is *'one of the primary assets of our nation'* and *'we must re-position health as an investment'*.

> Health and a sustainable economy are also intimately linked – and sustainable prosperity must be an important part of human flourishing.

Making economic growth sustainable is, of course, essential for tackling the climate crisis. Here, Kate Raworth's doughnut economics, mentioned in Chapter 3, can be helpful in helping balance *'the social foundation of wellbeing that no one should fall below'* and *'the ecological ceiling of planetary pressure that we should not go beyond'*.[10]

## PLANETARY HEALTH

The discussion in Chapter 3 brought out the intimate links between human and planetary health. It described how climate change is already impacting health and how we can expect the impact to grow as temperatures rise and 'once-in-a-lifetime' events happen more and more regularly. This will lead to greater migration and growing conflicts over natural resources.

The health industry is also contributing to climate change an estimated 4.4% of emissions in carbon equivalent terms. These need to be brought down. Moreover, as Sonia Roschnik argues, actions to improve health – more primary care, better diets, healthy cities – will all contribute to slowing down climate change. There are a range of actions at all levels that can reinforce each other in very positive ways.

Human flourishing and living well are dependent on our health as individuals and the health of our communities, societies and planet. In each area, it is about balances between, for example, independence and interdependence, or between sustainable growth and planetary sustainability. Health and care systems and health and care professionals have an important part to play in achieving this.

## HEALTH AND CARE SYSTEMS FOR THE FUTURE

It is very likely, given the importance of context, that health and care systems will develop very differently in different countries. There are, however, two things that we can expect will be common to them all.

First, they will be concerned with each of the three activities outlined in Chapter 9: service provision, the protection of health and prevention of disease, and health creation. They are closely linked, and all are important. Everyone from the professionals to government and civil society to public authorities have their roles to play.

Ideally, the health and care systems of the future will be built explicitly around these three areas, all of which will be invested in and developed. Civil society and communities will have their roles in creating the conditions for people to be healthy, supported and enabled by professionals from different sectors working collaboratively to create health. Government and national and local authorities will provide the legislative and regulatory frameworks that protect citizens and enable the professionals to prevent disease. The health and care services will provide the professional interventions and care needed by the ill, injured and infirm.

Secondly, health and care systems will depend for at least the foreseeable future on four driving factors: the continuing development of the professions and their expertise, scientific and technological advances across the natural and social sciences, commercial activity to promote innovation and build capacity (with perhaps a few exceptions in countries where the state controls everything), and the search for economic and social value.

As described in Chapter 11, all these core features need to be turned upside down to make them relevant and effective in today's circumstances. Professional competence is enhanced through working with patients and communities; scientific and technological advances need to work within the wider societal context; commercial innovation needs to link with wider social goals; and measures of cost and productivity need to be replaced by measures of value. Western scientific medicine will not be replaced but enhanced.

These adaptations are shown in Figure 12.1.

The precise way in which health and care systems develop will, however, depend very much on local context, culture and history as well as on the economic capacity of the country. There will be big differences.

- Greater professional competence is achieved through patients and communities empowering and being empowered by the professionals together with a greater emphasis on teamwork.
- Scientific discovery is made relevant by our understanding of society and cultures and of how to apply it. It also requires public support and needs to be accountable publicly for its activity and applications.
- Commercial innovation is at its most effective when it is undertaken in partnership with health systems, properly regulated, and linked with wider societal goals which promote health alongside human rights and the rule of law.
- Measures of input spending and activity need to be replaced by measures of the social and economic value achieved and the impact on population as well as individual health.

**Figure 12.1** The core features of western scientific medicine need to be turned upside down to improve health and health systems.

Examples in Chapter 8 and elsewhere describe ways in which inspirational people in low- and middle-income countries who don't have the resources or the baggage of history and vested interests of high-income countries are innovating and developing different approaches.

BRAC, for example, uses business methods to achieve social goals, works with communities and especially women, empowers people by helping them become economically independent, and deals with health as part of peoples' lives and not as something completely separate. They and others have developed new ways of training and deploying health staff, bring public health and clinical medicine closer together, and make the best use of whatever resources are to hand.

Combinations of these seven ideas are already proving vital in many countries and could have an impact elsewhere depending on context. Figure 12.2 shows the seven key features that distinguish the approaches being adopted so successfully in many countries.

- Developing social enterprises using business methods to achieve social goals
- Working with communities and especially women
- Empowering people by helping them become economically independent as well as having rights and a voice
- Dealing with health as part of peoples' lives and not as something completely separate.
- Training health workers to meet local needs and not just for the professions
- Bringing public health and clinical medicine together
- Making best use of the resources to hand

**Figure 12.2** A different set of ideas that can enhance western scientific medicine.

There is also a great deal to learn about behaviour from the health creators in our own countries, some of whom were described in Chapter 9. Figure 12.3 lists ten behaviours which are very different from the way health systems normally work but which can complement formal health and care systems.

The health creators think about health in broad, holistic terms and not just about how the health and care system works. They almost always link physical and mental health together, whereas health systems typically treat them separately, and they generally focus on communities or groups of people not just individuals.

1. Taking off our health system spectacles
2. Addressing physical and mental health together
3. Starting by building relationships not systems
4. Building on strengths not focusing on weaknesses
5. Recognising the importance of communities
6. Imbuing actions with meaning and purpose
7. Connecting and communicating
8. Recognising the importance of the natural environment
9. Learning by doing
10. Taking control and helping others to take control

**Figure 12.3** The health creators – ten behaviours that can complement health systems.

One very distinctive feature is how the health creators start with a vision or purpose and bring people together around it, connecting and communicating, and begin by building relationships rather than systems. Successful health creators build on the strengths of individuals and communities rather than concentrating on deficits and weaknesses and very often make use of the natural environment to create health and promote well-being. Their activities are imbued with meaning and purpose rather than just being steps in a plan. They learn by doing, being entrepreneurial and creative, and – perhaps most importantly of all – take control, act and help others to do the same.

This description of these behaviours shows how different they are from the behaviours within a large and structured organisation or health system and show why clinicians and planners can find it very difficult to work with the more freewheeling health creators and vice versa. We need both, of course.

## AGENTS OF CHANGE

Science, technology and data will undoubtedly help transform health systems in the future and are already doing so in many ways and many places. Health and care professionals, however, hold the key to linking everything and everyone together.

> Health and care professionals, however, hold the key to linking everything and everyone together.

How health and care professionals see the world – how they understand it and how they behave are fundamentally important. This is why the idea of the professionals as agents of change, as described in Chapter 10, is so important and potentially very radical. They can reach out to others across society to work with them on preventing disease and creating health as well as on providing care. And they can reach out to each other around the world as well as locally, crossing professional boundaries and working with non-professionals.

They will require new competences and skills if they are to do this truly effectively.

## REFERENCES

1. https://www.who.int/about/governance/constitution (Accessed 25 November 2021).
2. Huber M, Knottnerus JA, Green L, van der Horst H *et al*. How should we define health? *BMJ*, 2011; **343**: d4163.
3. Orrow G. All flourishing is mutual: cultivating personal, population and planetary health. *BMJ*, 2021, p. 375. doi: https://doi.org/10.1136/bmj.n2827.
4. Aristotle. *Nicomachean Ethics*.
5. Sen A. *Development as Freedom*. New York: Knopf, 1999.
6. Campbell J. Lecture, Cambridge University, 2008.
7. Crisp N. *Health is Made at Home, Hospitals are for Repairs: Building a healthy and health-creating society*. Billericay: SALUS, 2020, p. 71.
8. Marmot M. *The Health Gap*. London: Bloomsbury, 2015.
9. https://www.wto.org/english/res_e/booksp_e/wtr20_e/opinionpiece_by-emily-j-blanchard_e.pdf (Accessed 25 November 2021).
10. Raworth K. *Doughnut Economics*. London: Penguin Random House, 2017.

# Action

We live our own lives and the lives of our times.[1] Our beliefs, attitudes and behaviour are all shaped by the times we live in. Our times are changing fast, and we need to help shape these changes or they will shape us – and we may not like the result.

This chapter is not about the action that governments and politicians need to take. There is plenty for them to do and a great deal has been written about it which I don't need to add to here. The SDGs, the Paris Accord on climate, COP26 and 'leaving no one behind' have set out a very clear agenda. We don't need much more in the way of analysis and recommendations, but we do need a sense of urgency, long-term commitment and practical action. And governments and international institutions need to be held to account for their promises.

My focus here is on the people at the forefront of change who don't have the formal power but do have the energy, motivation and, in large part thanks to social media and the internet, the connections to make change happen. This should include all of us.

I wrote 12 years ago that there was a movement of people and ideas which was developing a new global outlook on health. There were many people and organisations starting to make connections globally who were inspired by the possibilities of making a difference in the world. Looking back, there was a positive and dynamic feeling, despite the credit crunch and financial crisis which were still unfolding at the time. Things seemed possible.

Today, the pandemic, climate change and political turmoil are shaking our worlds and our expectations. Old, trusted structures are falling away, and many people are disoriented, some are badly hurt, and many are feeling alienated by where they see their societies and their leaders going. It is a much less hopeful time.

We are also going through a long-overdue period of righting old wrongs – facing up to racism, the legacy of colonisation, the degradation of the environment, the continuing discrimination and violence against women, and the other inequalities structured into our societies – all of which impact on the health and well-being of millions.

The shocks to the system are, however, unfreezing attitudes and letting new ideas bubble up. There is a rich medley of different ideas appearing: new knowledge of how society and

DOI: 10.1201/9781003267706-13

politics affect health, a resurrection of older ideas from traditional societies, an exploration of the possibilities of science and technology, and a deepening understanding of ecology and the environment.

There is as yet no clear shared vision and perhaps there never should be. My vision for health is about promoting human flourishing. Our health is about our physical, mental and social well-being, our relationships with our communities, wider society and the planet, and our ability to self-manage and exercise control over our lives. And just as health professionals and health creators can help us to heal our minds and bodies, intervening where necessary, professionals in other areas can help communities, societies and the planet to adapt and heal.

One of the things I learned from the Nursing Now campaign, however, was that people adopt and adapt a vision for themselves. They may use the same words, but they internalise the vision differently, making it relevant to their reality and their circumstances – and they need to do so if they are going to own it. In the Nursing Now campaign, the vision was about raising the profile and status of nurses. It meant different things in different circumstances but, because people owned it, they were able to make changes locally and connect with others around the world in ways which proved influential and helped raise the profile and status of nursing.

A vision is not enough by itself. We also need data. This has been a continuing theme of this book. Without data and hard evidence, we can't understand diseases or – and this is becoming increasingly important – how they affect individuals and how treatments can be personalised. Without data, we can't understand – and sometimes can't even see – discrimination and how different people are affected by policy and practice. Without data, we can't understand the path that climate change or a pandemic is taking and what we may be able to do to arrest it.

It is vital, of course, that the data is accurate and fit for purpose. Data governance – who decides what data is collected and how – and accountability are central issues now and for the future. The same thing can be described in very different ways and lead to very different actions.

This is not about power and politics in a twentieth-century sense. We have been afflicted by the twin religions of the market and the party where market forces or party loyalties have been used to justify both outrageous actions and straight lies. We need markets and we need people to band together in common political causes, but we don't need to reify and deify them as though they should determine our actions whatever happens. Parties and party leaders need followers, and it is interesting that social media has adopted the word. The future, however, needs people who can and do think for themselves.

> The future . . . needs people who can and do think for themselves.

I would note in passing that religion itself, in all its richness and complexity, has too often been co-opted for other purposes, but that goes far beyond the scope of this book. The internet, too, that enables so much, can do great damage with its capacity to send a million lies around the world before the truth has even opened its app.

## PRACTICAL ACTION – THE CHANGE MAKERS

We need the new ideas and the new ways of doing things that will help us move on.

Many of them will, I believe, come from people outside the existing and traditional power structures; not just from low- and middle-income countries and communities in our own countries but from younger people, women, disabled people, migrants and others.

Migrant health workers and members of the diaspora are other groups of people who understand these issues well. One of the results of the large-scale migration of health workers is that there are now many thousands of people with a view of the world from at least two different national perspectives and, often, from several more. Many of them are professionally trained and they have moved to new homes where the science remains the same but where they need to learn to adapt their behaviours and adopt new practices.

Others include the health creators in our own countries, some of whom were described in Chapter 9, and the health and care professionals and all the paid and unpaid carers who on a daily basis may be constantly challenged by pain, suffering and loss.

I suggest that there are three groups of action that people may want to take. The first is simply to act on one or more of the things that they believe to be important, whether it is improving their community, climate change, inequalities in health, or data collection and education. We learn by doing. Protesting and campaigning can be important but the things that change the world are the things that people *do*.

Set up the gardening group, reach out to your neighbours, provide practical support to the health workers in Myanmar, help children or adults to read, set up the community interest group to learn together or whatever it is. Connect or reconnect with others. There are many examples in this book which show how major changes have come from small beginnings.

Professor Bas Bloem is the creator of Parkinsonnet and has developed innovative new services and new ways of relating to patients (who he doesn't call patients) with Parkinson's disease and professionals working with them.[2] He has a very useful way of thinking about change: *'Start small, think big, go fast.'*

> Start small, think big, go fast.
>
> *Professor Bas Bloem*

Start small because then you can really understand the issue involved; if something doesn't work at the small scale, it won't work at the large scale. Too many policymakers start with the big picture and then don't understand why it doesn't work. Start small but think big about the possibilities for the future. Go fast because you will build up momentum and 'they' won't be able to catch up with you and stop you.

The second group of actions is to build partnerships. We live in a polarising world where the internet can act simply as an echo chamber that separates us from our neighbours, and it has never been more important to reach out to others. Several partnerships focused on health and communities have already been mentioned in this book and there are many more.

Some partnerships are focused on diseases or conditions such as the multi-country partnership organised by Rifat Atun and colleagues from Harvard, which shares learning about diabetes in low- and middle-income countries, or the palliative care partnership run by Liz Grant and colleagues from Edinburgh, which engages with Africa countries and provides opportunities for mutual learning and support, or the Global Learning Laboratory run as a collaborative by Shams Syed from the WHO.

There are whole-country partnerships such as that between Kings College London and Somaliland, which for more than 20 years has supported developments and professional education in the country. More recently, the Uganda UK Health Alliance was set up by Ged Byrne from Health Education England with the Government of Uganda to help coordinate the activities of the many UK teams who are working with Ugandan partners on health and development.[3] It reduces wasteful duplication and helps focus all the effort on priorities and maximising the impact of the collective efforts. The Kenyan President launched a Kenya UK Health Alliance in partnership with the UK Government and the University of Manchester in July this year, and there are plans for a Tanzania UK one to come.[4]

THET, mentioned in earlier chapters, supports many UK partnerships with health workers and institutions around the world including the work in Myanmar described in Chapter 3. Elsewhere, other organisations such as the ESTHER Alliance for Global Health Partnerships and Memisa have played similar roles.[5,6]

Universities and institutions from high-income countries have traditionally carried out a great deal of research in lower-income ones but are increasingly starting to do this in partnership with institutions within the countries themselves. There is still a very long way to go in moving towards more equal partnerships where more of the principal investigators are local people and where more of the money is invested in local institutions; however, progress is being made.

Sir Mark Walport, formerly the UK Government's chief scientific adviser, was the chief executive of the Wellcome Trust when this policy was instituted. He told me that they had insisted that governments contributed to the costs of the research so as to ensure there really was local ownership of the shared programmes. It is an important point; nothing will change if it doesn't fully take root in the country. It will just be another group of foreigners doing something in your country.

COVID-19 is moving this issue and so many others on, and we are already seeing countries planning their own research and vaccine development and manufacturing facilities. A new focus on science and technology will surely follow.

It is also important that partnerships are not just built among the like-minded but are diverse and enable different people and groups to bring different things to the party. Andrew Mawson, some of whose work was described in Chapter 9, talks about 'joining the dots' and bringing people together who don't normally meet, whether they are from education, health, the police, voluntary organisations or businesses. He has been sharply critical of groupthink in the public and voluntary sector that only sees one set of issues and one set of partners. The same can be said of many private businesses which take very narrow view of the world. Great gains can be made by them all working together. Partnerships need a shared purpose but will benefit from a diversity of partners who think and behave differently and can open up new and creative opportunities.

> Partnerships need a shared purpose but will benefit from a diversity of partners who think and behave differently and can open up new and creative opportunities.

The third area for action is the development of health and care professionals as agents of change, people who can not only discharge their own role as experts and professionals but also facilitate, enable and influence others. Individual professionals have always done this, of course, but it needs to be seen now as a core part of the professional's role.

Change needs to take place in the most important place of all, the minds of the professionals in every field who shape so much of our lives. When they internalise and own ideas, things can happen.

We can see this, for example, in the way Sam Everington and, more recently, Gill Orrow – whose work was described in Chapters 9 and 10 – are working outside their surgeries as well as in them as GPs in England and are actively redefining what it is to be a GP. At the same time, nurses are taking on bigger and more central roles in primary care and, as described in Chapter 8, the Brazilian model of community health workers is being trialled in London. Primary care is being radically reshaped in England, not as a result of the decisions of policymakers and politicians, but because of the actions and insights of professionals themselves.

There are many people all over the world taking other radical new approaches. I wrote, for example, in Chapter 8 about Fazle Abed's injunction to *'empower the women'*. It is a powerful point which BRAC acted on and which brought about enormous improvements in the health of individuals and communities.

Professionals from different backgrounds working together can have an enormous impact when they all own a shared set of ideas. I described in Chapter 9 how Hazel Stuteley and a group of professionals from different sectors worked with residents on a troubled estate to bring about change with dramatic and measurable improvements in postnatal depression, asthma, educational achievement, crime and employment, among other things. It is worth looking back on these results if you doubt the value of this approach.

These sorts of approach need to become mainstream.

## TURNING THE WORLD UPSIDE DOWN AGAIN

Politics can bring about long-term change, as can new ideas and technologies, and the professionals can facilitate, but long-term and sustainable change needs to be owned and internalised by populations. And the professionals, policymakers and politicians need to become better at listening.

I recall Sir Maurice Shock telling me 20 years ago about the 'scorched earth' approach of some governments. They flatten everything in front of them, imposing change on the population but, when eventually the regime falls (as it always does) and the pressure is removed, the people return to the old ways. They never owned the change.

I am reminded, too, of Hugh Ellis, a very experienced planner, talking to me about 'the other England'. It is still there under all the noise created by politics, marketing and fashion.

The Scottish poet Hamish Henderson spoke in similar terms about 'the carrying stream', the continuity of life and culture that endures.[7]

Finally, I return to the words of the three women from a housing estate in southern England who I mentioned in Chapter 1. When asked by a researcher how they described themselves, their reply was straightforward and to the point.

*We are kind, members of the community, we look out for each other, and we want to make the place better.*

## REFERENCES

1. From Penny Jones who derived it from a saying by Laurens van der Post.
2. https://www.parkinsonnet.com/ (Accessed 29 November 2021).
3. https://uukha.org/ (Accessed 29 November 2021).
4. https://www.president.go.ke/2021/07/29/kenya-and-the-uk-sign-two-key-health-agreements-in-london/ (Accessed 29 November 2021).
5. https://esther.eu/ (Accessed 29 November 2021).
6. https://memisa.be/en/ (Accessed 29 November 2021).
7. Bort E (ed). *Borne on the Carrying Stream: The legacy of Hamish Henderson.* Edinburgh: Grace Note Publications, 2010.

# Appendix

This is an example Community Health Worker (CHW) job description from the pilot in Westminster begun in 2021.

| Job Summary |
|---|
| As Community Health Worker (CHW) you will be a frontline primary care and public health worker employed from the local community. The outreach work of a CHW is essential in addressing the rising inequalities in health and social care and in identifying unmet need in the community. The CHW performs a variety of duties with the aim of improving the health and wellbeing of the communities they serve. They play a significant role in increasing health promotion, through a range of activities including outreach assessments, community education, signposting, informal counselling, and advocacy. Their bridging role between health and social services and the community facilitates improved access and supports the provision of services that meet the needs of the local community. This is an exciting opportunity to shape a new job role new to the UK. |

| Main Duties and Responsibilities |
|---|
| Monthly household visits (or more frequent if the household need requires it) within a defined geographical area (up to a maximum of 120 households within defined Output Areas) to assess the health and social needs of everyone within a household, adopting a proactive and holistic approach when supporting the local community. |

Educational

- Deliver personalised health promotion to families whilst providing health literacy support
- Provide lifestyle advice such as smoking cessation, alcohol consumption, healthy diet and physical exercise
- Provide up-to-date messaging on COVID-19 immunisation, testing and social distancing measures
- Provide basic health education around breastfeeding, immunisation and screening

Clinical

- To identify those eligible for childhood immunisations and adult health and cancer screening appointments and encourage the uptake of missed appointments
- To support chronic disease diagnosis and management through improved adherence to medication and early identification of signs and symptoms of chronic disease and its complications
- To identify household determinants of ill health and health seeking behaviour and play an active role in resolving these through linkage in to the health and social care system

Navigational

- Support households to navigate the health and social care system and access the appropriate services for their needs
- Signpost and refer on to other existing community services

Support

- Develop meaningful therapeutic relationships with the local community
- Offer informal counselling and empathetic listening
- Adopt health coaching and motivational approaches including problem solving and goal setting

Research

- Keep digital records that reflect household and community need and progress via secure tablet that will be linked to the clinical system used by the General Practice
- Complement GP records with the collected community outreach data
- Contribute your work and findings to the local GP and multidisciplinary team

# Index

Note: Page numbers in **bold** refer to tables or figures